Mapping Global Racisms

Series Editor
Ian Law
School of Sociology and Social Policy
University of Leeds
Leeds, UK

There is no systematic coverage of the racialisation of the planet. This series is the first attempt to present a comprehensive mapping of global racisms, providing a way in which to understand global racialisation and acknowledge the multiple generations of different racial logics across regimes and regions. Unique in its intellectual agenda and innovative in producing a new empirically-based theoretical framework for understanding this glocalised phenomenon, Mapping Global Racisms considers racism in many underexplored regions such as Russia, Arab racisms in North African and Middle Eastern contexts, and racism in Pacific contries such as Japan, Hawaii, Fiji and Samoa.

More information about this series at
http://www.palgrave.com/gp/series/14813

Riccardo Armillei

The 'Camps System' in Italy

Corruption, Inefficiencies and Practices of Resistance

Riccardo Armillei
Alfred Deakin Institute for Citizenship
and Globalisation (ADI)
Deakin University
Burwood, VIC, Australia

Mapping Global Racisms
ISBN 978-3-319-76317-0   ISBN 978-3-319-76318-7   (eBook)
https://doi.org/10.1007/978-3-319-76318-7

Library of Congress Control Number: 2018935400

© The Editor(s) (if applicable) and The Author(s) 2018
This work is subject to copyright. All rights are solely and exclusively licensed by the Publisher, whether the whole or part of the material is concerned, specifically the rights of translation, reprinting, reuse of illustrations, recitation, broadcasting, reproduction on microfilms or in any other physical way, and transmission or information storage and retrieval, electronic adaptation, computer software, or by similar or dissimilar methodology now known or hereafter developed.
The use of general descriptive names, registered names, trademarks, service marks, etc. in this publication does not imply, even in the absence of a specific statement, that such names are exempt from the relevant protective laws and regulations and therefore free for general use.
The publisher, the authors, and the editors are safe to assume that the advice and information in this book are believed to be true and accurate at the date of publication. Neither the publisher nor the authors or the editors give a warranty, express or implied, with respect to the material contained herein or for any errors or omissions that may have been made. The publisher remains neutral with regard to jurisdictional claims in published maps and institutional affiliations.

Cover photograph: Candoni 'Solidarity Village' 2012 © Riccardo Armillei

Printed on acid-free paper

This Palgrave Macmillan imprint is published by the registered company Springer International Publishing AG part of Springer Nature.
The registered company address is: Gewerbestrasse 11, 6330 Cham, Switzerland

To Antonio and Romana
I owe you everything. I wish you were still here; you left too early, but you will always be in my heart!

Foreword

One of the key moral failures and policy challenges of our increasingly globalised world is how the notion of free movement of goods and services has not translated to free mobility for people. Human mobility is certainly increasing as a result of new regional blocs, temporary labour needs, international students markets and other forms of forced migration. Yet this supposed human mobility becomes constrained when it involves individuals from the global South or those minorities living in the global North but who unfortunately are not considered to be ethnonationals of the states where they happen to live.

The problem these new forms of mobility and diversity raise concern how we treat people and how we regulate social relations within our multicultural societies. Unfortunately, the framework of national citizenship which has traditionally served to indicate membership of a socio-political community with associated rights and obligations has not necessarily caught up or reflected the new lived reality of mobility and diversity. This contributory understanding of such citizenship approaches has been enshrined by the now outdated Westphalian conception of the nation-state and its tendency to govern social relations within fixed and defined territorial borders.

The contemporary challenge in our increasingly globalised world, however, is that many individuals including migrants, asylum seekers, people from indigenous backgrounds and other categories of marginalised groups

vii

and individuals are experiencing new forms of systematic oppression and exclusion. These new manifestations of oppression hegemonic state policies are impacting negatively on struggles and aspirations for cultural rights, socio-economic equality and active political participation.

It is a fact that some Western Governments have adopted various social policies to deal with rising levels of diversity ranging from multiculturalism to national citizenship frameworks. Yet, a common feature across these state-centric policies has been that ethnic and other minority groups have largely been constructed as collectives representing reified and essentialised cultures that needed to adapt and in some cases gradually assimilate within dominant mainstream cultural norms. And nowhere are these struggles and contestations more apparent that the situation of the Romani people across Europe and in particular in Italy. Armillei's book is a timely and important intervention that brings fresh empirical evidence on how state policies have deliberately contributed to the social political exclusion of the Romanies, who find themselves today at once spatially segregated and socially marginalised.

What is perhaps most disturbing about the findings of Armillei's research is how racist state policies deliberately work towards rendering the already deplorable conditions within the Romani urban camps even more inhumane and inhospitable. Ultimately, these practices highlight not only institutional and systematic racism, but more worryingly the failure of democratic ethos at various levels of governance. The book should not be viewed as simply about the plight of the Romani people in Italy and across Europe. Rather, it offers hope for resistance politics, hope for civil society activism and hope for the emerging global discourse on ethical solidarity and intercultural understanding.

UNESCO Chair, Cultural Diversity   Fethi Mansouri
and Social Justice, Alfred Deakin Institute
for Citizenship and Globalisation, Deakin University
Australia

Acknowledgements

This book draws on research supported by a Chancellor's Research Scholarship offered by the Swinburne University of Technology. Without this financial support, it would have been impossible to accomplish.

I would like to express my deepest gratitude to my supervisors, Lorenzo Veracini, Michael Leach and Linda Briskman, for their invaluable guidance during the drafting of my PhD dissertation, on which this book is based.

The completion of this undertaking would not have been possible without the participation and assistance of so many people whose names may not all be enumerated. Their contributions are sincerely appreciated and gratefully acknowledged. However, I would like to express my deepest appreciation and indebtedness particularly to the following:

All the people and interviewees I have met during my fieldwork in Italy. In particular, I owe a big debt of gratitude to Nazzareno Guarnieri, Carlo Stasolla, Marco Brazzoduro and Nicolae Gheorghe.

Robin Carballido, Jeff Bartram and Michele Giordano for their support in copyediting the final manuscript.

x   Acknowledgements

My parents, my sweet little sisters Manuela, Silvia and Sara, my aunties Angela and Irene, and my friends, who in one way or another shared their support, whether morally, financially and physically.

Special thanks go to Zsofia Samu. Without you I would have not been able to cope with the loss of my mum and dad. You are an angel!

Riccardo Armillei

Contents

1 Inside *campi nomadi*: The Italian Approach to the Global
Shanty Town Development 1

2 The Institutional and Spatial Segregation of Romanies
in Italy 41

3 The Paradoxes of the Italian Approach Towards
the Romani People 79

4 The Business of the Camps During the 'Nomad
Emergency' 113

5 Between Self-Determination and 'Collective-Identity
Closure' 161

6 Conclusions 209

Bibliography 225

Index 263

Acronyms and Abbreviations

AIZO	Associazione Italiana Zingari Oggi (Italian Association Gypsies Today)
ASGI	Associazione per gli Studi Giuridici sull'Immigrazione (Association for Juridical Studies on Immigration)
CDS	Casa dei Diritti Sociali (House of Social Rights)
CERD	Committee on the Elimination of Racial Discrimination
CIR	Consiglio Italiano per i Rifugiati (Italian Council for Refugees)
CoE	Council of Europe
COHRE	Centre on Housing Rights and Evictions
CRI	Croce Rossa Italiana (Italian Red Cross)
CSOs	Civil Society Organisations
DAST	Document Authorising Temporary Stay
ECRI	European Commission against Racism and Intolerance
ERRC	European Roma Rights Centre
ERTF	European Roma and Travellers Forum
EU	European Union
FRA	European Union Agency for Fundamental Rights
IFRC	International Federation of Red Cross and Red Crescent Societies
IRU	International Romani Union
ISMU	Fondazione Iniziative e Studi sulla Multietnicità (Foundation for Initiatives and Studies on Multi-Ethnicity)
ISTAT	Istituto Nazionale di Statistica (National Institute for Statistics)
MIUR	Ministero dell'Istruzione, dell'Universita e della Ricerca (Ministry of Education, Universities and Research)

xiv Acronyms and Abbreviations

NFP	National Focal Point
ODIHR	Office for Democratic Institutions and Human Rights
OSCAD	Observatory for Security against Acts of Discrimination
OSCE	Organisation for Security and Co-operation in Europe
PON	National Operational Program
RAXEN	EU Commission's Network of National Focal Points
RSC	Roma, Sinti and Camminanti communities
SCPPHR	Commissione straordinaria per la tutela e la promozione dei diritti umani (Special Commission for the Protection and Promotion of Human Rights)
UN	United Nations
UNAR	Ufficio Nazionale Antidiscriminazioni Razziali (National Office against Racial Discrimination)
UNHCR	United Nations High Commissioner for Refugees

1

Inside *campi nomadi*: The Italian Approach to the Global Shanty Town Development

Global 'Slummification', Romani People and the EU's Response

The development of urban slum areas is a global phenomenon and one of the major issues of the twenty-first century: a sad reflection of the dire living conditions and sense of abandonment experienced by its inhabitants. Aggravated by the global economic crisis, the foci of poverty have been shifting to cities, with the formation of 'shanty towns' representing an evident sign of this process (Gago-Cortés and Novo-Corti 2015: 2). According to the UN-Habitat (2016), urban areas around the world are facing greater challenges (demographic, environmental, economic, social and spatial) than ever before, largely due to a continuous rural–urban migration. Today, more than a half (54 per cent) of the world's population lives in urban areas, and this is a figure that is expected to grow larger by 2030. While cities keep sprawling, they have also faced growing difficulties integrating migrants and refugees. Unable to keep up with the growing demand, particularly from the neediest, the dominant model of urbanisation has generated multiple forms of inequality, exclusion and deprivation, with spatial inequalities and divided cities as an unwelcome side effect (e.g. gated communities and slum areas).

© The Author(s) 2018

R. Armillei, *The 'Camps System' in Italy*, Mapping Global Racisms,
https://doi.org/10.1007/978-3-319-76318-7_1

1

Already in 2001, UN-Habitat had estimated that '924 million people, or 31.6 percent of the total urban population in the world, lived in slums' (UN-Habitat 2016: 13). The absolute number of slum dwellers has continued to increase since then, with one in eight people across the world today, living in areas whose defining characteristics are their 'precarious legality and almost non-existent level of services such as community facilities, potable water, and waste removal' (ibid.). Though this is clearly a phenomenon affecting the developing world, the rising presence of housing deprivation can be observed in the developed world as well (58). In Europe, for instance, migrant slums sprang up in some of the major capital cities (Madrid and Paris, just to name a few). *Canada Real Galiana*, only a 15-minute drive from the centre of Madrid, is believed to be Europe's largest shanty town, with around 30,000 people (many from North Africa or Eastern Europe) living here illegally (Keller 2016). In Paris, the derelict *Petite Ceinture* railway, once known for its hipster cafe and beer garden, is now home to a squatter camp. Home to an estimated population of 350 people (mainly Romanies from Romania and Bulgaria), it also houses refugees from the Middle East (Azadé 2016).

With an estimated population of 10–12 million, the Romani people make up Europe's largest ethnic minority (European Union Agency for Fundamental Rights [FRA] 2017a). They have been subjected to social exclusion and marginalisation for centuries and are still today one of the poorest and most discriminated against groups on the continent (e.g. securing access to health, education, employment and housing is extremely difficult). According to data collected by the EU Commission's network of National Focal Points (RAXEN), many Romani people live in informal settlements or unauthorised housing. As the Fundamental Rights Report 2017 shows, around 80 per cent of Romani people 'live below their country's at-risk-of-poverty threshold, one in three live in housing without tap water and one in 10 live in housing without electricity' (FRA 2017b: 18). People living in such conditions are also under the constant threat of forced evictions (Council of Europe [CoE] 2016). There are thus a number of obstacles that prevent Romanies from accessing basic goods and services, such as securing equal rights to housing, health care, education and work. In addition, 'throughout Europe, the Roma are poorly represented in political and administrative structures and face considerable difficulties in integrating into mainstream society' (Renzi 2010: 40).

In the last few decades, European institutions have increasingly raised their concern about the situation of Romani communities throughout the continent. The emergence of this new interest can be better understood if placed within the perspective of two major events: the collapse of the Eastern European Communist regimes in 1989 and, later, the eastward enlargement of the European Union (EU). The presence of a large Romani population in Central and Eastern Europe, whose lived environment was one of severe discrimination and marginalisation, was perceived with fear by the more prosperous Western European countries. They feared being 'invaded' by poor and desperate waves of Romani migrants, whose situation had worsened after the economic and political collapse of the former Soviet bloc (Bartlett et al. 2011). The situation of the Romani minority groups ceased to be treated as a mere 'external affair' (Pogány 2004: 2): this increased its political salience within the European agenda. With the aim of creating a new and united community, the EU became a fertile ground for the promotion of human rights.

Clearly, the plight of Europe's biggest and most marginalised ethnic minority group could no longer be ignored. Throughout the process of consolidation of the EU and of its institutions and mechanisms, Romani-related issues were now considered to be one of its major concerns, and improvement of Romani living conditions became a pre-requisite for joining the EU (Rövid 2011). In 2008, the *European Platform for Roma Inclusion* was launched during the first *European Roma Summit* held in Brussels (European Commission 2013). A year later, the *Ten Common Basic Principles on Roma Inclusion* was adopted as a tool for both policy-makers and practitioners managing programmes and projects designed to support Romani inclusion (European Commission 2009). In 2011, the European Commission introduced the *EU Framework for National Roma Integration Strategies up to 2020* aimed at improving the economic and social situation of this minority through the implementation of 'common European goals'. This communiqué marked a joint effort by European institutions and EU member states to achieve by 2020, the social inclusion and integration of Romani people by developing targeted measures in four crucial areas: education, employment, health care and housing (European Commission 2011: 4–7).

Nevertheless, many Romani advocates have strongly criticised this strategy, because it neither introduced real measures to combat a widespread anti-Romani sentiment nor did it involve the Romani communities themselves in the elaboration of inclusion policies directed specifically towards these people (European Public Health Alliance 2011). A critical aspect of the new EU approach is that social inclusion would merely imply a 'top-down process'. Drawing on Musgrave and Bradshaw's work (2014), EU institutions continue to use a model, the outcomes of which view inclusion as 'assimilation' to a mainstream: 'Decisions about what an individual can be included in are made on this normative basis and are not negotiable by those who are to be included' (ibid.: 198). In a way, this conceptual change would seem to reflect the new global 'tendency to split societies and people into "included" and "excluded"' (Molero-Mesa and Jiménez-Lucena 2013: 13). Social inclusion-related issues point to complex contextual questions that researchers and policymakers should pay attention to. For example, who defines inclusion? And what does inclusion signify for those in different social and economic positions? (Wotherspoon and Hansen 2013: 34). These are questions that are generally ignored. In other words, instead of challenging the status quo and raising awareness as to how society might be made more inclusive, discourses of social inclusion/exclusion served to normalise and unquestioningly strengthen existing arrangements.

The Politics of the Romani People in Contemporary Italy

Romanies from Central and Eastern Europe have moved to and from Italy for centuries. The first settlements can be traced back to around the fourteenth century; part of migratory flows from South-Eastern Europe during the expansion of the Ottoman Empire into the Balkan region (Bellucci 2007). The Romanies in Italy represent a very small minority group. According to the most recent figures, between 120,000 and 180,000 Romani are living in Italy. This corresponds to 0.25 per cent of the national population. It is also estimated that 28,000 of them live in emergency housing conditions. This figure includes around 18,000 Romanies living in *villaggi della solidarietà/villaggi attrezzati*[1] (solidarity/equipped villages; Associazione 21 Luglio 2016). In the city of Rome alone, 9 of these institutional camps host 4500 Romanies (Comune di Roma 2017), while 1145 live in 11 'tolerated' areas (La Stampa 2017). But there are also around 200 small and medium 'illegal' camps scattered throughout the city (Fiaschetti 2017). Generally speaking, there are no precise data on Italy's Romanies. One reason for this is that Romanies usually adopt mimetic strategies to better assimilate to the rest of the population, thus reducing the risk of potential discrimination (Commissione straordinaria per la tutela e la promozione dei diritti umani [SCPPHR] 2011). This attitude has generated a knowledge gap about Romanies. Another important reason for the imprecision of data on the Romani is that no country in Europe, except for Britain and Ireland, gathers ethnic data (Simon 2012).

As in the rest of Europe, where nomadism was considered an element of asociality to be suppressed through policies of forced 'sedentarisation' (Silverman 1995: 8), in Italy Romanies were 'treated as a public danger and subjected to bans throughout the Italian peninsula' (Clough Marinaro 2009: 271). The height of these practices of exclusion and marginalisation was reached under the Fascist regime in the 1940s. Only from the 1970s, did the Italian Government start to experiment with new forms of cultural protection explicitly directed at the Romani communities. These approaches were based on the premise that Romanies were a nomadic people and their supposed nomadism was addressed as a problem (Bravi and Sigona 2006). It is in this period that the modern 'camps strategy' can be seen in its embryonic stage, soon to give birth to the stereotypical association of Romanies and camps. At the same time, at the end of the economic and urban boom of the 1950s and 1960s, Italy had moved from being a net exporter of migrants to a net importer (Bonifazi et al. 2009). The growing economic prosperity which characterised those years saw also the emergence of new problems such as illegal

---

[1] 'Solidarity Villages' can be described as camp structures built by public institutions on 'the military camp model, with residents allotted a numbered place with a caravan or, sometimes, a prefabricated container' (Sigona 2005: 748). These facilities are commonly fenced, equipped with video surveillance and patrolled by security officers at the entrance and inside the camp. There is also a second type of institutional camp, *Centro di accoglienza* (refuge shelter), which accommodate evicted Romanies and provide a form of temporary assistance similar to the Solidarity Villages. At the end of 2016, three of these shelters were still active in Italy (Associazione 21 Luglio 2016).

immigration and the 'racialisation' of politics, a consequence of the clash between an increasingly diverse population and the monocultural dominant discourse (Allievi 2010). Attracted by the prospect of permanently settling in Italy, there were new waves of Romani immigrants (mainly from the Balkans).

Their arrival took place at different stages. This became more significant especially at the time of the dissolution of the former Yugoslavia and later of the EU enlargements, as it compromised the very delicate balance that over the centuries well-established Romani communities had been trying to create with non-Romani people (Fiorucci 2010). Within this context, the trend to represent Romanies through the conceptual prism of cultural, political and economic 'insecurity' was exacerbated in 2008, after a number of high-profile crimes allegedly committed by people of Romani ethnicity (Amnesty International 2012b). In clear continuity with previous left-wing Governments (Clough Marinaro 2009; Lunaria 2011), the Berlusconi right-wing coalition implemented an extraordinary measure, the so-called *Emergenza Nomadi* (Nomad Emergency). This state of emergency aimed to solve an issue that had been categorised in the 1970s as the *Problema Nomadi* (nomad problem) (Ministero dell'Interno 2006: 16). Now it was described and handled as a 'natural disaster' (Fiorucci 2010: 34). Being mainly directed against the Romani 'camp inhabitants/dwellers', this approach fuelled widespread racism against them, while reinforcing the stereotypical binomials 'nomad/foreign' and 'Romani/crime'.

Although in November 2011, the 'emergency' was eventually declared 'unfounded and unsubstantiated' by the Italian Council of State (Amnesty International 2012a: 8), in February 2012 a new Government, led by Mario Monti, had been trying to re-endorse the same decree that in May 2008 had introduced the intervention (Associazione 21 Luglio, Associazione per gli Studi Giuridici sull'Immigrazione [ASGI], Amnesty International, Human Rights Watch, & Open Society Justice 2012). Paradoxically, the Monti Government had also launched a *National Strategy for the Inclusion of Roma, Sinti and Camminanti Communities* (throughout the book I will simply refer to it as the 'National Strategy'). As stated by the *Ufficio Nazionale Antidiscriminazioni Razziali* (the National Office against Racial Discrimination, also known by its acronym UNAR), which is the relevant National Focal Point (NFP) designated for the elaboration and co-ordination of this strategy, one of its aims was 'to definitively overcome the emergency phase, which had characterised the past years' (UNAR 2014: 3). On May 2, 2013, the Court of Cassation, Italy's highest court, rejected the Government's appeal against the Council of State's finding from November 2011, thus upholding the unlawfulness of the *Emergenza Nomadi* (European Roma Rights Centre [ERRC] 2013).

Nevertheless, since then, political and ideological attacks on Romani people have remained at frightening levels, 'with several politicians openly supporting policies of segregation in housing and education' (European Commission 2016: 5). Most importantly, an emergency approach, based on 'camps policy' and forced evictions, is still in place today. In addition, as conveyed in a recent report issued by the ERRC (2017: 4), 'no national desegregation plans have been drawn up', with housing, employment, education and health projects being inadequate to the challenge of achieving the authentic inclusion of Romanies, as the 'National Strategy' prescribes. This document surely signified an unprecedented attempt at the inclusion of these minority groups. Despite the official pledge to turn over a new leaf in its stance on social inclusion, Italy's own strategy towards Romani people 'proved a short-lived hope' (Amnesty International et al. 2016: 2). Instead of building capacity and autonomy for this minority groups, Italian institutions (and their subcontracted Third Sector organisations) keep adopting an approach that produces and entrenches the exact opposite effect. While the 'State of emergency' aggravated the already poor living conditions of the Romani population, the 'National Strategy' reconfirmed a well-established top-down Government-knows-best attitude that dismissed the notion of directly involving the 'target group' itself in any policy deliberations.

Why a Book on the 'Nomad Camps' in Italy?

The Romani experience in Italy constitutes a case unique in the European context, as Italy was until recently the only country, whose official policy was to institutionalise its Romani population inside urban 'ghettos'

(ERRC 2000; Clough Marinaro 2009).[2] Analysing this context reveals a series of anomalies resulting from the simultaneous interplay of several agencies. The growing attention to Romani-related issues, both nationally and internationally, led to the establishment of a complex system that a range of actors benefitted from private and public, left- and right-wing and Romanies and non-Romanies. Together with a political vacuum, the Romani issue is commonly ascribed to an institutional mechanism of repression. In the course of this book I will argue that the current situation of the Romanies has been created by a mix of interrelated factors, including a highly politicised issue characterised by bipartisan convergence; the Third Sector's (or 'civil society' organisations [CSOs]) dependence on welfare and an incapacity to act in the interests of its Romani beneficiaries; and, finally, a failure to understand the attitude of the Romani people as an act of 'resistance', in the sense that they have learned to take advantage of their marginal conditions.

By studying the case of the Romani people, this book aims to answer the following two major questions:

1. What role has the Italian Government and its subcontracted CSOs played in marginalising and disempowering Romanies?
2. Should Romanies be construed as victims or agents in representation of the 'Romani problem' in Italy?

The main argument is that the decision to declare a 'state of emergency', which defined Romanies as 'nomads' and a 'natural disaster' (Fiorucci 2010: 34), was used by the Government merely as a way to acquire more power and take an authoritarian approach towards Romani individuals and communities. The declaration of the 'Nomad Emergency', in fact, brought a reinforcement of the security measures. Besides which, the 'state of exception' has gradually become the rule, as posited by Agamben (1998), serving to cover a prolonged situation of institutional abandonment and

---

[2] At the beginning of the 2000s, similar institutional camps (called villages d'insertion or 'inclusion villages') have been endorsed by French local Governments. Although they are officially aimed at all marginalised populations, regardless of their ethnicity (Délégation Interministérielle à l'hébergement et à l'accès au lodgement, 2011), these 'Urban and Social Organisation Programs' (Maitrises D'œuvre Urbaine et Sociale) are currently inhabited by Romani migrants only (Doytcheva 2016).

neglect. This in turn became the pretext for implementing emergency measures—disproportionate to the severity of the threat—while blaming the Romanies themselves. The contemporaneous commitment of the Italian Government to a 'National Strategy' for improving Romani living conditions not only failed to empower them, it instead had the opposite effect.

This book will deliver a new perspective on the Romani issue by arguing that the 'camp' is a tool not only for institutional control and segregation but also for 'resistance', as well as a huge business in which everyone plays their part. The experience of the Romani people in the city of Rome demonstrates a very complex set of relationships in what I termed the 'camps system'. This definition differs substantially from the one used by Associazione 21 Luglio, one of the leading advocacy organisations in Rome. According to them, this system is a segregational practice which aims to 'manage and control Romani people within institutional settlements' (Scutellà 2016). The use I make of this term has a broader connotation and consequences, implying a more composite make-up. Here different agents (local authorities, Third Sector organisations and the Romanies themselves) have been involved, to differing degrees, in reifying the marginalised position of this minority. The in-depth analysis of this specific socio-political context shows the existence of a democratic deficit in the way these stakeholders operate and co-operate with each other: competition and antagonisms, corruption and lack of transparency, and accountability and inefficiencies—these have all contributed over the years to producing and maintaining the present living conditions of the Romani people.

By providing a clearer picture of the complex system that surrounds Romani-related issues in Italy, this book will suggest possible courses of interventions that could make existing policy initiatives more effective. At the same time, the findings of this study can deepen our understanding of similar liminal situations, particularly where the 'slummification' of urban areas can potentially be turned into a lucrative business. The exploitation of the Romanies and immigrants in Italy is part of a global trend within the 'poverty aid system', where the constant input of the giver and the constant poverty of the poor create a vicious cycle which is more about profit, than solving the problem (Otieno 2015). The camps are a particular form of 'inclusion sites' which are characteristic of Italy but the topics under discussion are of much wider importance. Presenting and analysing the Italian experience can shed light on processes which are starting to emerge in other member states of the EU. Moreover, issues relating to the management of cultural diversity, combating discrimination/exclusion and addressing xenophobia as a consequence of European Unification are some of the topical areas where this book can make a contribution.

The Governance of the 'Camps System' in Rome

The alarming proliferation of *campi nomadi* in Italy intensifies the urgency of analysing their internal mechanisms and the complex relationships between the parties involved in them. Thus, this study attempts to delineate a novel way of understanding the relationship between 'camp-dwellers', Government agencies and CSOs, whose interactions produced and reified the 'camps system'. The book is focused on the *campi nomadi* in the city of Rome, particularly the institutional ones, also known as 'solidarity villages', and the social exclusion of their inhabitants. My investigation is placed within the context of the recent governmental implementation of the 'Nomad Emergency' and the 'National Strategy'. A range of theoretical frameworks have been drawn upon that were useful in making sense of the interview material, participant observation and documents collected. Many social scientists have dealt with issues of citizenship rights, irregular migration, ethnicity, social exclusion, poverty and sovereign power. Their contributions have been significant for my study, supporting me in the construction of an analytical framework for interpreting the contemporary conditions of Romanies in Italy. Yet, the lack of a synthetic discussion on the phenomena connected to the emergence and maintenance of this form of social exclusion institution inspired the making of this book.

This study contends that the present conditions of the Romanies in Italy and their liminal status put them at the nexus of differing theoretical interpretations. To arrive at an adequate appreciation of this nexus, the three components of the 'camps system' have been analysed separately. This approach helped to pinpoint how they have combined to produce a hegemonic perspective on Romani issues, which yields a simplistic binary interpretation of a complex and dynamic phenomenon: Romanies are generally viewed as either victims or threats, narrowing the range of responses to charity or hostility. In this context, current research stands on the side of the subjugated and against a hierarchy which produces and reproduces injustice. Only in recent years, has a growing awareness regarding the agency of the camps' inhabitants re-emerged. This was after a period in which the encamped life of these individuals was at times associated with Agamben's (1998) notion of 'bare life' and Foucault's (1977) concept of 'biopolitics', stressing the importance of sovereign agencies in producing the exceptionality of the camp space and its population. Nevertheless, scholars have not yet analysed the camps as 'resistance sites' and 'all-inclusive systems' where interacting and interdependent agents form an integrated whole.

This research thus aims to uncover the hidden mechanism underlying the 'camps system', which involves a host of different stakeholders, Romani individuals included. In order to promote a better understanding of its functioning, I have employed a multitheoretical framework to model multiple facets for each of its constituents. According to scholars who have adopted this approach (e.g. Berman 2013; Mills and Bettis 2015), by drawing together the multiple theories involved in the reality under investigation, it will be possible to produce a broader conceptualisation of human behaviours within the social environment of the 'camps system'. Each agent has, in fact, its own effect on the reification of this mechanism and can be conceptualised differently, but their combination is allowed to form a unified and all-encompassing theoretical framework. After having analysed each subject separately, I have focused my attention on the multiple relationships existing between them. Another way to think about this process is to consider the 'nomad camp' at the conjunction of different type of discourses. This multilayered framework will provide a basis for theorising (Smyth 2004, cited in Berman 2013) and for generating new knowledge. This way the theory, as Wexler (1992, cited in Mills and Bettis 2015: 116) argued, will come out as 'a "fusion of horizons" between the elements of the analytical fields'.

The first layer of my analysis (Chaps. 1 and 2) looks at the Government's approach towards Romani communities. In this part, I outline the situation of the Romani 'camp-dwellers' in Rome by looking at current theories on the use of 'emergency' as a frame for political action (e.g. Honig 2009, 2014; Sigona 2011; Walters 2011; van Baar 2014, 2015). In doing so, this study also offers important analyses of the historical, racial and legal issues surrounding the treatment of this population. The second layer (Chap. 4) is dedicated to understanding the Third Sector's role in the 'camps system'. Here I use theories on institutional isomorphism (resource dependence theory and institutional theory; Di Maggio and Powell 1991) to explain how increasing rationalisation and bureaucratisation has transformed these organisations in ways that replicate the State they criticise. In the context of competitive marketplaces, CSOs (chiefly those contracted by Government to work inside institutional camps) implemented coercive institutionalised models. Finally, the third layer of my work (Chap. 5) is devoted to the Romanies living in the camps. Foucault's writing (1977, 1990), in particular, has been used to interpret the fieldwork data collected from encamped communities. This helps to understand the Romanies' response to the *politica dei campi* (camps policy) as an act of 'resistance'. While exclusionary policies have been implemented by the Government, with indirect complicity of its subcontracted agents, thus paralysing any possibility of dialogue with Romani 'camp-dwellers', these people were not mere voiceless spectators.

The Italian Government

Instead of building capacity and autonomy among the Romani minority groups, the Italian institutions chose to adopt an approach that produced and replicated the opposite effect, implementing policies which were completely centred on the institutionalisation of the Romanies in 'camps' (Piasere 1985; Sigona 2002, 2005, 2009). A number of scholars have already criticised this strategy, arguing that the situation of the Romanies (both locally and nationally) is an issue characterised by political bipartisanship. Work by Clough Marinaro (2003, 2009, 2014, 2015), Daniele (2010, 2011a, b) and Solimene (2013), for instance, specifically focussed on the city of Rome. But scholarly papers by Italian academics based in other cities have also pointed out the same ambiguity of the politics on Romanies: Bontempelli (2006, 2012) in Pisa; Brunello (1996) documenting numerous cases of this kind in Milan, Padua, Florence and Rome; Lintner (2014) in Bolzano; Peró (1999, 2007) in Bologna; Picker (2010, 2011) in Tuscany and nationally; Saletti-Salza (2003) in Turin; Sigona (2005, 2008, 2011) in Naples and nationally; and Solimano and Mori (2000) in Florence to name a few.

'Camp-dwellers' and *campi nomadi* can be understood as liminal subjects and spaces, whose relationship with institutions, Third Sector and mainstream society is best characterised by Agamben's (1998) notion of 'inclusive exclusion': Romanies are neither included nor absolutely excluded. They have a distinctive place within Italian society. By spending millions of euros every year on Romani-related issues, this has become a huge business involving hundreds of employees, in public and private sectors alike (Armillei 2014). Consequently, instead of merely thinking about 'Othering', marginalisation or exclusion, my analysis comes to grips with the approach adopted by Italian institutions in terms of 'inclusive exclusion'. On the one hand, the Government invests significant sums in supposed 'inclusion' projects; on the other, it keeps promoting the 'camps policy', forced evictions and emergency measures. Using Cemlyn and Briskman's (2002: 49) definition of 'dyswelfare', it can be argued that service providers failed 'to understand, respect and respond to different cultural values, lifestyles and strengths', which in turn had damaging impacts on the Romanies. Zygmunt Bauman's (2007) interpretation of modernity contends that the authorities have consigned Romanies to the status of 'human waste', excluded from competing in the job market and relegated to marginalised areas.

Hannah Arendt's (1962) analysis of the legal and political paradoxes of the Rights of Man can help to frame the presence of people forced to live within a society but with no recognised right of belonging. The essence of superfluity explained by Arendt in the closing pages of *The Origins of Totalitarianism* equates with the living conditions of Romanies in camps and forms a continuing theoretical thread throughout the thesis. The Romani/'abjected' is never utterly irrelevant or absolutely useless and maintains a crucial relationship with the society/'abjector'. It constitutes the antithetical 'Other' in relation to which the abjector self is defined. The perception of Romanies as a threat was not caused by their presence or by their arrival from foreign shores, but was actively fostered by the Government through a process of dehumanising each Romani in society's midst. As Hepworth (2012) argued, they are constructed as 'permanent migrants', which normalise their confinement in the abject space of the 'nomad camp'. In this context, they become 'abjects', neither subjects nor objects, living 'inexistent states of transient permanence' (Isin and Rygiel 2007: 198). It was the institutional immobility and indifference to their living conditions that turned the Romanies into *popoli delle discariche* (peoples of the rubbish dumps) (Piasere 2005). Decay and abandonment, which by now constitute a common feature in these encampments, then created the 'emergency' and the pretext for extraordinary measures.

The 'Nomad Emergency' and 'National Strategy' represent the clearest examples of the contradictory approach adopted by public institutions. The Italian Government, responding to an EU request, introduced several measures to tackle the causes of marginalisation and social exclusion of Romanies. Their condition was defined as a 'humanitarian emergency' (Sigona 2009: 277) and a 'humanitarian problem' (Clough Marinaro and Daniele 2011: 621), conceptualisations which match with what Walters (2011: 138) calls the 'emergence of the humanitarian border'. The humanitarian construction of the measures towards the Romanies thus turned them into something acceptable within strategies of control. This goes well together with van Baar's (2014) 'reasonable anti-Gypsyism'. In other words, the belief that they would otherwise be involved in 'illegal' practices that could harm 'our' rights and freedoms justifies a differential treatment of the Romanies (van Baar 2015). The implementation of these state policies, though, was in the end rather ineffective or even counterproductive. The first type of intervention portrayed Romani issues merely as a security matter. This kept reviving old stereotypes, legitimising discriminatory and even violent, actions against them. The second type, which aimed at transcending the emergency phase and finding valid alternatives to the 'camps policy', neither had any influence over institutional attitudes nor did it increase the involvement of Romani representative bodies.

Agamben's (1998) work is again useful here when it comes to interpreting Government strategy. Declaring a state of emergency not only tightened the security measures, but the 'state of exception' has gradually become the norm. Sigona (2005) used the expression of 'permanent emergency', as a new political category to describe it. Clough Marinaro (2009: 270–271), instead, portrayed the Romanies as forced into a condition of 'perpetual nomadic outsiderness', which justified the constant construction of a state of emergency. At the same time, 'nomad camps' became spaces suspended in a state of 'permanent temporaneity' (Clough Marinaro 2015: 370). In other words, the 'emergency' was designed to contain a problem rather than to solve it definitively, and in so doing it established a permanent practice of exclusion and marginalisation. This involves a sovereign decision to suspend the law and Agamben here follows Carl Schmitt (2005) in declaring that this power places the sovereign at once inside and outside the legal order. As Agamben further notes, through the state of exception, the sovereign has created and guaranteed the situation that the law needed for its own validity. The fact that in May 2013 the Italian Supreme Court declared the *Emergenza Nomadi* unlawful, but did not eliminate emergency approaches towards the Romanies is a sign of that.

Honig's work (2009, 2014) helps to make this point much clearer, reminding us that emergencies are more common than we think. In this context, by 'de-exceptionalising the exception', she argues that the camps stop being exceptions to the legal–political normality of liberal democracy, and become 'significant markers of the fundamentally postpolitical and biopolitical condition of late modernity's normality/emergency' (Honig 2014: 46–47). In addition, as Honig (2009) further states, political emergencies are not just the result of sovereign state power but reflect and constitute the character of a people. Sovereignty, in fact, is only effectual if there is popular support for the decision. In fact, mainstream society's negative perception of migrants provides an adequate back-up to the implementation of repressive measures. According to a recent survey conducted by Istituto per gli Studi di Politica Internazionale (2015), 67 per cent of the people interviewed shared the opinion that immigrants pose a threat to national security. Only a small minority of the respondents (2 per cent) considers immigration as a resource for the country. Another study confirms the existence of a widespread anti-immigration sentiment in Italy (Eumetra Monterosa 2016).

'Terzo Settore'/Third Sector/CSOs

Distinct from the 'business or private sector' (market) and the 'public sector' (State), 'civil society'—*Terzo Settore* (Third Sector)[3] the definition commonly adopted within the Italian context—it may also be understood as an 'intermediate space of society' (Patanè 2003: 2). It constitutes a complex system, composed of a wide range of actors from various organisational and juridical settings 'that seek to bring about positive social and environmental change' (United Nations Global Compact 2010: 10). It is today a highly debated concept which 'has many different definitions and interpretations spanning across time' (Boose 2012: 310). The European roots of this term are traceable to the late eighteenth century and early nineteenth century. According to Keane (2010: 461), it is particularly during the industrial revolution period 1750–1850 that

> the traditional language of civil society (*societas civilis*), which had until then referred to a peaceful political order governed by law, underwent a profound transformation. Contrasted with government, civil society meant a realm of social life – market exchanges, charitable groups, clubs and voluntary associations, independent churches and publishing houses – institutionally separated from territorial state institutions. This is the sense in which civil society is still understood today.

For a long period of time, from 1850 up until the last few decades, the concept disappeared from political theory, becoming 'arcane'. In the 1980s, though, 'civil society' was revitalised 'by the Polish opposition movement and the subsequent wave of democratisation around the world' (Howard 2010: 186). It is particularly during the last couple of decades that we can attest to an exponential growth of this sector. The definition of 'civil society' adopted by the World Bank (2013), which was developed by a number of leading research centres, refers to

---

[3] Because of its specificity, the Third Sector 'is always spelt with capital letters' (FrancoAngeli 2011: 8). Throughout the book when referring to Third Sector organisations I will also use the acronym CSOs.

the wide array of non-governmental and not-for-profit organisations that have a presence in public life, expressing the interests and values of their members or others, based on ethical, cultural, political, scientific, religious or philanthropic considerations. Civil Society Organisations (CSOs) therefore refer to a wide of array of organisations: community groups, non-governmental organisations (NGOs), labour unions, indigenous groups, charitable organisations, faith-based organisations, professional associations, and foundations. (para. 5)

Until recently, the Third Sector was 'relatively unknown to a large share of the population, to the media and probably to the legislator himself' (Barbetta 2000: 136), and it still enjoys no accepted definition in the Italian legal system (Benvenuti and Martini 2017). According to the latest census, released by the Italian National Institute for Statistics in 2011 ([ISTAT] 2016), the Third Sector counts 301,191 non-profit institutions. This represents an increase of 28 per cent compared to that of the 2001 census. It is a sector which employs more than 681,000 workers, producing 4 per cent of the Italian gross domestic product (GDP) (La Repubblica 2017). In the last two decades neither the 'State' nor the 'market' has coped with changes in the demographic structure, which has generated demands for new services (Barbetta 2000). This can explain the Third Sector organisations springing up in response to these demands (which usually involved health care, educational, recreational and cultural services) coming mainly from local public authorities but also, to some extent, from private citizens.

Rossi (2010: 218) uses the expression 'social emergencies' when referring to these different issues. This definition relates more closely to the main feature of the Italian approach to collective needs and public services, as well as to the topic of this research project. During the 1990s, the rise of what has been defined as a 'welfare mix' brought about not only greater involvement of non-profit organisations in welfare politics, but also the establishment of informal arrangements between public authorities and CSOs which were mediated by political patronage (Ranci 1994: 247). Despite the fact that these organisations are contracted by local Governments through a system of public bidding which in the 2000s became more transparent (Patanè 2003), a proportion of public procurement notices continues to conceal the existence of special agreements rooted in political patronage (Fazzi 2011; Springhetti 2009; Stasolla 2017). More recently, for instance, a police inquiry known as *Mafia Capitale* (capital mafia) revealed a series of anomalies resulting from the simultaneous interplay of Government agencies and CSOs, a 'mutual accommodation system' as Ranci (2015: 2313) would define it.

The employment of the institutional theory helps to highlight how this tendency within the non-profit sector is particularly evident when there is funding dependence from the Government (Townley 1997), which is at times the most important source of income (Anheier and Salamon 2006). In the case of the subcontracted agents working within 'nomad camps', a dichotomous behaviour resulted from the constraining influences of isomorphic mechanisms: on the one hand, contestation of Government policies, and on the other hand, compliance with Government requirements. In other words, CSOs are subject to coercive institutionalised models, in the sense that their choices are limited by external pressures (Verbruggen et al. 2011). At the present time, there is no study specifically focusing on the controversial relationship between Third Sector and the 'nomad camps'; this research sheds light on the ways in which they operated. More in general, although the Italian Third Sector constitutes the driving force of welfare development and social change, there is still very little empirical evidence regarding how innovative they are (Fazzi 2011). There is rather evidence of the impact of public policies on Third Sector's internal dynamics (Vitale and Caruso 2009).

Because of the financial and economic crisis of the last decade in particular, public resources towards the social sector have been constantly decreasing at the expense of service quality. This had direct repercussions for Third Sector organisations, since local institutions kept outsourcing their work to them. For instance, in 2007, almost 50 per cent of municipal expenditure for social services was subcontracted externally (Springhetti 2009: 39). By 2013, it was estimated that the Municipality of Rome spent more than €24 million running its 'camps policy'. A big part of this investment went to subcontracted CSOs, as shown in the report entitled 'Campi Nomadi s.p.a.' (Nomad Camps Ltd.) produced by Associazione 21 Luglio (2013: 66–67). Fazzi (2011) argues that this situation, together with increasing pressure towards cost rationalisation and growing competition (often as a consequence of lowest bid auction mechanisms; Springhetti, 2009), confirmed this about the Third Sector's dependency on public institutions, with isomorphic behaviours as side effects (Barbetta et al. 2003; Lori 2010; Federico 2012). The recent *Mafia Capitale* investigation provides the clearest example of the level of isomorphic degeneracy that can be reached by the non-profit sector (Conclave 2017). On that occasion, a number of key figures involved in the working of the local administration and Third sector management of 'nomad camps' in Rome were arrested for corruption (Teolato 2016).

In particular, forms of coercive and mimetic isomorphism could be observed during the fieldwork. For instance, both the CSOs dealing with Romani-related issues (mainly those involved in the 'camps system') and the city council departments seldom publish the results of their activities or try to generate a better understanding of the Romanies' plight. It was very difficult to gain a clear understanding of the way in which institutions and CSOs operate. A lack of official reports, and other studies detailing budgets, objectives, strategies and outcomes, made it impossible to evaluate these organisations scientifically, via the elaboration of empirical indices. Another problem was the extreme difficulty of making contact with them. Public offices either did not answer phone calls or did not reply to emails requesting formal interviews. In the rare instances when they made representatives available, they insisted on anonymity. On approaching the representatives of the organisations hired by councils to administer the *campi nomadi*, a similar situation emerged. It was generally unclear what public agencies and CSOs did, why they did it, how they did it and with what results for the Romani people. An atmosphere of secrecy and scarcity of material complicated the collection of data on the management of the camps.

The Romani 'Camp-Dwellers'

A number of authors have described the condition of the 'Romanies of the camps' in Italy as institutionalised within a system of 'patrol and surveillance', developing a sociology of camps which mainly draws on Agamben's work (1998). Rossi (2010: 3) conceptualised the encampments as physical spaces where Roma were 'forced to live'. Bravi and Sigona (2006) analysed the camp as *non luogo* (no man's land), a place whose purpose was to confine the 'Other' and where individuals lost their sense of self. Ronald Lee (2002), a Canadian Romani, used the expression *Kalisferia*, which in Romanes (the Romani language) means 'a place between Earth and Heaven', to describe the camp. Nicola (2011) termed it a 'total institution' that dehumanised Romanies, leaving them with no real opportunity to be included within Italian society. Nicola's intuition is a clear adaptation to the contemporary situation of the 'nomad camps' of Erving Goffman's 1961 work on totalitarian social systems. Clough Marinaro (2009), instead, described Romanies by often using Agamben's (1998) conceptualisation of the concentration camp, reduced to a 'bare life' upon which the state can inscribe its sovereign power without restriction.

The camp thus produces and replicates the idea of the Romanies as 'a "monstrous hybrid" of humanity and bestiality' (Todesco 2004; Piasere 2006, cited in Solimene 2013: 171) which in turn has served the purpose of justifying the implementation of exceptional measures. This study argues that the 'camp' is not just an exogenous institutional means of control and segregation but also an endogenous tool of 'resistance' to Government assimilative efforts, which produce self-ghettoisation as a side effect. As a consequence, my analysis sheds new light on the experience of 'camp-dwellers'. Over the years the *campi nomadi* have become a 'battlefield', an arena of conflict between Romanies and non-Romanies; not a productive space for conflict, as Solimano (1999) posited, from which valid solutions could emerge, but rather a site where 'oppressor' and 'oppressed' form and crystallise their own identities as homogenous entities, each in opposition to the other. The picture that emerges from the work of Asséo (1989), Piasere (2005) and Calabrò (2008), and more recently from Armillei (2016, 2017a, b), Clough Marinaro (2014, 2015), Sigona (2015), Daniele (2010, 2011a, b), Solimene (2013) and Maestri (2016, 2017), reminds us that Romanies should not be regarded merely as voiceless and passive victims of a hostile society.

By drawing upon Wacquant's (2011) analysis of the 'ghetto' as a Janus-faced institution of ethnoracial closure, Clough Marinaro (2015: 11) recognises Rome's institutional camps' function as a protective shield, which fosters 'active forms of identification, resistance, and mobilisation from within'. This is clearly in opposition to previous one-dimensional views of camps as isolating and confining spaces for an unwanted ethnic group (Clough Marinaro 2009). Sigona (2015) uses Levy's (2010) work on refugee camps in order to distance himself from Agamben's previous interpretation of the camp (Sigona 2005; Bravi and Sigona 2006). In this new work, Sigona (2015) acknowledges, more vigorously than in the past, the strategies of resistance, adaptation and contestation that 'camp-dwellers' develop in their everyday lives. Active resistance is also documented by Solimene (2013) in his work, which specifically refers to the Bosnian Xoraxané Romá living in illegal encampments.

Already by 1989 Asséo had coined the term *peuples-Résistances* (Resistance-peoples), which described how Romani people resisted assimilation and expressed what she calls an 'internal counter-hegemony'. Later, in 2011, Carrasco used the concept of 'warriors' to underline the fact that for centuries the Romanies resisted the 'colonisation of their way of life by any means necessary' (para. 6). A number of Romani intellectuals referred to the 'Romanies of the camps' in Rome as 'fighters' or 'warriors' (their contribution relies more on personal interviews and will be dealt specifically in Chap. 5). According to them, Romanies have learned to take advantage of their marginal condition. They have been exploiting the old 'Gypsy' stereotypes for their personal gain, mainly as a way of obtaining welfare aid, while simultaneously blaming others: Governments, CSOs and mainstream society. They basically occupy an 'in-between' position, partly imposed on them by outside forces and partly of their own volition. This also shows the Romanies' ability to simultaneously transcend and reinforce existing social and cultural boundaries (Marotta 2011: 193). At the same time, Rivera (2003) maintains that determination to resist is a sign of an isolationist and ethnocentric culture (Uzunova 2010).

This book places the analysis of the Romani issue in the context of a deeply rooted opposition between a majority group and a minority one. For the dominant culture the 'Other', *par excellence*, is the *Zingaro* (Italian term for 'Gypsy'), while for the Romanies this corresponds to the *Gadje*, which in Romanes stands for the entire non-Romani population (Benedetto 2011). Both these terms are derogatory and reflect a deep-rooted mutual antagonism between the groups. This manifests itself in each of them in two different, and opposing, ways: an assimilationist approach adopted by mainstream society and an attitude of refusal and rejection on the part of the minority group's members. The strong sense of cultural belonging and superiority on both sides of today's divide represents an obstacle to mutual understanding and positive dialogue. The existence of this separateness between Romani communities and mainstream societies led Gheorghe and Acton (2001: 55) to coin the term 'Gypsy archipelago'. On the one hand, this expression describes the diversity of various sub-groups and meta-groups, with their cultural, religious, linguistic and geographical affiliations. On the other, despite the great internal diversity that characterises Romani communities around the world, a unifying factor could be found in their blunt opposition to the 'Gadje world' (Fischer 2011).

Contradicting Agamben's categories, camp-dwelling Romanies have not been reduced to a 'bare life', which denotes a state of complete submission where the state can exert its sovereign power unfettered. The meeting of state and 'camp-dwellers' has not actually produced a definite seat of all powerful object and passive subject, respectively. Most writing on the topic emphasises the superior power of the State and its subcontracted CSOs, which in effect exercise sovereignty over the population and civic status of the 'Romanies of the camps'. However, this addresses only one aspect of the power relationship. Foucault's (1977, 1990) reconceptualising of power was particularly useful in understanding how power flowed through and between Romani individuals, groups, institutions and Third Sector agencies. The 'Romanies of the camps' and their 'Gadje' antagonists will not be presented as part of a 'powerful'/'powerless' dichotomy, where actors are fixed and polarised in restrictive categories. Using the work of Foucault, it is possible to see how 'subjugated' knowledge can challenge the strategy enacted by the dominant elite to establish, renew and maintain the hierarchy underpinning their privilege. Although relations between the State, the CSOs and the Romani residents are shaped by an unequal struggle, the opposition between 'rulers' and 'ruled' gives rise to a cycle of power and resistance. Using Foucault's (1990: 95) words: 'Where there is power, there is resistance'.

A 'Contentious Space'

The intertwined relationship between different agents involved in the 'camps system' can be summarised as follows: administrations carry out forced evictions, breed new camps and violate human rights, instead of implementing real social inclusion policies. At the same time, as recent studies have pointed out, there is evidence showing a 'mutual accommodation' structure of relation between the non-profit and the public sector. The main tendency, in fact, is for the State to vacate its responsibility to non-profit organisations, while exerting coercive pressure through stringent and non-transparent funding regulations. Resource dependence and coercive isomorphism have prevented the Third Sector from being fully independent. This situation also reveals the incapacity of both public institutions and the Third Sector to find a more constructive dialogue with Romani agencies. But, as well as the top-down approach adopted by the Government and CSOs, this study also confirms a recent trend to describe Romani communities living in camps as actively performing a bottom-up opposition. 'Nomad camps' should be thus conceived as contentious spaces, which generate both active and passive forms of 'resistance' (Barry 2006) whereby a plethora of players have antagonistic interactions with one another and with other players (Verhoeven and Bröer 2015). In line with Ramadan's (2013) interpretation of the 'camp as an assemblage' of people, institutions and organisations, the interplay of these heterogeneous components crystallised within the context of the 'camps system'. Just like in medicine, where a 'systemic disease' (an illness that affects multiple organs) requires a holistic treatment, the 'nomad camps' in Italy need to be analysed and handled as a whole. Only then, can we understand its complexity in relation to all aspects of their functioning. Implemented temporarily, camp space has become a permanent–temporary reality, a time-space of dislocation (a space displacement and a time of interruption) awaiting resolution which can come only through its dissolution (Ramadan 2013).

Research Design

This study consists of two interlocking phases: background analysis and empirical research.

During the first phase, the existing legislative and policy framework was mapped and analysed. This process is based mainly on different types of documentary research sources (McCulloch 2004). These include policy reports, committee papers, published treatises, newspapers and magazines. The background analysis was essential for the preliminary collection of contextual information. This included the following: analysis of EU level policy alongside national and local legislation; identification of research already carried out by international organisations, various agencies, national and local associations; examination of social inclusion projects (focusing on employment, education, health and housing) carried out by the local administration and Third Sector organisations, particularly in the city of Rome; and identification of the existing literature on interculturalism and the examination of Romani-oriented projects promoted by the city council and Third Sector organisations.

The second phase consisted of empirical research. Although fieldwork has been carried out using many of the classical tools that can be identified as ethnographic (such as the use of qualitative data, based on structured and semi-structured interviews, field notes, direct and participant observation of contexts), this did not lead to the production of classic ethnography as theorised by authors such as Malinowski (2002) or Geertz (2001). The object of this study was not specifically the Romani as a group or an ethnic community. Neither was my aim to take up full-time residence in a *campo nomade* in order to study its population. Rather, I sought to gain a closer understanding of the camps' administrative machinery and relations among the agencies operating in it within a metropolitan and national context. This involved consultation with experts, institutions and associations (both Romani and non-Romani) that dealt with Romani-related issues on the ground.

By drawing upon Shore and Wright's (1997: 11) definition of 'anthropology of policy', I moved through "'the field" […] as a social and political space articulated through relations of power and systems of governance'. Although this study aims to go beyond the conceptualisation of policies as constructing their subjects as mere objects of power, it acknowledges them as fundamentally ideological devices. By codifying social norms and values, policies also contain implicit (in the Romani case explicit) models of society. As instruments of governance they aim to organise people within systems of power and authority, empowering some while silencing others. Using what Reinhold (1994, as cited in Shore and Wright 1997: 11) calls 'studying through', I sought to conduct multisite ethnographies by exploring policy connections between different organisational and everyday worlds.

Before beginning to collect data, I mapped the organisations (private and public, Romani and non-Romani, independent and social advocacy, local and national) as well as individuals (activists, academics, local politicians, journalists, schoolteachers, social workers) engaged in these issues. Participant observation was carried out in a number of Romani encampments: four *solidarity villages* (Candoni, Castel Romano, Camping River and Cesare Lombroso); two 'tolerated encampments' (Tor de' Cenci and Torraccio di San Basilio); and Metropoliz/Città Meticcia, an abandoned pork-meat factory occupied in 2009 by more than 200 people from different parts of the world, including Romanies, with the support of two non-profit organisations (Blocchi Precari Metropolitani and Popica Onlus). I collected information through repeated visits not only inside these encampments but also outside, using methods that included email correspondence, phone conversations, participation at public conferences, official events, unofficial assemblies, cultural exhibitions, meeting informants in their households and attending private celebrations.

The project used a composite methodology to create a comprehensive picture of both the situation of Romani people living in the metropolitan target area and the challenges this group posed to service providers (Creswell and Plano Clark 2011). This aim was achieved by combining theoretical conceptual analysis, qualitative empirical and exploratory analysis, social documents analysis, quantitative data analysis and critical analysis of public policies. The data collection also relied on the contributions of sundry community-based and advocacy organisations. The roles of partner organisations included the provision of support during the fieldwork to forge links with relevant communities; logistical guidance with regard to meetings, conferences and interviews; provision of feedback on interim reports and other project materials; and assistance in exploring the project's policy implications.

Target Group, Sample Size and Recruitment Methods

The present research focuses not only on selected Romani communities living in Rome but also on official agencies, Third Sector organisations and other privileged informants directly or indirectly involved in Romani issues, both nationally and locally. The interviews were carried out using research templates specifically tailored to each of the identified groups and categories. Since I had been working with Romanies in the Italian capital from 2006 until 2008, and remained in touch with a number of them, I already had an extensive pre-existing network of contacts in the field. My choice, though, was not to approach those with whom I had an ongoing friendship or anyone I had helped as a social worker. With few exceptions, in fact, I approached individuals I had no previous contact with. My intention was to gather information spontaneously, avoiding possible contamination of the process owing to the existence of prior association.

Initially, the Internet enabled me to identify Rome-based organisations—both Romani and non-Romani—together with all the institutional actors that had been dealing with this issue. I then sent them emails asking if they were interested in participating in my research project. At the same time I listed all the camps (spontaneous, tolerated and equipped) within the city limits. The camps' residents and social workers were then visited a number of times. Despite the number of interviewees, the amount of data collected and the breadth of issues discussed, only the most relevant aspects were analysed in detail. These were the themes most often reiterated by participants that could provide a theoretical insight and a contribution to understanding Romani issues (Bryman 2012). The selection of statements quoted in this book was dictated by the quality of the information contained in them and how well they clarified the topic under investigation. The most significant statements were given priority (Mason 2010).

The fieldwork was conducted in two different stages in the city of Rome. The capital city functioned as a magnifying lens through which the social exclusion of Romani people could be investigated. As Clough Marinaro and Daniele (2011: 621) argue, the condition of Romanies living in Rome 'holds the potential to directly affect future approaches to policy across Italy'. Rome is also where more Romanies reside than anywhere else in Italy. The first data collection took place between 2011 and 2012 during the so-called Nomad Emergency. In late 2016, a new set of interviews were conducted with key institutional and Third Sector representatives, as well as 'camp-dwellers'. This allowed us to understand if the conditions of the Romani people had improved since the first round of data collection. During the fieldwork phase I interviewed 90 informants. The key themes of my interview questions differed according to the subject interviewed. Romani people, for instance, were asked about their family details, life memories, relations with their culture and community including Italian culture and the host society; the settlement process and any problems encountered therein. Interview themes for Government and Third Sector representatives were job description and role, type of approach and service provided, goals and expected outcomes, problematics, analysis and reporting on achievements.

Bibliography

Agamben, G. (1998). *Homo Sacer: Sovereign power and bare life* (trans: Heller-Roazen, D.). Stanford: Stanford University Press. (Original work published 1995).

Allievi, S. (2010). Immigration and cultural pluralism in Italy: Multiculturalism as a missing model. *Italian Culture, 28*(2), 85–103. https://doi.org/10.1179/016146210X12790095563020.

Amnesty International. (2012a). Italy: Briefing to the UN Committee on the Elimination of Racial Discrimination 80th session February 2012. Retrieved from http://www2.ohchr.org/english /bodies/cerd/docs/ngos / AI_Italy_CERD80.pdf

Amnesty International. (2012b). On the edge: Roma forced evictions and segregation in Italy. Retrieved from http://www.amnesty.ch/de/laender/ europa-zentralasien/italien/dok/2012/amnesty-fordert-das-ende-der-diskri-minierung-von-roma/bericht-on-the-edge-roma-forced-evictions-and-segregation-in-italy.-september-2012.-16-seiten

Amnesty International, Associazione 21 Luglio, & European Roma Rights Centre (2016). Italy: The national strategy for Roma Inclusion: A short-lived hope for Roma in Italy. Retrieved from https://www.amnesty.org/en/documents/ eur30/3520/2016/en/

Anheier, H. K., & Salamon, L. M. (2006). The nonprofit sector in comparative perspective. In W. W. Powel & R. Steinberg (Eds.), *The non-profit sector. A research handbook* (pp. 89–116). New Haven/London: Yale University Press.

Arendt, H. (1962). *The origins of totalitarianism.* Cleveland/New York: Meridian Books.

Armillei, R. (2014). Neither included, nor excluded: The paradox of government approaches towards the Romanies in Italy. *Citizenship and Globalisation Research Paper Series, 5*(3), 1–22.

Armillei, R. (2016). Reflections on Italy's contemporary approaches to cultural diversity: The exclusion of the 'Other' from a supposed notion of 'Italianness'. *Australia New Zealand Journal of European Studies, 8*(2), 34–48.

Armillei, R. (2017a). The 'Piano Nomadi' and its pyramidal governance: The hidden mechanism underlying the 'camps system' in Rome. *Romani Studies, 27*(1), 47–71.

Armillei, R. (2017b). The Romani 'camp-dwellers' in Rome: Between state control and 'collective-identity closure'. In C. Agius & D. Keep (Eds.), *Identity making, displacement and rupture: Performing discourses of belonging, being and place* (pp. 107–122). Manchester: Manchester University Press.

Asséo, H. (1989). Pour une histoire des peuples-Résistances [For a history of resistance-peoples]. In P. Williams (Ed.), *Tsiganes: identité, évolution* (pp. 121–127). Paris: Syros.

Associazione 21 Luglio. (2013). Campi Nomadi s.p.a. [Nomad Camps Ltd.]. Retrieved from http://www.21luglio.org/21luglio/campi-nomadi-s-p-segregare-concentrare-allontanare-i-rom-i-costi-roma-nel-2013-giugno-2014/

Associazione 21 Luglio. (2016). Rapporto annuale 2016 [Annual report 2016]. Retrieved from http://www.21luglio.org/21luglio/wp-content/uploads/2017/04/RAPPORTO-ANNUALE_2016_WEB.pdf

Associazione 21 Luglio, Associazione per gli Studi Giuridici sull'Immigrazione, Amnesty International, Human Rights Watch, & Open Society Justice. (2012). Italy: Leave 'Nomad Emergency' in the past. Retrieved from http://www.statewatch.org/news/2012/may/italy-nomad-emergency-press-release.pdf

Azadé, A. (2016). Life in the new shanty town taking root on Paris's abandoned railway. Retrieved from https://www.theguardian.com/cities/2016/jan/05/life-shanty-town-paris-abandoned-railway-petite-ceinture

Barbetta, G. P. (2000). Italy's third sector on consolidation course. *German Policy Studies, 1*(2), 136–160.

Barbetta, G. P., Cima, S., & Zamaro, N. (2003). *Le istituzioni nonprofit in Italia: Dimensioni organizzative, economiche e sociali* [Not-for-profit institutions in Italy: Organisational, social and economic dimensions]. Bologna: Il Mulino.

Barry, A. (2006). Technological zones. *European Journal of Social Theory, 9*(2), 239–253.

Bartlett, W., Benini, R., & Gordon, C. (2011). Measures to promote the situation of Roma EU citizens in the European Union. Brussels: European Union. Retrieved from http://www2.lse.ac.uk/businessAndConsultancy/LSEConsulting/pdf/Roma.pdf

Bauman, Z. (2007). *Consuming life.* Cambridge: Polity Press.

Bellucci, P. (2007). *Rom e Sinti in Italia: Profili storici e culturali* [Roma and Sinti in Italy: Historical and cultural profiles]. Urbino: Università degli Studi di Urbino.

Benedetto, I. (2011). Le minoranze Rom e Sinte: Alla ricerca di uno status giuridico [Roma and Sinti minorities: The pursuit of legal status]. Doctoral dissertation. Retrieved from http://www.stranieriinitalia.it/briguglio/immigrazione-e-asilo/2011/dicembre/tesi-irene-benedetto.pdf

Benvenuti, S., & Martini, S. (2017). La crisi del welfare pubblico e il "nuovo" Terzo settore [The crisis of the welfare state and on the 'new' Third Sector]. Retrieved from http://www.osservatorioaic.it/la-crisi-del-welfare-pubblico-e-il-nuovo-terzo-settore-la-via-tracciata-dalla-legge-delega-n-106-2016.html

Berman, J. (2013). Utility of a conceptual framework within doctoral study: A researcher's reflections. *Issues in Educational Research, 23*(1), 1–18.

Bonifazi, C., Heins, F., Strozza, S., & Vitiello, M. (2009, March). Italy: The Italian transition from an emigration to immigration country. Idea working papers. Retrieved from http://www.idea6fp.uw.edu.pl/pliki/WP5_Italy.pdf

Bontempelli, S. (2006). La tribù dei gagè: Comunità Rom e politiche di accoglienza a Pisa (1988–2005) [The tribe of the Gadje people: Romani communities and integration policies in Pisa (1988–2005)]. *International Journal of Migration Studies, 43*(164), 947–967.

Bontempelli, S. (2012). Roma policies in Italy: Good practices for housing. Retrieved from https://www.academia.edu/3279580/Roma_policies_in_Italy_Good_Practices_for_Housing

Boose, J. W. (2012). Democratization and civil society: Libya, Tunisia and the Arab Spring. *International Journal of Social Science and Humanity, 2*(4), 310–315.

Bravi, L., & Sigona, N. (2006). Educazione e rieducazione nei campi per 'nomadi': Una storia [Education and re-education inside camps for 'nomads': An overview]. *International Journal of Migration Studies, 43*(164), 857–874.

Brunello, P. (Ed.). (1996). *L'urbanistica del disprezzo. Campi rom e società Italiana* [The urban scorn. Romani camp and Italian society]. Roma: Manifestolibri.

Bryman, A. (2012). *Social research methods* (4th ed.). Oxford: Oxford University Press.

Calabrò, A. R. (2008). *Zingari: Storia di un'emergenza annunciata* [Gypsies: The history of an announced emergency]. Naples: Liguori.

Cemlyn, S., & Briskman, L. (2002). Social (dys)welfare within a hostile state. *Social Work Education, 21*(1), 49–69.

Clough Marinaro, I. (2003). Integration or marginalization? The failures of social policy for the Roma in Rome. *Modern Italy, 8*(2), 203–218.

Clough Marinaro, I. (2009). Between surveillance and exile: Biopolitics and the Roma in Italy. *Bulletin of Italian Politics, 1*(2), 265–287.

Clough Marinaro, I. (2014). Rome's 'legal' camps for Roma: The construction of new spaces of informality. *Journal of Modern Italian Studies, 19*(5), 541–555.

Clough Marinaro, I. (2015). The rise of Italy's neo-Ghettos. *Journal of Urban History, 41*(3), 368–387.

Clough Marinaro, I., & Daniele, U. (2011). Roma and humanitarianism in the Eternal City. *Journal of Modern Italian Studies, 16*(5), 621–636.

Commissione straordinaria per la tutela e la promozione dei diritti umani. (2011). Rapporto conclusivo dell'indagine sulla condizione di Rom, Sinti e Camminanti in Italia [Final report of the survey on the status of Roma, Sinti and Travellers in Italy]. Retrieved from http://www.senato.it/service/PDF/PDFServer/DF/233751.pdf

Comune di Roma. (2017). Campi rom: al lavoro per superamento villaggi Monachina e La Barbuta [Romani camps: Work is underway to close the Monachina and La Barbuta villages]. Retrieved from https://www.comune.roma.it/pcr/it/newsview.page?contentId=NEW1428937

Conclave, M. (2017). La vera valutazione dell' impresa sociale [The real evaluation of the social enterprise]. Retrieved from http://www.nuovi-lavori.it/index.php/sezioni/502-la-vera-valutazione-dell-impresa-sociale

Council of Europe. (2016). Stop evictions of Roma and Travellers. Retrieved from https://www.coe.int/en/web/portal/roma-latest-news/-/asset_publisher/Wf2OtrKpyHUY/content/stop-evictions-of-roma-and-travelle-3?_101_INSTANCE_Wf2OtrKpyHUY_languageId=en_GB

Creswell, J. W., & Plano Clark, V. L. (2011). *Designing and conducting mixed methods research* (2nd ed.). Thousand Oaks: Sage.

Daniele, U. (2010). Zingari di carta: Un percorso nella presa di parola rom ai tempi dell'emergenza [Paper Gypsies: A route towards the empowerment of Romanies during the emergency]. *Zapruder, 22*, 56–72.

Daniele, U. (2011a). 'Nomads' in the eternal city. *Géocarrefour, 86*(1), 15–24. Retrieved from http://geocarrefour.revues.org/8230

Daniele, U. (2011b). *Sono del campo e vengo dall'India: Etnografia di una collettività rom ridislocata* [I live in a camp and I come from India: Ethnography of a re-displaced Romani community]. Rome: Meti Edizioni.

Délégation Interministérielle à l'hébergement et à l'accès au lodgement. (2011). French government strategy for Roma integration within the framework of the communication from the Commission of 5 April 2011 and the Council conclusions of 19 May 2011. http://ec.europa.eu/social/BlobServlet?docId=8969&langId=en

Di Maggio, P. J., & Powell, W. W. (1991). The iron cage revisited: Institutional isomorphism and collective rationality in organizational fields. In W. W. Powell & P. J. Di Maggio (Eds.), *The new institutionalism in organizational analysis* (pp. 63–82). Chicago: University of Chicago Press.

Doytcheva, M. (2016). Between infra-right and public hospitality: Ambiguity in local policies towards Roma migrant families in France. *International Journal of Migration and Border Studies, 2*(4), 365–381.

Eumetra Monterosa. (2016). L'opinione degli italiani sull'arrivo degli immigrati [The opinion of Italians on the arrival of immigrants]. Retrieved from https://www.eumetramr.com/it/lopinione-degli-italiani-sullarrivo-degli-immigrati

European Commission. (2009). Vademecum: The 10 common basic principles on Roma inclusion. Retrieved from http://www.coe.int/t/dg4/youth/Source/Resources/Documents/2011_10_Common_Basic_Principles_Roma_Inclusion.pdf

European Commission. (2011). An EU framework for national Roma integration strategies up to 2020. Retrieved from http://ec.europa.eu/justice/policies/discrimination/docs/com_2011_173_en.pdf

European Commission. (2013). Roma platform. Retrieved from http://ec.europa.eu/justice/discrimination/roma/roma-platform/index_en.htm

European Commission. (2016). Country report non-discrimination Italy. Retrieved from http://www.equalitylaw.eu/downloads/3736-2016-it-country-report-nd

European Public Health Alliance. (2011). European Commission adopts EU Framework for National Roma Integration Strategies. Retrieved from http://www.epha.org/spip.php?article4500

European Roma Rights Centre. (2000). Campland: Racial segregation of Roma in Italy. Retrieved from http://www.errc.org/cms/upload/media/00/0F/m0000000F.pdf

European Roma Rights Centre. (2013). End of the road for Italy's illegal state of emergency. Retrieved from http://www.errc.org/article/end-of-the-road-for-italys-illegal-state-of-emergency/4137

European Roma Rights Centre. (2017). Parallel report: For Consideration by the Human Rights Committee at its 119th session (6 – 29 March 2017). Retrieved from http://www.errc.org/cms/upload/file/italy-iccpr-8-february-2017.pdf

European Union Agency for Fundamental Rights. (2017a). Fundamental Rights Report 2017. Retrieved from http://fra.europa.eu/en/publication/2017/fundamental-rights-report-2017

European Union Agency for Fundamental Rights. (2017b). Roma. Retrieved from http://fra.europa.eu/en/theme/roma

Fazzi, L. (2011). L'innovazione nelle cooperative sociali in Italia [Innovation in social cooperatives in Italy]. Retrieved from http://www.forumterzosettore.it/multimedia/allegati/Innovazione%20nelle%20cooperative%20sociali.pdf

Federico, V. (2012). Impresa sociale e terzo settore: esperienze europee [Social enterprise and Third Sector: European experiences]. In V. Federico, D. Russo, & E. Testi (Eds.), *Impresa sociale, concorrenza e valore aggiunto. Un approccio europeo* (pp. 89–131). Lavis: LEGO spa.

Fiaschetti, M. E. (2017, September 28). Dieci campi rom (legali) da chiudere [Ten Romani (legal) camps need to be closed]. *Corriere della Sera*. Retrieved from http://roma.corriere.it/notizie/cronaca/17_settembre_28/dieci-campi-rom-legali-chiudere-piano-comune-appena-partito-9a49eda0-a3ba-11e7-a066-220c02125bda.shtml

Fiorucci, M. (2010). Un'altra città è possibile. Percorsi di integrazione delle famiglie Rom e Sinte a Roma: Problemi, limiti e prospettive delle politiche di inclusione sociale. [Another city is possible. Integration trajectories of Roma and Sinti families in Rome: Problems, limitations and perspectives of social inclusion policies]. Roma, Italia: Geordie onlus.

Fischer, A. M. (2011). Between nation and state: Examining the International Romani Unions. Senior Projects Spring, Paper 12. Retrieved from http://digitalcommons.bard.edu/senproj_s2011/12

Foucault, M. (1977). *Discipline and punish* (trans: Sheridan, A.). London: Allen Lane.

Foucault, M. (1990). *The history of sexuality: An introduction* (trans: Hurley, R.). New York: Vintage Books.

FrancoAngeli. (2011, February). Norme redazionali [editorial rules]. Sociologia e Politiche Sociali. Retrieved from https://www.francoangeli.it/riviste/NR/Sp-norme.pdf

Gago-Cortés, C., & Novo-Corti, I. (2015). Sustainable development of urban slum areas in Northwestern Spain. *Management of Environmental Quality: An International Journal, 26*(6), 891–908.

Geertz, C. (2001). *The Interpretation of cultures*. New York: Basic Books.

Gheorghe, N., & Acton, T. (2001). Citizens of the world and nowhere: Minority, ethnic and human rights for Roma. In W. Guy (Ed.), *Between past and future: The Roma of Central and Eastern Europe* (pp. 54–70). Hatfield: University of Hertfordshire Press.

Goffman, E. (1961). *Asylums: Essays on the social situation of mental patients and other inmates*. New York: Doubleday Anchor.

Hepworth, K. (2012). Abject citizens: Italian 'nomad emergencies' and the deportability of Romanian Roma. *Citizenship Studies, 16*(3-4), 431–449.

Honig, B. (2009). *Emergency politics: Paradox, law, democracy*. Princeton: Princeton University Press.

Honig, B. (2014). Three models of emergency politics. *Boundary 2, 41*(2), 45–70.

Howard, M. M. (2010). Civil society and democracy. In H. K. Anheier & S. Toepler (Eds.), *International encyclopedia of civil society* (pp. 186–192). New York: Springer.

Isin, E. F., & Rygiel, K. (2007). Abject spaces: Frontiers, zones, camps. In E. Dauphinee & C. Masters (Eds.), *Logics of biopower and the war on terror* (pp. 181–203). Houndmills/Basingstoke: Palgrave.

Istituto per gli Studi di Politica Internazionale. (2015). Gli italiani e le migrazioni: percezione vs realtà [Italians and migration: perception vs. reality]. Retrieved from http://www.ispionline.it/it/articoli/articolo/emergenzesviluppo-europa-italia-global-governance/gli-italiani-e-le-migrazioni-percezione-vs-realta-13562

Italian National Institute for Statistics. (2016). La rilevazione sulle istituzioni non-profit: un settore in crescita [The survey of non-profit institutions: A rising sector]. http://www.istat.it/en/files/2013/07/05-Scheda-Non-Profit_DEF.pdf

Keane, J. (2010). Civil society, definitions and approaches. In H. K. Anheier & S. Toepler (Eds.), *International encyclopedia of civil society* (pp. 461–464). New York: Springer.

Keller, R. (2016). Cañada Real Galiana, Madrid the largest slum in Europe. Retrieved from https://www.ethz.ch/content/dam/ethz/special-interest/con-ference-websites-dam/no-cost-housing-dam/documents/Keller_final.pdf

La Repubblica. (2017, January 27). Italia non-profit, arriva la piattaforma per far conoscere gli enti del Terzo settore [Italian non-profit, soon the launch of the platform to know Third Sector organization]. *La Repubblica*. Retrieved from http://www.repubblica.it/economia/miojob/2017/01/27/news/italia_non_profit_arriva_la_piattaforma_per_far_conoscere_gli_enti_del_terzo_settore-156861576/

La Stampa. (2017, May 11). Rom e Sinti in Italia. *La Stampa*. Retrieved from http://www.lastampa.it/2017/05/11/multimedia/italia/cronache/rom-e-sinti-in-italia-DQyWN5m5PGilUEqGhvnzJK/pagina.html

Lee, R. (2002). Roma ande Kalisferia: Roma in limbo. In S. Montesi (Ed.), *Terre Sospese: Vite di un campo rom* [Suspended Worlds: Lives of a campo rom]. Roma: Prospettiva Edizioni Srl. Retrieved from http://kopachi.com/articles/

Levy, C. (2010). Refugees, Europe, camps/state of exception: 'Into the Zone', the European Union and extraterritorial processing of migrants, refugees and Asylum-Seekers (theories and practice). *Refugee Survey Quarterly, 29*(1), 92–119.

Lintner, C. (2014). Overcoming the "nomad camps" by initiating a new learning process on the example of Bolzano (Italy). *Procedia – Social and Behavioral Sciences, 116*, 775–779.

Lori, M. (2010, July). Autonomous or dependent: Isomorphic effects of public regulation on voluntary organisations. Paper presented at 9th International Conference of the International Society for Third Sector Research (ISTR), Istanbul. Retrieved from http://www.istr.org/?WP_Istanbul

Lunaria. (2011). *Chronicles of ordinary racism: Second white paper on racism in Italy* (trans: Di Pietro, D. & Marshall, C.). Rome: Edizioni dell'Asino.

Maestri, G. (2016). Persistently temporary. Ambiguity and political mobilisations in Italy's Roma camps: A comparative perspective. Durham theses, Durham University. Retrieved from Durham E-Theses Online: http://etheses.dur.ac.uk/11881/

Maestri, G. (2017). Struggles and ambiguities over political subjectivities in the camp: Roma camp dwellers between neoliberal and urban citizenship in Italy. *Citizenship Studies, 21*(6), 640–656.

Malinowski, B. (2002). *Argonauts of Western Pacific*. London: Routledge & Kegan Paul Ltd.

Marotta, V. (2011). The idea of the in-between subject in social and cultural thought. In M. Lobo, V. Marotta, & N. Oke (Eds.), *Intercultural relations in a global world* (pp. 179–199). Champaign: Common Ground Publishing LLC.

Mason, M. (2010, September). Sample size and saturation in PhD studies using qualitative interviews. *FQS, 11*(3), art.8. Retrieved from http://www.qualitative-research.net/index.php/fqs/article/view/1428/3027

McCulloch, G. (2004). *Documentary research in education, history and the social sciences*. London/New York: Routledge Falmer.

Mills, M. R., & Bettis, P. J. (2015). Using multiple theoretical frameworks to study organizational change and identity. In V. A. Anfara Jr. & N. T. Mertz (Eds.), *Theoretical frameworks in qualitative research* (pp. 96–118). Thousand Oaks: SAGE Publications.

Ministero dell'Interno. (2006). La pubblicazione sulle minoranze senza territorio [The publication on stateless minorities]. Retrieved from http://www1. interno.gov.it/mininterno/export/sites /default/it/assets/files/13/La_pubblicazione_sulle_minoranze _senza_territorio.pdf

Molero-Mesa, J., & Jiménez-Lucena, I. (2013). (De)legitimizing social, professional and cognitive hierarchies. Scientific knowledge and practice in inclusion-exclusion processes. *Dynamis: Acta Hispanica ad Medicinae Scientiarumque Historiam Illustrandam, 33*(1), 13–17.

Musgrave, S., & Bradshaw, J. (2014). Language and social inclusion: Unexplored aspects of intercultural communication. *Australian Review of Applied Linguistics, 37*(3), 198–212.

Nicola, V. (2011). *I ghetti per i rom. Roma, via Di Salone 323. Socianalisi narrativa di un campo rom* [The ghettos for Romani people. Rome, Di Salone road, 323. Socio-analysis account of a Romani camp]. Cuneo: Sensibili alle Foglie.

Otieno, M. (2015, December 8). Poverty is big business in the West: A new documentary savages the philosophy of foreign aid. *MercatorNet.* Retrieved from https://www.mercatornet.com/harambee/view/poverty-is-big-business-in-the-west/17311

Patanè, S. (2003). The Third Sector in Italy. EuroSET Report, Rome: European Social Enterprise Training, Centro Italiano di Solidarietà di Roma.

Peró, D. (1999). Next to the dog pound: Institutional discourses and practices about Rom refugees in left-wing Bologna. *Modern Italy, 4*(2), 207–224.

Peró, D. (2007). *Inclusionary rhetoric/exclusionary practices. Left-wing politics and migrants in Italy.* New York: Berghahn Books.

Piasere, L. (1985). Les pratiques de voyage et de stationament des nomades en Italie [Travel and short-stay practices of the nomads in Italy]. In A. Reyniers (Ed.), *Les pratiques de deplacement, de halte de stationament des populations tsiganes et nomades en France* (pp. 143–195). Paris: Centre de Recherches Tsiganes.

Piasere, L. (2005). *Popoli delle discariche: Saggi di antropologia zingara* [Peoples of the dumps: Essays in Gypsy anthropology] (2nd ed.). Rome: CISU.

Picker, G. (2010). Nomad's land? Political cultures and nationalist stances vis-à-vis Roma in Italy. In M. Steward & M. Rovid (Eds.), *Multidisciplinary approaches to Romany studies* (pp. 211–227). Budapest: Central European University Press.

Picker, G. (2011). Welcome 'in'. Left-wing Tuscany and Romani migrants (1987–2007). *Journal of Modern Italian Studies, 16*(5), 607–620.

Pogány, I. (2004). Legal, social and economic challenges facing the Roma of Central and Eastern Europe. Queen's Papers on Europeanisation, 2, Queen's University Belfast, Belfast.

Ramadan, A. (2013). Spatialising the refugee camp. *Transactions of the Institute of British Geographers, 38*(1), 65–77.

Ranci, C. (1994). The third sector in welfare policies in Italy: The contradictions of a protected market. *International Journal of Voluntary and Nonprofit Organizations, 5*(3), 247–271.

Ranci, C. (2015). The long-term evolution of the government – Third Sector partnership in Italy: Old wine in a new bottle? *VOLUNTAS: International Journal of Voluntary and Nonprofit Organizations, 26*(6), 2311–2329.

Renzi, L. (2010). Roma people in Europe: A long history of discrimination. European Social Watch Report 2010. Retrieved from http://www.social-watch.eu/wcm/documents/Roma_a_long_history_of_discrimination.pdf

Rivera, A. (2003). *Estranei e nemici* [Aliens and enemies]. Rome: DeriveApprodi.

Rossi, M. (2010). The city and the slum: An action research on a Moroccan and a Roma Xoraxanè community in Rome. Doctoral dissertation. Retrieved from http://etheses.bham.ac.uk/1263/

Rövid, M. (2011). Cosmopolitanism and exclusion: On the limits transnational democracy in the light of the case of Roma. Doctoral dissertation. Retrieved from http://pds.ceu.hu/doctoral-school-phd-dissertations

Saletti-Salza, C. (2003). *Bambini del campo nomadi: Roma´ bosniaci a Torino* [*Children of the nomad camps: Bosnian Romanies in Turin*]. Roma: CISU.

Schmitt, C. (2005). Political theology: Four chapters on the concept of sovereignty. Edited and translated by Schwab, G. Chicago: University of Chicago Press.

Scutellà, A. (2016, October 5). Rom, i campi non chiudono [Romanies, camps are not shut down]. *La Repubblica*. Retrieved from http://www.repubblica.it/solidarieta/diritti-umani/2016/10/05/news/rom_i_campi_non_chiudono_21_luglio_ecco_il_sistema_a_5_stelle_-149182944/

Shore, C., & Wright, S. (1997). *Anthropology of policy*. London: Routledge.

Sigona, N. (2002). *Figli del ghetto: Gli italiani, i campi nomadi e l'invenzione degli zingari* [Sons of the ghetto: Italians, nomad camps and the invention of the Gypsies]. Civezzano: Nonluoghi.

Sigona, N. (2005). Locating 'The Gypsy problem'. The Roma in Italy: Stereotyping, labelling and 'nomad camps'. *Journal of Ethnic and Migration Studies, 31*(4), 741–756.

Sigona, N. (Ed.). (2008). The 'latest' public enemy: Romanian Roma in Italy. The case studies of Milan, Bologna, Rome and Naples. Retrieved from http://www.osservazione.org/documenti/OSCE_publicenemy.pdf

Sigona, N. (2009). The 'Problema Nomadi' vis-à-vis the political participation of Roma and Sinti at the local level in Italy. In N. Sigona & N. Trehan (Eds.), *Romani politics in contemporary Europe: Poverty, ethnic mobilization, and the neoliberal order* (pp. viii–xiii). New York: Palgrave Macmillan.

Sigona, N. (2011). The governance of Romani people in Italy: Discourse, policy and practice. *Journal of Modern Italian Studies, 16*(5), 590–606.

Sigona, N. (2015). Campzenship: Reimagining the camp as a social and political space. *Citizenship Studies, 19*(1), 1–15.

Silverman, C. (1995). Persecution and politicization: Roma (Gypsies) of Eastern Europe. *Cultural Survival Quarterly, 19*(2), 43–49. Retrieved from http://www.culturalsurvival.org/publications/cultural-survival-quarterly/albania/persecution-and-politicization-roma-gypsies-eastern

Simon, P. (2012). Collecting ethnic statistics in Europe: A review. *Ethnic and Racial Studies, 35*(8), 1366–1391.

Solimano, N. (1999). Immigrazione, convivenza urbana e conflitti locali [Immigration, urban coexistence and local conflicts]. *La Nuova Citta, 2*(4), 135–140.

Solimano, N., & Mori, T. (2000, June). A Roma ghetto in Florence. *The UNESCO Courier.*

Solimene, M. (2013). Undressing the gağé clad in state garb: Bosnian xoraxané romá face to face with the Italian authorities. *Romani Studies, 23*(2), 161–186.

Springhetti, P. (2009). Le zone grigie del Terzo Settore [The grey area of the Third Sector]. Retrieved from http://www.volontariato.lazio.it/documentazione/documenti/RetiSolidali_2_09_ZoneGrigieDelTerzoSettore.pdf

Stasolla, C. (2017, September 28). Roma, il campo rom deve chiudere? Il Comune gli cambia nome e gli ospiti restano lì. *Il Fatto Quotidiano.* Retrieved from http://www.ilfattoquotidiano.it/2017/09/28/roma-il-campo-rom-deve-chiudere-il-comune-gli-cambia-nome-e-gli-ospiti-restano-li/3882570/

Teolato, L. (2016, June 24). Roma, arrestato per corruzione su appalti gestione campi nomadi [Rome, arrested for bribery in relation to tender procurement contracts for the management of nomad camps]. *Il Fatto Quotidiano.* Retrieved from http://www.ilfattoquotidiano.it/2016/06/24/roma-arrestato-per-corruzione-su-appalti-campi-nomadi-aveva-affidato-bene-sequestrato-alla-mafia/2857090/

Townley, B. (1997). The institutional logic of performance appraisal. *Organization Studies, 18*(2), 261–285.

Ufficio Nazionale Antidiscriminazioni Razziali. (2014). Strategia Nazionale d'inclusione dei Rom, dei Sinti e dei Caminanti: Attuazione comunicazione commissione europea n.173/2011 [National Strategy for the inclusion of Roma, Sinti and Camminanti communities: European Commission communication no. 173/2011]. Retrieved from http://www.unar.it/unar/portal/wp-content/uploads/2014/02/Strategia-Rom-e-Sinti.pdf

UN-Habitat. (2016). Urbanization and development: Emerging futures. Retrieved from http://wcr.unhabitat.org/wp-content/uploads/2017/02/WCR-2016-Full-Report.pdf

United Nations Global Compact. (2010). Civil society. Retrieved from https://www.unglobalcompact.org/howtoparticipate/civil_society

Uzunova, I. (2010). Roma integration in Europe: Why minority rights are failing. *Arizona Journal of International and Comparative Law, 27*(1), 283–323. Retrieved from http://academos.ro/sites/default/files/biblio-docs/845/roma_integration_in_europe.pdf

van Baar, H. (2014). The emergence of a reasonable Anti-Gypsyism in Europe. In T. Agarin (Ed.), *When stereotype meets prejudice: Antiziganism in European societies* (pp. 27–44). Stuttgart: Ibidem.

van Baar, H. (2015). The perpetual mobile machine of forced mobility: Europe's Roma and the institutionalization of rootlessness. In Y. Jansen, J. de Bloois, & R. Celikates (Eds.), *The irregularization of migration in contemporary Europe: Deportation, detention, drowning* (pp. 71–86). London/New York: Rowman & Littlefield.

Verbruggen, S., Christiaens, J., & Milis, K. (2011). Can resource dependence and coercive isomorphism explain nonprofit organizations' compliance with reporting standards? *Nonprofit and Voluntary Sector Quarterly, 40*(1), 5–32.

Verhoeven, I., & Bröer, C. (2015). Contentious governance: Local governmental players as social movement actors. In J. W. Duyvendak & J. M. Jasper (Eds.), *Breaking down the state protestors engaged* (pp. 95–110). Amsterdam: Amsterdam University Press B.V..

Vitale, T., & Caruso, L. (2009). Conclusioni. Ragionare per casi: dinamiche di innovazione nelle politiche locali con i Rom e i Sinti [Conclusions. Case by case analysis: Innovation dynamics in local politics with Rom and Sinti]. In T. Vitale (Ed.), *Politiche possibili: Abitare le città con i rom e i Sinti* (pp. 265–288). Rome: Carocci editore.

Wacquant, L. (2011). A Janus-Faced institution of ethnoracial closure: A sociological specification of the ghetto. In R. Hutchison & B. Haynes (Eds.), *The ghetto: Contemporary global issues and controversies* (pp. 1–31). Boulder: Westview Press.

Walters, W. (2011). Foucault and frontiers: Notes on the birth of the humanitarian border. In U. Bröckling, S. Krasmann, & T. Lemke (Eds.), *Governmentality: Current issues and future challenges* (pp. 138–164). New York: Routledge.

World Bank. (2013). Defining civil society. Retrieved from http://web.worldbank.org/WBSITE/EXTERNAL/TOPICS/CSO/0,,contentMDK:20101499~menuPK:244752~pagePK:220503~piPK:220476~theSitePK:228717,00.html

Wotherspoon, T., & Hansen, J. (2013). The "Idle No More" movement: Paradoxes of First Nations inclusion in the Canadian context. *Social Inclusion, 1*(1), 21–36.

2

The Institutional and Spatial Segregation of Romanies in Italy

Romani People/Romanies/Roma: A Kaleidoscope of Definitions

The Romani population comprises a multitude of groups and sub-groups scattered across all continents. Since their first appearance in Europe, which can be dated *circa* the tenth century AD (Matras 2004), these peoples have been generally identified by non-Romanies in derogatory terms (i.e. *Gypsies*, *Zingari*, *Zigeuner*, *Gitanos*, *Cigani*). These definitions are all 'exonyms', given to the Romanies by outsiders and dominant groups. Since 1971, after the First World Romani Congress was held in London in 1971, they agreed on the dissemination of the term 'Roma'. As Rövid (2011) argues though, it is only after the collapse of the Communist Block in 1989 that the term 'Roma' came to the fore. Particularly in Europe, where they are concentrated and constitute the largest ethnic minority, the terminology used to describe them has varied considerably since 1969, the date of the first text relating to the Roma communities. This was clearly acknowledged by the CoE (2012: 3) in a recent report entitled 'Descriptive Glossary of terms relating to Roma issues':

© The Author(s) 2018
R. Armillei, *The 'Camps System' in Italy*, Mapping Global Racisms,
https://doi.org/10.1007/978-3-319-76318-7_2

'Gypsies and other travellers', 'Nomads' (1975 and 1983), 'populations of nomadic origin' (1981), 'Gypsies' (1993), 'Roma (Gypsies)' (1995), 'Roma' (1997, 2002), 'Roma/Gypsies' (1995, 1998, 2000), 'Roma/Gypsies and Travellers' (2001), 'Roma and Travellers' (between 2004 and 2010), and 'Roma' since 2010.

While the use of the term 'Roma' has experienced an exponential growth, it is not embraced universally by all Romani communities.

According to Hancock (2010), the word 'Rom' originally meant 'married Romani male', but after they arrived in Europe, it diverged in two directions. Some kept this meaning but confined it to themselves; for the others, it came to denote only 'husband'. The Sinti, for example, or the Romanichals or the Manouches/Manush use the word only with this narrower meaning, not when referring to the broader group. The adjective 'Romani' has instead a much wider ethnonymic application (Rövid 2011: 48). In fact, as Hancock (2010: xix) argues, all Romani groups use it to describe themselves: 'A Sinto or a Romanichal readily admit to being a Romani person, to speaking the Romani language and maintaining the Romani culture'. As a consequence, following Hancock, I will employ the term 'Romani' (plural Romanies) throughout this book, thus keeping the common practice of using adjectival forms as nouns (e.g. she is a Bulgarian, he is Hungarian). Even though the above-mentioned terms are based upon mistaken assumptions and carry offensive meanings, they continue to be used. Regrettably, the transition to the endonym 'Roma(nies)' has not yet been successful (Hancock 2010). The term 'Romani' was the product of elites that started to emerge in the 1950s within the Romani diaspora. For this reason, it is an unfamiliar concept and one not universally accepted by Romani people. As Klímová-Alexander (2005: 13) observed, 'the homogeneous Romani identity is a political project rather than a reality'. It may be rare but there are also Romanies who proudly define themselves as *Zingari*, consciously appropriating a term imposed upon them (Bellucci 2007; UNAR 2011b).

Romanies living in Italy can be divided into three major groups: *Rom*, *Sinti* and *Caminanti* (or *Camminanti*).

Rom is an endonym commonly used as a cover term for all groups (Rom, Sinti, Kalé, Manouches/Manush, Romanichals, Camminanti, Jenisch) living in Italy (Marzoli 2012; Vitale 2010). Italy's 'Rom' constitutes a specific category, which divides into several sub-groups. These generally differentiate themselves from one another by profession, region of origin or residence, or religion (Marzoli 2012). They arrived in Italy by sea from the Balkans, settling predominantly in its central and southern regions and incline to a sedentary life (Sigona 2007).

Sinto (plural 'Sinti') is another endonym. Presumably it stems from 'Sindh', a southern province of present-day Pakistan bisected by the Indus River (Bellucci 2007; Marzoli 2012). This cluster of peoples constitutes probably the oldest Romani settlement in Italy and has maintained a 'semi-nomadic' lifestyle. They live predominantly in the central and northern regions, but in summer they move south and to the islands for reasons of work. Italy has at least ten groups of Sinti, all of whom differ according to their region of origin or their speech dialect, which has largely replaced the Romani language (SCPPHR 2011).

The *Camminanti* (literally travellers) are a distinct group of Romani who settled principally in Sicily. To this day their origin remains a matter of debate (Sigona 2007). According to Cellai (2003), 'they consider themselves a nomadic or semi-nomadic group, but they refuse to be associated with the "Zingari", though they do not deny the fact they may have become related by marriage to Sinti groups during their travels' (para. 1). They are the smallest community numbering only a few hundred (Bellucci 2007). The term which is used to describe this group probably derives from their nomadic lifestyle (Cellai 2003).

These three groups, *Rom*, *Sinti* and *Camminanti*, are commonly recognised as the longest-established Romani communities in Italy. The Romani communities of Italy can be subdivided by their citizenship status as well as by period of immigration. It is estimated that the majority of them are Italian citizens. According to a recent report published by UNAR (2014: 16), around 70,000 are from families that have been in Italy for more than 600 years and spread all over the national territory. The 90,000 who came from the Balkans in the 1990s after Yugoslavia collapsed are classified as *extra-comunitari* (non-EU citizens) and live mainly in the north, while the arrivals from Romania and Bulgaria are EU citizens and live predominantly in the major metropolitan areas (Milan, Turin, Rome, Naples, Bologna, Bari, Genoa). To these groups one should also add the unknown number of *rom irregolari* (illegal

Romanies) (UNAR 2014). The complexity of the Romani condition in Italy is reinforced by the heterogeneity of their legal status. In fact, as UNAR (2014: 16) states,

> When we talk about the Romani communities we refer to: Italian citizens; foreign citizens belonging to other EU member states; foreigners who are citizens of non-EU countries; foreigners granted asylum-seeker status or temporary protection; *de facto* stateless, born in Italy from *de facto* stateless parents.

A further distinction can be made in describing the Romani presence in Italy. It is possible to distinguish *Rom e Sinti autoctoni* (autochthonous or native groups) from *Rom e Sinti stranieri* (immigrants or foreigners). When referring to these groups, Fiorucci (2010) appeals to two categories, those who have lived in Italy for a long time and those who arrived after 1945. The distinction Fiorucci draws is of relevance today. Over the years, and especially after the break up of Yugoslavia, Romanies in these categories came into conflict with each other. The arrival, in subsequent stages, of other Romani groups from elsewhere in Europe has often been perceived by the 'Italian-Romani' as an intrusion and a threat. In the last two decades the presence of new 'foreigner-communities', and their criminalisation, affected public perceptions of the whole Romani population. Romanies who arrived from the Balkans in the 1980s and 1990s, and those who left Romania at the time of EU enlargement in January 2007, have been accused of compromising the fine balance developed over the years between 'Italian-Romanies' and non-Romanies. At the same time, most of the economic resources were realigned towards these 'alien' groups, forgetting that concrete problems among the Italian-Romanies still needed tackling (Converso 1996, as cited in Fiorucci 2010). This is not the only such rivalry within Italy's Romani population. In fact, there is strong opposition among 'foreigner-communities' as well. Typically, the latest arrivals are being blamed (Centre on Housing Rights and Evictions [COHRE] et al. 2008).

This minority can be described and classified in other ways besides these 'Italian-Romanies'. For instance, they have also been labelled *rom invisibili* (invisible Romanies). Those who belong to this group generally have Italian surnames, live in houses, have regular jobs and prefer to hide their cultural background to avoid potential discrimination (Ricordy et al. 2012). The 'foreign Romanies', instead, are typically addressed as *rom dei campi* (Romanies of the camps), although a consistent number of Italian-Romanies live there also. According to Associazione 21 Luglio (2016: 12), around 37 per cent of the institutional camps' inhabitants hold Italian citizenship. As for the informal settlements, 92 per cent are Romanian Romanies. Paradoxically, the invisibility of Italian-Romanies is a direct consequence of the conspicuous visibility (albeit unwelcome) that those in the second category have attained in public discourse over recent decades. In turn, due to the complexity of the Romani population, the notion that mainstream society has of them is still hedged about with mystery, fear and stereotypical misconceptions. The Italian Senate's Human Rights Commission noted that 'on the one hand, many Romani people with Italian citizenship are commonly considered immigrants. On the other, many foreign Romanies were born in Italy they are still not recognised as Italian citizens' (SCPPHR 2011: 20).

A 2007 survey of a 'mainstream' population sample revealed that only 1 in 1000 had a complete knowledge of Italy's Romani communities (Arrigoni and Vitale 2008). Many do not even know that most of them are Italian citizens (Istituto per gli Studi sulla Pubblica Opinione 2008) and think they should all be expelled (Kington 2008), or subjected to such practices as fingerprinting and DNA profiling (AnalisiPolitica 2008). Despite all the differences, Italian media and mainstream society have only recently begun using the term *Rom* to refer to all the Romani communities living within the national borders. This is leading to their definition and classification as a homogeneous population, although many Romanies do not even define themselves as such (Bellucci 2007). Open confrontation exists between 'Rom' and 'Sinti' groups. Yet it is still very common to hear epithets such as *Zingaro* (Gypsy) or *nomade* (nomad). Such derogatory terms have the effect of generalising a very diverse population. According to a report by the ERRC (2000: 11), 'the Italian media use "nomad", "Gypsy" and "Rom" interchangeably, but "nomad" generally appears in headlines'. 'Nomad' was considered a 'catchier' term in the news, said an Italian journalist interviewed by the ERRC. This remains a common tendency, as reported by the Associazione Carta di Roma (2014), which was founded in 2011 to address the often discriminatory representation of new migrants in the Italian media.

Until recently, the Italian Ministero dell'Interno/Ministry of Interior (2009a, 2012) used the term *Zingaro* in an indiscriminate reference to all the Romanies living in Italy. On a section of its website that was dedicated to 'Communities with no Territory', the Ministero dell'Interno was equally indiscriminate in branding Rom, Sinti and Camminanti all as *Zingari*. Other subsections were also dedicated to the *campi nomadi*, which tended to imply that people living in these areas are nomadic. The updated version of the Ministero dell'Interno's (2017) website contains a section which broadly refers to the category *Minoranze* (minorities). On this page, Romanies are still defined as 'stateless communities' that 'are not settled within a delimited territory' (para. 6), despite the fact that some communities have been rooted in specific Italian regions for centuries. In Abruzzo, for instance, Romanies started to settle there around the fourteenth century (Solopescara n.d.). Interestingly, despite acknowledging the fact that they are no longer 'nomads' but mainly sedentary, the Ministero dell'Interno (2017) continues to use the term 'nomad'. As stated on its website: 'In Italy the most common *nomad groups* are "Rom", mainly settled in the Centre and South of Italy, 'Sinti' in the North of Italy and Caminanti in Sicily' (para. 5). This terminology perpetuates inaccurate and misleading information about these people. It also encourages the perception that Romanies who live in *campi nomadi* do so because they are 'stateless' and 'nomads'.

The Making of the 'Camps Policy'

From Protection to Segregation

In a work published in 2000 by the ERRC, Italy was iconically defined as 'Campland', the only country in Europe promoting a policy of segregating its Roma population inside 'ghetto-like urban camps' (Clough Marinaro 2009: 265). Almost two decades later, herding of Romani people into camps remains the dominant means used by the Italian Government to ensure the social 'inclusion' of this minority group, as highlighted in a recent report published by Associazione 21 Luglio (2016). According to Clough Marinaro and Sigona (2011: 587), the camps

The Institutional and Spatial Segregation of Romanies in Italy   **47**

are the most visible expression of Roma's social exclusion and are consequently the primary focus both of popular anti-Gypsism and institutional repression and control. While many camps are being demolished because of dire living conditions, others are being built by the same authorities to continue ware-housing an ethnic group for which few alternative policy approaches are devised.

The institutional policy of using camps to suit a supposedly 'nomadic lifestyle' has been defined by UNAR (2011b) as a completely 'made in Italy' solution. This particular approach places Italy in the unique position as 'precursor' within a European context. In 2006, for instance, the French Government also started supporting the construction of *villages d'insertion* ('integration villages'). Although they are officially aimed at all marginalised populations, regardless of their ethnicity (Délégation Interministérielle à l'hébergement et à l'accès au lodgement 2011), they are currently inhabited by Romani migrants only (Doytcheva 2016).

According to Piasere (2004, as cited in SCPPHR 2011), the 'politics of the camps' can be dated back to the mid-twentieth century, corresponding with the arrival of Romani people from the then Yugoslavia. Piasere explains that this Government policy was not rolled out as the result of a specific national choice, but could rather be described as 'a local policy which, from the northern [Italian] cities, developed and contaminated the rest of the country' (49). From the 1980s onwards, this approach gained support and funding from a number of *Regioni*.[1] It is because of this political process (ranging from local experiments to national policy) that Italy has slowly turned into a *paese dei campi* or 'Campland'. In other words, what could be initially described as a generic *consuetudine* (custom) later became a political practice sanctioned by law. The institution of the *campo nomade* as we know it today finds its very origins in the *Leggi Regionali* (Regional Laws) issued during the 1980s. The idea of the Romani people as 'nomadic' and the creation of camps as an institutional measure to 'protect' this alleged 'cultural trait' were the main features of these laws (Fiorucci 2010). Enactment of this legislative framework was significant for two reasons. One, it represented a belated

---

[1] The Italian state is administratively subdivided into 20 regions, each characterised by a local regional administration endowed with some legislative powers.

attempt to respond to the Romani presence in Italy, an embryonic mechanism for regulating the discriminatory episodes affecting them. Two, it reinforced stereotypical ideas, laying down the association between Romanies and camps.

On this point, a social worker operating inside one of the *campi nomadi* was adamant:

> In the Italian mainstream mentality, the '*Zingari*' (Gypsies) were always considered nomads. Before the Second World War, though, only a proportion of them were still nomadic or semi-nomadic. These people, in particular, were devoted to the '*spettacolo viaggiante*' (travelling exhibitions and performances), horse-trading, metal handicrafts and were defined as '*girovaghi*' (itinerants/vagrants) by mainstream society. After the war, a process of settlement took place, and an economic boom, until the first influx of Romani people from Yugoslavia began. When the Italian Government issued the Regional Laws, it was with the earlier nomadic or semi-nomadic Romanies in mind. The government was trying to solve a problem, such as the need for housing policy, but without seriously thinking about a reality that had been changing. Those laws were thus not able to deal with the situation as it evolved and to respond properly to it. Those people were no longer nomads. Yet, institutions continue to implement, in the best case, the 'camps' solution. (As cited in Fiorucci 2010: 35)

Indeed, although only a fraction of the Romani people live in camps today—between one-quarter and one-sixth of the entire population of this minority (Associazione 21 Luglio 2016) —the '*Rom/nomade/Zingaro* that policymakers have in mind is an abstract person created around the use of stereotypical images' (Sigona 2007, as cited in Fiorucci 2010: 35).

According to Bravi and Sigona (2006), the very first form of recognition and protection of the 'right to live nomadically' harks back to October 1973, when the Ministero dell'Interno issued the *Circolare* (internal memorandum) MIAC no. 17/73. This document was directed at Italy's mayors, especially those from the northern regions, who had started to enforce *divieti di sosta* (no-parking zones) against Romani groups.[2] The Sinti were the sub-group particularly affected by these repressive measures, since their usual activities implied frequent relocation throughout the country. Although this Act required local administrations to abolish discriminatory

---

[2] This practice persists in several urban areas (U Velto 2008; Francese 2015).

bans and allow Romani people the right to a temporary stay in designated areas (Maggian 2011), it also had repercussions. Firstly, it started to contextualise these people as a *Problema Nomadi* (Ministero dell'Interno 2006). Secondly, the recommendations contained in the MIAC no. 17/73 were also sowing the seeds of a future 'camps strategy'. In fact, it led to the creation of special campsites, which had to be equipped with all modern conveniences (Ministero dell'Interno 2006; Sigona 2002). The principles advanced in 1973 were reinforced in 1985 with the issuing of a new *Circolare* (MIAC no. 15185/85). On this occasion, the inappropriateness of forced evictions of Romani people being carried out by local administrations was again highlighted (Ministero dell'Interno 2006).

Nevertheless, as argued by Sigona (2002), the 'expulsion policy' adopted by many Italian local authorities even in the 1970s forced part of the Romani population to be constantly on the move. This repressive approach was responsible for rotating the 'Romani problem', by exporting it from one urban area to the next. This had also strengthened prejudices and fixed ideas about the Romanies as 'nomadic' (Bontempelli 2006). With the introduction of these new legislative measures, Romani people were given a chance to settle temporarily in specific areas. The characteristics of these early types of encampment already resembled today's *campi nomadi*. They were delimited areas located on the urban fringe in accordance with *piani regolatori comunali* (urban planning regulations) governing their location, size and settlement standards (Nessun luogo è lontano 2008). On top of that, the regulations were quite rigid, subjecting inhabitants of these embryonic camps to a range of restrictions. For example, school attendance for children was compulsory and truancy could result in the child's family being evicted from the camp; police had standing instructions to enforce special controls over the camp areas and residents had to carry identity papers at all times (Sigona 2002).

The Camp as a 'Civilising Site'

In the 1970s, the implementation of a new Government approach was spurred on by a progressive impetus, based on the view that this was the way that would best meet the needs of a 'non-sedentary, nomadic population'. Over the years, though, this political shift led to the exclusion of the Romani people from active citizenship, with all the rights attached to it (among other things housing, schooling, employment and health care). The camp evolved from the initially tenuous notion of *campo sosta* (halting site) to a more permanent concept of the *villaggio attrezzato* (equipped village). Still, the rootlessness attached to *nomade*, a term used in Italian political discourse on the false assumption that all Romani people are stateless and itinerant (Ciani 2011; UNAR 2011a), constitutes the main justification for the temporary character of this type of intervention. In the era when the Italian Government started regulating Romani policy, Opera Nomadi—a non-profit organisation established in the 1960s and one of the first to work at integrating the Romanies—played an important role in combating discrimination and prejudice.

But Opera Nomadi's efforts also had a downside. While advocating for Romani rights, it was also responsible for the spread of a certain perception that Romanies were exponents of nomadism. The organisation's self-denomination is telling: Opera Nomadi literally means 'activity (work) for nomads'. With that idea in mind from its earliest days, and its support of the first *campi sosta* designated for Romani caravans, Opera Nomadi helped normalise a kind of official intervention, and a rigid, narrowly defined understanding of what Romani culture was (Bravi and Sigona 2006; Sigona 2002). Ironically, Opera Nomadi was proactive in rejecting negative stereotypes attached to Romani communities, yet its own view of them, consistently iterated, was static and stereotyped. For instance, in 1965 when Opera Nomadi pushed for the introduction of 'special schooling' for Romani children living in camps, it laid the foundation for differential treatment and a two-tiered pedagogical system. At the same time, this initiative carried overtones of 'charity', centred as it was on the premise that these camps were to be a temporary solution.

This schools system, also known as *Lacio Drom*, was the fruit of mediation by Opera Nomadi between public authorities and Romani communities (Associazione 21 Luglio 2011b). The launch of this measure marked the first time that systematic schooling had been introduced for a minority group not previously involved in the Italian educational system (ISMU 2011). According to Bravi and Sigona (2006), the main idea behind this new Government intervention was not merely to give

Romanies the benefits of an Italian education but to sponsor their 're-education'. Together with their children, adults had to be imbued with a civic spirit aimed at forging a mutually positive society (Sigona 2002). In those years, the educational gap between mainstream Italians and Romanies was commonly explained as a result of adhering to their own culture. Rituals related to gender roles, treatment of the dead, funerals and religion were all considered to play a crucial role in inhibiting their social development. As a consequence, so it was thought, they had to be re-educated through a process of cultural change effected within their own communities. The *campi sosta* became instrumental towards this end (Azzolini 1971, as cited in Bravi and Sigona 2006).

The educational project for Romani children was fundamentally driven by a sort of 'religious or civilising mission'. In some cases, teaching staff looked upon Romani children as if they were primitive and savage. This attitude, Sigona argued (2002), was reinforced by the Catholic and missionary roots of Opera Nomadi volunteers. At the same time, the creation of a separate schooling system was a way of keeping Romani students out of Italian schools (Bellucci 2007). Only in 1982 was 'special schooling' at last abolished, but then supplementary teachers were introduced. This conveyed the impression that Romanies were afflicted with some kind of 'abnormality' compared to their Italian peers, and needed to be the objects of specific intervention. Despite the official suppression of separate schooling for Romanies, some principles have revived the practice (Associazione 21 Luglio 2011b). Nowadays, Opera Nomadi's long-established policy, as well as its controversial and often ill-defined relationship with the State bureaucracy, is regularly criticised by various Romani activists and intellectuals.

In Santino Spinelli's opinion (Italian Romani intellectual and internationally renowned musician), Opera Nomadi should be held

> responsible for the proliferation of nomad camps in Italy. For many years this organisation convinced both mainstream society and public institutions that Roma and Sinti are nomads [...] so they need nomad camps to be built for them. These spheres of activity cost the Italian society a lot of money, and Romani people became victims of this vulgar charity network. (Associazione Thèm Romanó 2010, para. 3)

Kazim Cizmic, a Romani from former Yugoslavia, president of the Unirsi Association (International and National Union of Roma and Sinti), is another who has accused Opera Nomadi of making money out of Romani people (Gruppo Intercultura CdB S. Paolo 2011). Interestingly, Cizmic was also vice-president of Opera Nomadi. According to research conducted by Monica Rossi (2010: 228),

> for a long time it had been the only organisation to benefit from the funds for schooling of Roma children until the year 2000, when the arrival of other associations such as ARCI, CDS and Ermes – Comunità Capodarco replaced it, winning all the Municipality bids concerning Roma schooling projects.

Opera Nomadi basically enjoyed an undisputed monopoly over Romani issues for many years. Only recently, partly due to internal divisions and partly to growing competition, were they coaxed into sharing the 'business' of the Romani people with other organisations. A negative opinion of Opera Nomadi and its president, Massimo Converso, also emerged from my interviews with the representatives of different 'pro-Romani' organisations in the city of Rome during 2012.

Condemnation of the organisation's ultra-conservative approach and its past political choices appeared unanimous. Today, Opera Nomadi, as a national unified body, no longer exists. The central headquarters, directed by Converso, in Rome recently collapsed. Only the branch offices in major cities have survived and continue to act independently (Bagnoli 2010). Yet, State agencies have been often giving preference to reports prepared by Opera Nomadi, rather than one's prepared by independent organisations or well-known academics. For instance, two of the major studies carried out by the Government in recent years—*The Publication on Stateless Minorities* issued in 2006 by the Ministero dell'Interno and the *Final report of the survey on the status of Roma, Sinti and Travellers in Italy* published in 2011 by the SCPPHR—rely extensively on Opera Nomadi's knowledge of Romani-related issues. Despite the widespread criticism mentioned earlier, a three-year agreement was signed between the Ministero dell'Istruzione (MIUR) and Opera Nomadi in 2009, covering the education of Romani children and the fight to bring down school dropout rates (MIUR 2009). It is worth noting that during a private meeting held in 2012, Romani intellectual Nazzareno Guarnieri (personal communication, February 26, 2012) accused Cizmic of corruption, arguing that he embezzled public funds that were to be directed to the schooling of Romani children living in the institutional camp 'Castel Romano'. Converso's image had also been surrounded by similar accusations. In 2016, these rumours were confirmed, when an investigation exposed the existence of systemic corruption and bribery within the *campi nomadi* involving (among others) Cizmic and Converso (Fiano and Sacchettoni 2016).

From Italian *'baraccati'* to Romani 'Camp-Dwellers'

This section presents the case of 'Casilino 900', a Romani camp in the suburb of Casilina on the south-eastern outskirts of the Italian capital— where former *baraccati* (shanty-dwellers) live. Camp Casilino 900 is not only a good example of the product of bipartisan strategy towards the Romani communities but also a forgotten relic of the nation's and city's historical memory. The problem of Rome's *baraccati* has a long history (Ministero del Lavoro e delle Politiche Sociali 2010). Immediately after the end of the Second World War, agglomerations of shanty dwellings spread throughout the capital city's environs. Mostly concentrated along the Tiber (the main river that runs through Rome), near parks and industrial zones, they provided shelter for all those who had lost their homes during the bombing of the city in 1943/1944 or had been displaced by the war. Casilino 900 was one of the areas that was occupied for decades by post-war Italian refugees. Later on, during the economic boom of the 1960s, Rome also became a destination for immigrants from the south of Italy in their quest for job opportunities and better living conditions. Many became 'squatters' in the abandoned shacks of citizens who had either received *alloggi popolari* (council houses) or found more permanent housing (Ministero del Lavoro e delle Politiche Sociali 2010).

In the 1980s, Italian groups from Naples, Sicily and Calabria occupied these same shacks. As often as not, their neighbours would be Romani immigrants, who had been settling in the capital region since the late

1960s (Associazione 21 Luglio 2011a). During the 1970s and 1980s a massive programme of council house construction undertaken by local administrations gave Italian citizens the opportunity to move into new accommodation. In 1981 the first council houses were granted to *Rom Napulengre* (Neapolitan Romanies) and *Rom Abruzzesi* (Abruzzi Romanies) from the shanty town in the inner suburb of Mandrione. A few years later, in 1987, the first three *campi sosta* were built (Rossi 2010). Since then, due to a lack of public investment, living in shacks or other makeshift shelter became a solution adopted mainly by foreign immigrants, not just Romanies (Ministero del Lavoro e delle Politiche Sociali 2010). Casilino 900 was inhabited until the end of the 1980s only by Romani residents, who had been migrating to Rome at different stages with most hailing from Yugoslavia. For a brief period in 2000 and 2001, the camp was home to 160 Moroccan immigrants. On February 18, 2001, a fire destroyed the area where they were located and two years later, they left (Associazione 21 Luglio 2011a).

When it comes to protecting and promoting their basic rights, such as the provision of adequate living conditions, Romani people are commonly regarded as 'second-class citizens'. To this day, the preference for official Romani camps rather than council houses remains the principal strategy. This is clearly evident, for example, in the following utterance by Rome's former Deputy Mayor Sveva Belviso: 'There is no valid alternative to the camps. It is not possible to fast-track the granting of council houses to Romani people. That would be to discriminate against Italians registered on the waiting lists' (as cited in Cucinotta 2012). In May 2017, the new mayor of Rome, Virginia Raggi, launched her strategy for the eradication of the camps for Romanies (Rainews 2017). However, in March 2017 the city council had also approved the creation of a new 'equipped camp', as a temporary measure for *apolidi* (stateless people), in the territory of the XV Municipal Hall (Bisbiglia 2017b). Despite making some reference to the possibility that the 4500 Romani people living in institutional camps might be deemed fit to apply for council houses (Bisbiglia 2017a), this plan is still largely unapplied. Besides which, it is not clear how the Raggi Mayorship will handle the 3000 Romani living in informal settlements (Per i Diritti Umani 2017). In other words, Italians still receive and retain priority for the allocation of tenement buildings.

The Institutional and Spatial Segregation of Romanies in Italy 55

This remains the case, in light of the fact that in Italy, and particularly in Rome, housing was the 'real emergency', as the then prefect of Rome, Giuseppe Pecoraro, declared, at a time when the Italian Government implemented extraordinary measures in order to deal with the Romani issue (Zema 2012). In 2017, housing remains a critical problem for many. In 2007 some 600,000 families across the Italian territory were under threat of eviction (Noi Consumatori 2007). A decade later, as stated by the Italian Ministry of Interior (2016), 61,718 evictions were issued. As for the city of Rome, while over 3200 families were forcibly evicted in 2016, only 200 council houses were allocated (Bisbiglia 2017c). At the same time, about 10,000 people are registered on a waiting list for public housing (Gaita 2017). Amnesty International (2012: 14) recently concluded: 'Social housing in Italy is scarce'. The sector is constantly shrinking, although the number of people in need of housing is actually rising (Riccardo and Gruis, 2007). Italy occupies one of the worst positions in Europe in terms of public-housing stock. Such stock accounts for about 5.4 per cent of all real estate in Italy, a low ratio compared to the Netherlands (33 per cent), Austria (20.1 per cent), Denmark (20 per cent) and Sweden (19 per cent), which have the four highest levels in the EU (Pittini et al. 2015).

The fact that these council houses are allocated according to discriminatory criteria makes it almost impossible for Romani individuals to access them, as Amnesty International (2016) recently reported. A 'points system' assigns a higher score to the most vulnerable families. Two big hurdles face Romani applicants, though. Firstly, to be registered, they must prove they have been evicted from private accommodation. Secondly, to be assessed, they must show they have the right of residency. On the first point, Amnesty International (2012: 14) notes how

> Roma who have always lived in camps will never be able to prove eviction from private accommodation, no matter how many forced evictions they may have endured, even though they are among the most in need of social housing. Camps are not regarded as private accommodation and eviction from camps does not follow the same safeguards as eviction from private accommodation.

As for the second point, Amnesty International notes that in order to register residency, an address is needed, with street name and house number. Romani families most in need of social housing often live in informal settlements with no street number. In other words, not only does Italian public opinion oppose the creation of an official camp or a 'parking zone' for Romani people: the suggestion of giving them council houses has the potential to provoke public unrest (Sigona 2002). In turn, public pressure influences the way policymakers develop their political strategy (Bontempelli 2006).

Today, there is only one regional law in the Lazio region specifically aimed at the inclusion of the Romani population, L.R. no. 82/85, *Norme in favore dei rom* (norms supporting Romani people), which dates back to May 24, 1985 (Quinto 2017). Although the law implies the possibility of Romanies who choose a sedentary life to have access to public housing, this is a commitment that remains mainly on paper. Other Italian regions, such as Umbria or Lombardy, seem to exclude *a priori* this option (Associazione 21 Luglio 2013). Its major weak points can be summarised as follows: the law makes constant use of the term 'nomad' and *campi sosta*, somehow generating a natural association between these two terms; it makes no mention of the complexity of the Romani population, and specifically to the Sinti, Camminanti Siciliani or Romanies from former Yugoslavia who have been residing in Italy, and in particular Rome, since the 1960s; it contradicts the 'National Strategy' main goal of dismissing the 'camps policy' as unable to meet the needs of a population which is no longer nomadic (Associazione 21 Luglio 2013; Fiorucci 2010). The dearth of council houses and inadequacy of the legislative framework designed to regulate this issue are significant impediments to a comprehensive policy of social inclusion.

The Legislative Framework on Romani Issues

'Legal Limbo'

Ghettoisation of the Romanies in authorised camps not only leads to their 'physical segregation from Italian society' but to 'their political, economic and cultural isolation as well' (OsservAzione 2006: 8). In a report released in March 2012 the Committee on the Elimination of Racial Discrimination ([CERD] 2012: 4) raised great concern over the fact that Italy continued to put Romanies 'in camps outside populated areas that are isolated and without access to health care and other basic facilities'. Its concluding remarks urged the Italian Government to desist from practising segregation, and instead encouraged it to find alternative housing solutions (CERD 2012: 4). Several few years hence, Italy has not gone any distance in implementing the *National Action Plan against Racism, Xenophobia and Related Intolerance*, and the *National Strategy for the Inclusion of Roma, Sinti and Caminanti Communities*, as stated by Gay Mcdougal, Committee Expert and Rapporteur for Italy: while the conditions of existing camps were shocking, new camps were still being opened (CERD 2016). According to a 2008 survey conducted by the Croce Rossa Italiana (CRI), 67 per cent of the Romani living in *campi nomadi* in Rome are from the former—and now non-existent—Yugoslavia (Pulzetti 2010). It is not surprising that in 2011 about 72.6 per cent of the Romanies in these camps were jobless (SCPPHR 2011). According to a recent report released by the European Roma and Travellers Forum (ERTF), 'it is estimated that only one out of ten Roma aged 20 to 64 has a paid job in Italy. Such high unemployment is typically 4-5 times higher than the non-Roma population' (ERTF 2015: 5).

In fact, one of the main issues many Romanies face in Italy is that they find themselves in a sort of 'legal limbo'. This denies the opportunity to fully participate in the social and political life of the country. Dire living conditions in the camps, often defined as *non luogo* (no man's land; Bravi and Sigona 2006), immediately conjures up another type of limbo, or *Kalisferia*, which in *Romanes* means 'a place between Earth and Heaven'. This term was used by Ronald Lee (2002), upon entering Camp Casilino 900 in Rome for the first time. The legal status of *apolidia* (statelessness) that characterises most camp-dwelling Romanies (mainly those coming from Bosnia and Herzegovina, Serbia and Kosovo; European Commission Against Racism and Intolerance [ECRI] 2016) today constitutes a formidable obstacle within a network of interventions undertaken by bureaucrats or Third Sector organisations. This obstacle has never allowed them to become self-sufficient. Uncertain legal status is a fundamental issue bearing on the right to participate in the civil and political life of the State without being discriminated against (Crepaldi and Boccagni 2009). This uncertainty is tantamount to 'indirect discrimination' by the Italian Government, which has never shown any determination to narrow the existing legislative gap between Romanies and Italians as a whole, thus minimising the prospect of equal treatment for Romani individuals.

This administrative barrier clearly falls within the remit of Article 2 of the European Council's Racial Equality Directive 2000/43/EC, which defines indirect discrimination:

> Indirect discrimination shall be taken to occur where an apparently neutral provision, criterion or practice would put persons of a racial or ethnic origin at a particular disadvantage compared with other persons, unless that provision, criterion or practice is objectively justified by a legitimate aim and the means of achieving that aim are appropriate and necessary. (Council of the European Union 2000: 3)

This situation can also be explained using the analysis by Clough Marinaro (2009) of Foucault's (1990) concept of 'biopolitics'. As Marinaro pointed out, it is possible to notice in the Italian context, the emergence of a new form of controlling one's internal 'enemies', in this case the Romanies—a feat achieved by taking charge of their lives (Foucault 1990; Marinaro 2009: 267). By applying administrative techniques, the Italian Government aims to control the existence of Romani individuals, thus factoring racism into the power equation (Cemlyn 2000). In turn, this allows the Government to avoid the use of physical violence in defence of society (Clough Marinaro 2009).

As Sigona and Monasta have observed (2006), the lack of personal documents and residency permits, a key priority for 'foreign Romanies', becomes a political tool that can be used to threaten individuals with expulsion. This condition 'heightens their social vulnerability and diminishes their hopes of integration and social inclusion' (ECRI 2016: 28). One of the main consequences of this 'biopolitics' is that today a vital part of the Romani population, mainly those living in official or unofficial camps, are virtually forced into succumbing to 'welfare dependency'. This leaves the principal causes of their marginalisation untouched, and forces them to survive on their wits (in casual and occasional employment, if

The Institutional and Spatial Segregation of Romanies in Italy 59

they can get it; in the worst cases, crime if they cannot). A report produced by the ERRC in 2000 portrayed this as the outcome of a policy that aimed to 'infantilise' Romani individuals (ERRC 2000: 12). Almost two decades later, the Italian Government is still using the same approach, which disempowers these people within a highly controlling system of marginalisation. The strongly criticised policy of housing Romanies in authorised and equipped camps, with their poor education and resultant high illiteracy rates—together with an indefinite legal status, the consequent unemployability and the denial of access to social security and healthcare system— keeps Romani communities on the margins of society and excludes them from public and political life.

Like *stranieri in patria*

To this day, the main 'legal reference points for statelessness are the 1954 Convention Relating to the Status of Stateless Persons, and the 1961 Convention on the Reduction of Statelessness' (Lynch 2005: 3). Italy is among the 80 signatories of the 1954 convention, which was ratified and entered into force under the title Law no. 1962/306. Only recently, on September 29, 2015, with Law no. 162/2015, has Italy ratified the 1961 convention (Senato della Repubblica 2015). According to the first convention, which provides general recognition to the condition of statelessness, a stateless person is defined as 'a person who is not considered a national by any State under the operation of its law' (United Nations [UN] 2011: 2). The second convention was introduced instead, with the goal being 'to avoid statelessness and resolve conflicts concerning nationality' (Parra 2011: 1674). Out of 193 UN members, only 68 states[3]—Italy finally among them—have acceded to it (United Nations High Commissioner for Refugees [UNHCR] 2017). As stated in the Explanatory Report of the European Convention on Nationality, 'only "*de jure* stateless persons" are covered and not "*de facto* stateless persons"' (CoE 1997: art. 4). The 1961 Convention 'recommends that persons who are *de facto* stateless should as far as possible be treated as *de jure*, to enable them to acquire an effective nationality' (Lynch 2005: 7).

---

[3] Correct as of June 7, 2017.

Ratification of this resolution should now provide a stronger protection for those persons who, for various reasons, do not fall into the *de jure* category. However, an organic law that can help stateless people to have their legal status recognised is still missing, as recently stated by the Italian Senate of the Republic (Senato della Repubblica 2016). A bill drawing up the principles of this important reform has been drafted, but it has been under consideration for almost two years by the Italian legislature (Paris 2017). At present, people without citizenship in Italy have two main procedural options to obtain the 'stateless' status: one administrative and the other judicial. In the first case, the individual need to submit an application before the Ministry of Interior. Due to the strict administrative requirements, this procedure has been harshly criticised (Chiodi and Latini 2016; Volpi 2017). The applicant must include a number of documents, such as birth certificate, a certificate proving residency in Italy, a copy of a residence permit, in order to prove his/her statelessness. It is obvious that this procedure is mainly directed to lawful residents, who represent a small minority. As for the judicial procedure, which follows the rules of the ordinary civil procedure, it also presents some disadvantages. As per the administrative procedure, the applicant carries the burden of proof. In addition, both procedures require a long processing time, such that applicants can remain in legal limbo for many years, without their basic rights being protected.

The existence of two types of statelessness (*de jure* and *de facto*), both displaying very different protection regimes, is a complex issue with significant political implications. This condition today affects most of the Romanies who arrived in Italy in the 1990s after the Balkans war. Although there are no official figures on these people in Italy, their number is somewhere between 3000 (Associazione 21 Luglio 2017) and 15,000 (Camera dei Deputati 2014). These individuals, together with their children—both those who were born on Italian territory and those who were not—are still deemed '*de facto* stateless'. That generally they have no documents proving their identity or place of origin makes it impossible for them to become '*de jure* stateless' (Sigona 2015). In some cases, this is due to the fact that 'the civil registries in their places of origin were destroyed during the conflicts in the former Yugoslavia' (ERTF 2015: 4).

As observed by David (2008):

> There is a catch-22 situation in Italy: The Interior Ministry requires a residency permit to recognise people as stateless. And a residency permit cannot be obtained without a valid passport, which stateless people do not have. The Interior Ministry declined to comment. The only alternative is to sue the ministry in a civil court, which can take at least three years. (Paras 18 & 19)

It is an invidious paradox that leaves today's Romanies very much 'caught in the middle'.

There is another aspect here to be considered. Italy's current citizenship policy (Law no. 91 of 1992) is mainly based on the *ius sanguinis* principle or law of blood, which relates to having Italian ancestry. According to this law, children born in Italy to stateless parents, to unknown parents or to parents who cannot transmit their nationality to their children should have the right to automatic citizenship. However, this depends on the legal position of their parents (Sigona 2015). As stated by Daniela di Rado, of the Consiglio Italiano per i Rifugiati (Italian Council for Refugees or CIR), these children can become Italian citizens only if their parents have been recognised as 'stateless' before they were born. The reality is that they are often denied citizenship because their parents are undocumented. Despite the fact they were either born in Italy or have been living there for decades, that 'they speak Italian, eat Italian and cheer for Italy's football stars' (David 2008: para. 1), these individuals are not officially 'Italians'. As recently stated in an appeal submitted by a group of Romanies to the President of the Italian Republic, Romanies feel like *stranieri in patria* (aliens in their homeland; Marcenaro 2012b). The lack of a legally defined position is generally understood to be one of the main reasons for their being considered 'nomads' or, in the worst cases, *intrusi e stranieri* (intruders and aliens) who should be removed (UNAR 2012: 14).

The Lack of National Legislation Regarding the Romani Issue

As previously mentioned, all Government interventions since the 1970s concerning the education, social life, health or employment of Romanies have been predicated on the existence of the 'camp'. Initially established as a means of affording this minority 'cultural protection', the camps gradually evolved into an official instrument of segregation and control. Within this context, the *Leggi Regionali* constituted a belated attempt to recognise and protect Romani language and culture. Different regions were slowly trying to fill what was a national legislative gap. This amounted to a clean break with the past, 'when the *"Zingari"* were merely considered a security and hygiene challenge, unworthy of protection' (Sigona 2002: 70). Nevertheless, the different degrees of autonomy granted by the national Government to the various regions created discrepancies and inequities in the enactment and enforcement of these laws over the years. Some laws are today more progressive than others: Tuscany and Emilia Romagna, for instance, focused on housing issues (Sigona 2002). In other cases, the regional laws only became effective long after their introduction. In Rome, a 1985 regional law was enforced only ten years afterwards (Clough Marinaro 2009: 273).

At the same time, the terms used by each region in reference to its Romani population are also quite varied: 'Nomad minorities' in Emilia Romagna; 'nomads' in Sardinia and Umbria; 'traditionally "nomads" and "semi-nomads"' in Lombardy; 'gypsies' in Piedmont; 'Rom' and 'Sinti' in Veneto, Tuscany and Trento; and 'Rom' in Lazio and Friuli Venezia Giulia (Associazione 21 Luglio 2013). It is clear that public authorities did not stand completely aloof, yet the existing legislative framework has mainly focused on recognising 'nomadism' as a characteristic cultural trait (Zincone 2001). Political recognition of this ethnic group has always been incomplete and piecemeal. If, on the one hand, the Government did not grasp this community's growing diversity, then the authorities' responses did not meet specific needs within a uniform legislative framework, on the other (Bonetti 2012). Not surprisingly, to this day, a comprehensive national law has not yet been enacted. Instead, there is a mosaic of regional laws (Forgacs 2015), all of which have led over the years, to great normative differences. After all, as Basso, Di Noia and Perocco (2016) argue, Romani people are recognised neither as an 'ethnic minority' nor as a 'linguistic one'.

In 2010, Olga Marotti, a lawyer and expert with the UNAR, stated that drafting a national law, with these people as its specific object of intervention, was considered a low priority by legislators. That year, for the very first time, a conference was held in the Italian Republic, entitled

The Legal Status of Roma and Sinti in Italy (ASGI 2010). The first-fruit of this international conference was the publication of a book that amounted to a unique work in this field (Bonetti 2011). It was actually the first legal text in the republic's 65-year history that extensively examined the condition of Italy's Romani minority. To this day, this remains the most comprehensive attempt to address this issue. It may be quite illuminating at this point to give an account here of renowned Italian jurist Paolo Bonetti's keynote speech:

> [...] an *ad hoc* law is required for the Romanies. This would not be to discriminate in their favour but to protect their cultural specificity. Certainly, the enactment of a national law by itself is not enough. It is necessary to modify a number of other national laws as well. The National Roma Integration Strategy is inadequate [...] The Regional Laws have failed: not only are they unequally disseminated, but they were not always implemented. The State of Emergency has failed. [...] It is therefore essential to have a long-term, specific law to protect this minority group. And it must be binding on all local authorities. [...] Complexity must be worked through from within, rather than using a bulldozer. Besides, the problem does not belong exclusively to the politics of the present. We need to look beyond today because coalitions change over time and problems remain unsolved. (Bonetti 2012)

The existence of a gap in the national legislative framework makes it impossible to define unambiguously, the status of individuals belonging to this ethnic group. This triggers a series of operational and bureaucratic reflexes that, till now, have prevented the Romani communities from taking an active part in any process of social inclusion. This has further reinforced the vicious circle of poverty, exclusion and discrimination whereby disadvantage in one area can lead to disadvantage in another. As stated by the Director of the EU Agency for Fundamental Rights, Morten Kjaerum (2012),

> exclusion from education leads to exclusion from employment, which leads to increased poverty, which forces people to live in poor or segregated housing which, in turn, affects their educational and employment opportunities, as well as their health. And the vicious circle starts again and again. (Para. 9)

The rule of law and an efficient legal system are crucial to removing social barriers and empowering the Romani communities. The lack of such a policy framework in Italy clearly contrasts with a recent resolution adopted by the Committee of Ministers of the CoE (2017) on the protection of national minorities by Italy. According to this document, the Italian Government is urged 'to elaborate and adopt without delay a specific legislative framework, at the national level, for the protection of the Roma, Sinti and Caminanti communities with due consultation of representatives of these communities at all stages of the process'.

Lack of Cultural Recognition and Cultural Misinterpretation

Since their arrival on the Italian peninsula, the *Zingaro* has always been characterised as the outsider *par excellence*, forced to play the role of 'guest' and live in a condition of perpetual *semi-clandestinità* (semi-illegality) (Tomasone 2012). Especially after the *Risorgimento*, the new unified Italian nation-state introduced policies specifically directed at controlling 'vagabonds' and, more broadly, 'socially dangerous' groups, such as the Romanies (Clough Marinaro 2009). They became the main catalyst for all the fears harboured by the Italian elite for the purity of a putative national identity. As in other parts of Europe, in Italy the pinnacle of segregational practices against Romanies was reached early in the 1940s when they were interned in concentration camps such as Agnone, Arbe, Boiano, Cosenza, Gonars, Perdasdefogu and Prignano (Bravi 2009; Bravi and Sigona 2006). According to a recent report by the SCPPHR (2011: 36), notwithstanding the terrible price paid by this population, 'there isn't much historical data about the persecution of the Romani people in Italy during the Fascist regime, and it is not possible to clearly determine the full dimension of the persecution they suffered'. Not until recently, as Clough Marinaro (2009) states, were the crimes against them committed by the Fascist regime during the Second World War disclosed.

In past decades, it was commonly believed that Fascism had 'targeted them exclusively as a problem of public order and not as a racial issue, unlike the Nazi regime' (Clough Marinaro 2009: 272). This assumption

The Institutional and Spatial Segregation of Romanies in Italy **65**

stemmed from a deep-seated belief in the legendary generosity of Italians. According to Favero (2010: 138), this misconception, which originated during the initial Italian colonial enterprises, has long been 'functioning as an ideological laundry for reformulating and then setting aside disquieting moments of national shame'. The growth of nationalist sentiments (Armillei 2016) is now playing a key role in entrenching a collective historical amnesia. Although to this day there are no precise figures regarding the actual number of victims, it is safe to say that between 500,000 and 1.5 million Romani individuals lost their lives during the Second World War (SCPPHR 2011). In the Romani language, this catastrophe is called the *Baro Porrajmos*, or 'Great Devouring' of human life (Hancock 2009). Jews were similarly subjected to discrimination, oppression, racial hatred and violence over centuries culminating in the dramatic events of their extermination under the Third Reich (Jones 2011: 233). Although both these peoples experienced huge losses during the Second World War, the Final Solution is mostly remembered today as the Holocaust of the Jewish people, while little space is generally given over to understanding the *Porrajmos* and the genocide of other victims.

Despite its alliance with Nazi Germany during the Second World War and its consistent contribution to the diffusion of Nazi-Fascist rule across Europe, Italy has not yet officially acknowledged its responsibility for the Holocaust of the Romanies (Armillei et al. 2016). Therefore, the Italian Government has not found itself able or willing to offer reparations to those incarcerated in Italian concentration camps or transferred to German-run extermination camps (Bravi 2006; Scutellà 2016). Commemoration of the Holocaust was established with the passing of Law no. 211/2000 which enshrines January 27 as the *Giorno della Memoria* (Remembrance Day) (Parlamento Italiano 2000). This Act does not mention the mass extermination of the Romani people or any other minority targeted by the Nazi-Fascist 'Racial Laws'. It contains a solitary reference to the Jewish people and the Italian politicians and soldiers that were deported to the Nazi camps. Only recently have some official documents specifically mentioned the *Porrajmos*, the need to promote awareness of it, commemorate it through meaningful initiatives and amend Italian legislation to extend official recognition to the historicity of the 'Great Devouring'.[4] Not surprisingly, Romani genocide is mainly forgotten in official history and collective memory (Armillei et al. 2016). In February 2011, an attempt was also made to change the relevant legislation through the draft Law no. 2558, which aimed to extend Holocaust Memorial Day to all Romani people (Ministero dell'Interno 2014). However, this was not successful, and since then, little has been done to address this.

A final point to be made is about the lack of formal recognition of the Romanies as a national minority. Nomadism has now almost disappeared in Italy, and Europe more broadly (Warmisham 2016). And yet, the Romanies still have a reputation as nomadic people. The major consequence for categorising the Romanies as 'nomads' is that they do not make it on to the list of non-native populations officially recognised by the Italian Government. Recognition of these minorities was restated by Law no. 482 of December 15, 1999, entitled *Provisions Concerning the Protection of Historico-Linguistic Minorities.* This Act had the merit of recognising, enhancing and protecting the language and culture of 12 minorities living on the peninsula: Albanians, Catalans, Germans, Greeks, Slovenes, Croats, as well as the speakers of French, Franco-Provençal, Friulian, Ladin, Occitan and Sardinian. However, the adoption of this law actually reinforced the exclusion of Romanies. The main reason for exempting Romani communities from the mandate of this legislation was that the Italian Government considered them 'not settled in a given territory' (Ministero dell'Interno 2009b: 4). In other words, they are still seen as 'non-sedentary and nomads' (Fiorucci 2010: 32).

The law established that recognition must be premised on four criteria. According to *The Publication on Stateless Minorities* issued by the Ministero degli Interni in 2006, the Romani minority meets only three of these: the State acknowledged that 'Rom, Sinti and Camminanti' had been living in Italy for the last 600 years (historical criterion), that they were defined as a specific ethnic group (ethnic criterion) and that they had their own language, *Romanes* (linguistic criterion), but they did not fulfil the fourth

---

[4] A couple of examples can be named here: the *Report to Parliament Concerning the Enforcement of the Principle of Equal Treatment and of the Effectiveness of Legal Mechanism* (UNAR 2011a) and the 'National Strategy' (UNAR 2014).

criterion (the link with a specific territory). The fact that the Romani communities were considered 'distributed throughout the entire territory' (Ministero dell'Interno 2009b: 20) precluded them from accessing legal protection. Exclusion of the Romani people was addressed merely as a bureaucratic and political issue rather than a linguistic and cultural one. Paradoxically, as argued by Spinelli (2012), *Romanes* is spoken by more people in Italy than some 'protected languages'. According to a recent document published by the CoE (2016), the Italian authorities have acknowledged this situation and have submitted numerous proposals in the Parliament to amend Law no. 482/1999 with the aim to address the identified shortcomings. To this day, though, no progress overall has been observed regarding the opportunity for the Romani communities to be granted linguistic and cultural minority status.

Bibliography

Amnesty International. (2012). On the edge: Roma forced evictions and segregation in Italy. Retrieved from http://www.amnesty.ch/de/laender/europa-zentralasien/italien/dok/2012/amnesty-fordert-das-ende-der-diskriminierung-von-roma/bericht-on-the-edge-roma-forced-evictions-and-segregation-in-italy.-september-2012.-16-seiten

Amnesty International. (2016). Roma on the margins: Housing rights denied. Retrieved from https://www.amnesty.org/en/latest/campaigns/2016/04/roma-on-the-margins-housing-rights-denied/

AnalisiPolitica. (2008). I campi nomadi? Gli italiani li vogliono chiudere. Il sondaggio di AnalisiPolitica. [Nomad camps? Italians want to shut them down. A survey by AnalisiPolitica]. Retrieved from http://affaritaliani.libero.it/static/upll/sond/sondaggio-analisi-politica-campi-nomadi.pdf

Armillei, R. (2016). Reflections on Italy's contemporary approaches to cultural diversity: The exclusion of the 'Other' from a supposed notion of 'Italianness'. *Australia New Zealand Journal of European Studies, 8*(2), 34–48.

Armillei, R., Marczak, N., & Diamadis, P. (2016). Forgotten and concealed: The emblematic cases of the Assyrian and Romani Genocides. *Genocide Studies and Prevention: An International Journal, 10*(2), 98–120.

Arrigoni, P., & Vitale, T. (2008). Quale legalità? Rom e gagi a confronto. [Which legality? A comparison between Romani and Gadje peoples]. *Aggiornamenti Sociali, 59*(3), 182–194.

Associazione 21 Luglio. (2011a). Casilino 900, parole e immagini di una diaspora senza diritti [Casilino 900, words and images of a diaspora with no rights]. Retrieved from http://www.21luglio.org/index.php/report/13-casilino-900

Associazione 21 Luglio. (2011b). Linea 40: Lo scuolabus per soli bambini rom [Line 40: The school bus for Romani children only]. Retrieved from http://www.21luglio.org/index.php/notizie/9-lassociazione-21-luglio-presenta-la-ricerca-qlinea-40q

Associazione 21 Luglio. (2013). Questione rom: Dal silenzio dello Stato alle risposte di Regioni e Province [The Romani issue: From the government's silence to the responses of the regions and provinces]. Retrieved from http://www.21luglio.org/wp-content/uploads/2013/10/QUESTIONE-ROM.-Dal-silenzio-dello-Stato-alle-risposte-di-Regioni-e-Province.pdf

Associazione 21 Luglio. (2016). Rapporto annuale 2016 [Annual report 2016]. Retrieved from http://www.21luglio.org/21luglio/wp-content/uploads/2017/04/RAPPORTO-ANNUALE_2016_WEB.pdf

Associazione 21 Luglio (2017). 21 Luglio: ecco la situazione di Rom e Sinti in Italia [21 Luglio: The situation of the Rom and Sinti in Italy]. Retrieved from https://cild.eu/blog/2017/04/07/titolo-21-luglio/

Associazione Carta di Roma. (2014). Zingaro chi? Rom, romeni e rom romeni nei media [Who's the Gypsy: Rom, Romanians and Romanian Romanies in the media]. Retrieved from https://www.cartadiroma.org/news/zingaro-chi-rom-romeni-e-rom-romeni-nei-media/

Associazione per gli Studi Giuridici sull'Immigrazione. (2010). Convegno internazionale: La condizione giuridica di Rom e Sinti in Italia [International conference: The legal status of Roma and Sinti in Italy]. Retrieved from http://www.asgi.it/home_asgi.php?n=918

Associazione Thèm Romanó. (2010). Un evento da non sottovalutare [An event which is not to be underestimated]. Retrieved from http://www.associazione-themromano.it/albumquattrosettembre.htm

Bagnoli, L. (2010, September 7). Opera Nomadi, il teatrino dell'indecenza continua... [Opera Nomadi, the indecency farce continues...]. U Velto. Retrieved from http://sucardrom.blogspot.it/2010/09/opera-nomadi-il-teatrino-dellin-decenza.html

Basso, P., Di Noia, L., & Perocco, F. (2016). Disuguaglianze combinate: Il caso dei Rom in Italia. In L. Di Noia (Ed.), *La condizione dei Rom in Italia*. Venice: Edizioni Ca' Foscari.

Bellucci, P. (2007). *Rom e Sinti in Italia: Profili storici e culturali* [Roma and Sinti in Italy: Historical and cultural profiles]. Urbino: Università degli Studi di Urbino.

The Institutional and Spatial Segregation of Romanies in Italy   69

Bisbiglia, V. (2017a, May 31). Campi rom, Raggi presenta "piano di superamento" [Romani camps, Raggi launches her plan]. *Il Fatto Quotidiano.* http://www.ilfattoquotidiano.it/2017/05/31/campi-rom-raggi-presenta-piano-per-il-superamento-patto-di-responsabilita-su-servizi-e-casa-prime-chiusure-in-24-mesi/3627998/

Bisbiglia, V. (2017b, March 13). Roma, dal comune ok a un nuovo campo rom [Rome, the city council approves the building of a new camp]. *Il Fatto Quotidiano.* Retrieved from http://www.ilfattoquotidiano.it/2017/03/13/roma-dal-comune-ok-un-nuovo-campo-rom-campidoglio-misure-temporanee-obiettivo-e-superare-villaggi/3447711/

Bisbiglia, V. (2017c, August 26). Roma, i numeri dell'emergenza abitativa [Rome, the figures about the housing emergency]. *Il Fatto Quotidiano.* Retrieved from https://www.ilfattoquotidiano.it/2017/08/26/roma-i-numeri-dellemergenza-abitativa-la-regione-al-comune-avete-40-milioni-ma-non-ci-avete-mai-risposto/3816067/

Bonetti, P. (Ed.). (2011). *La condizione giuridica di Rom e Sinti in Italia: atti del convegno internazionale. Università degli studi di Milano-Bicocca.* Milano: Giuffrè Editore.

Bonetti, P. (2012, April 24). Launch of the book 'The legal status of Roma and Sinti in Italy'. Speech presented at the Fondazione Adriano Olivetti, Rome.

Bontempelli, S. (2006). La tribù dei gagè: Comunità Rom e politiche di accoglienza a Pisa (1988–2005) [The tribe of the Gadje people: Romani communities and integration policies in Pisa (1988–2005)]. *International Journal of Migration Studies, 43*(164), 947–967.

Bravi, L. (2006). *Porrajmos, altre tracce sul sentiero di Auschwitz* [Porrajmos, new traces along the path towards Auschwitz]. Mantova: Istituto di Cultura Sinta.

Bravi, L. (2009). The history of the Roma and Sinti in Nazi-Fascism. Retrieved from http://www.theforgotten.eu/index.php?option=com_content&view=article&id=58%3Ala-storia-dei-rom-e-sinti-nel-nazi-fascismo-di-luca-bravi&lang=en

Bravi, L., & Sigona, N. (2006). Educazione e rieducazione nei campi per 'nomadi': Una storia [Education and re-education inside camps for 'nomads': An overview]. *International Journal of Migration Studies, 43*(164), 857–874.

Camera dei Deputati. (2014). Adesione della Repubblica italiana alla Convenzione delle Nazioni Unite sulla riduzione dei casi di apolidia, fatta a New York il 30 agosto 1961 [Accession of the Italian Republic to the convention on the reduction of statelessness, adopted in New York on 30 August 1961]. Retrieved from http://www.camera.it/_dati/leg17/lavori/schedela/apriTelecomando_wai.asp?codice=17PDL0028110

Cellai, F. (2003). Camminanti siciliani [Sicilian Travellers]. Città di Torino, Rivista Informagiovani, 4. Retrieved from http://www.comune.torino.it/infogio/rivista/archivio/04_03/a0403p34.htm

Cemlyn, S. (2000). Assimilation, control, mediation or advocacy? Social work dilemmas in providing anti-oppressive services for traveller children and families. *Child & Family Social Work, 5*(4), 327–341.

Centre on Housing Rights and Evictions, European Roma Rights Centre, Open Society Institute, Roma Civic Alliance in Romania, Romani Criss. (2008). Security a la Italiana: Fingerprinting, extreme violence and harassment of Roma in Italy. Retrieved from http://www.errc.org/cms/upload/file/m00000428.pdf

Chiodi, A., & Latini, M. (2016). Promessa cittadinanza [Promising citizenship]. Retrieved from http://reportage.corriere.it/cronache/2016/promessa-cittadinanza/

Ciani, P. (2011). I rom e i sinti in Italia: Una foto in corsa [Roma and Sinti in Italy: A picture in motion]. In T. Santoriello (Ed.), Ho visto anche degli zingari felici: Di chi parliamo quando parliamo di rom [I've also seen happy Gypsies: Who we mean when we speak of the Romanies]. Retrieved from http://www.associazionegiornalisti.it/public/files/rom_vademecum.pdf

Clough Marinaro, I. (2009). Between surveillance and exile: Biopolitics and the Roma in Italy. *Bulletin of Italian Politics, 1*(2), 265–287.

Clough Marinaro, I., & Sigona, N. (2011). Introduction Anti-Gypsyism and the politics of exclusion: Roma and Sinti in contemporary Italy. *Journal of Modern Italian Studies, 16*(5), 583–589.

Commissione straordinaria per la tutela e la promozione dei diritti umani. (2011). Rapporto conclusivo dell'indagine sulla condizione di Rom, Sinti e Camminanti in Italia [Final report of the survey on the status of Roma, Sinti and Travellers in Italy]. Retrieved from http://www.senato.it/service/PDF/PDFServer/DF/233751.pdf

Committee on the Elimination of Racial Discrimination. (2012, March). Eightieth session. Consideration of reports submitted by States parties under article 9 of the convention. Concluding observations of the Committee on the Elimination of Racial Discrimination: Italy. Retrieved from http://www2.ohchr.org/english/bodies/cerd/docs/CERD.C.ITA.CO.16-18.pdf.

Committee on the Elimination of Racial Discrimination. (2016). Committee on the Elimination of Racial Discrimination examines the report of Italy. Retrieved from http://www.ohchr.org/EN/NewsEvents/Pages/DisplayNews.aspx?NewsID=20978&LangID=E

Council of Europe. (1997). European convention on nationality: Explanatory report. Retrieved from http://conventions.coe.int/Treaty/EN/Reports/Html/166.htm

Council of Europe. (2012). Descriptive glossary of terms relating to Roma issues. Retrieved from http://a.cs.coe.int/team20/cahrom/documents/Glossary%20Roma%20EN%20version%2018%20May%202012.pdf

Council of Europe. (2016). Fourth opinion on Italy adopted on 19 November 2015. Retrieved from https://rm.coe.int/16806959b9

Council of Europe (2017). Resolution CM/ResCMN(2017)4 on the implementation of the Framework Convention for the Protection of National Minorities by Italy. Retrieved from https://search.coe.int/cm/Pages/result_details.aspx?ObjectId=090000168073038c

Council of the European Union. (2000). Council Directive 2000/43/EC of 29 June 2000: Implementing the principle of equal treatment between persons irrespective of racial or ethnic origin. Retrieved from http://eur-lex.europa.eu/LexUriServ/LexUriServ.do?uri=OJ:L:2000:180:0022:0026:EN:PDF

Crepaldi, C., & Boccagni, P. (2009). The Roma in Europe: Socio economic condition and policies of integration. Paper presented at the 7th ESPAnet conference 2009 Session 11 – Migrants and the Welfare State. Retrieved from http://www.espanet-italia.net/conference2009/paper/11%20-%20Crepaldi.pdf

Cucinotta, G. (2012, September 11). 'Case popolari ai Rom? Se le scordino': Belviso infiamma la querelle sgomberi ['Council house to Romani people? They can forget about it': Belviso sets the dispute about evictions on fire]. Corriere della Sera. Retrieved from http://roma.corriere.it/roma/notizie/cronaca/12_settembre_11/nomadi-case-popolari-belviso-2111775738259.shtml

David, A. (2008, September 21). Thousands without a country make Italy their home: Lack of papers places lives in limbo. *The Washington Post*. Retrieved from http://www.unhcr.org/cgi-bin/texis/vtx/refdaily?pass=463ef21123&date=2008-09-22&cat=Europe

Délégation Interministérielle à l'hébergement et à l'accès au logement. (2011). French government strategy for Roma integration within the framework of the communication from the Commission of 5 April 2011 and the Council conclusions of 19 May 2011. http://ec.europa.eu/social/BlobServlet?docId=8969&langId=en

Doytcheva, M. (2016). Between infra-right and public hospitality: Ambiguity in local policies towards Roma migrant families in France. *International Journal of Migration and Border Studies, 2*(4), 365–381.

European Commission Against Racism and Intolerance. (2016). ECRI report on Italy (fifth monitoring cycle) Adopted on 18 March 2016. Retrieved from https://www.coe.int/t/dghl/monitoring/ecri/Country-by-country/Italy/ITA-CbC-V-2016-019-ENG.pdf

European Roma and Travellers Forum. (2015). Fact sheet on the situation of Roma and Sinti in Italy. Retrieved from http://barabal.eu/images/The_situation_of_Roma_in_Italy_13062015.pdf

European Roma Rights Centre. (2000). Campland: Racial segregation of Roma in Italy. Retrieved from http://www.errc.org/cms/upload/media/00/0F/m0000000F.pdf

Favero, P. (2010). Italians, the 'good people': Reflections on national self-representation in contemporary Italian debates on xenophobia and war. *Outlines – Critical Practice Studies, 2*, 138–153.

Fiano, F., & Sacchettoni, I. (2016, June 16). Tangenti sui campi rom [Bribes regarding the Romani camps]. *Corriere della Sera*. Retrieved from http://roma.corriere.it/notizie/cronaca/16_giugno_29/tangenti-campi-rom-indagati-15-dirigenti-campidoglio-819c44c6-3d66-11e6-922f-98d199acd386.shtml#

Fiorucci, M. (2010). Un'altra città è possibile. Percorsi di integrazione delle famiglie Rom e Sinte a Roma: Problemi, limiti e prospettive delle politiche di inclusione sociale. [Another city is possible. Integration trajectories of Roma and Sinti families in Rome: Problems, limitations and perspectives of social inclusion policies]. Roma, Italia: Geordie onlus.

Forgacs, D. (2015). *Margini d'Italia: l'esclusione sociale dall'Unità a oggi* [Italian margins: Social exclusion from political unity now]. Gius: Laterza & Figli Spa.

Foucault, M. (1990). *The history of sexuality: An introduction* (trans: Hurley, R.). New York: Vintage Books.

Francese, I. (2015, April 8). Il sindaco veneto vara il "divieto di sosta ai nomadi" [The Venetian Mayor launches 'no-parking zones' for nomads]. *Il Giornale*. Retrieved from http://www.ilgiornale.it/news/cronache/sindaco-veneto-vara-divieto-sosta-ai-nomadi-mio-paese-non-li-1114331.html

Gaita, L. (2017, January 29). Emergenza abitativa, in Italia nel 2015 oltre 57mila sfratti per morosità [Housing emergency in Italy, in 2015 more than 57,000 evictions for rent arrears]. *Il Fatto Quotidiano*. Retrieved from http://www.ilfattoquotidiano.it/2017/01/29/emergenza-abitativa-in-italia-nel-2015-oltre-57mila-sfratti-per-morosita-roma-in-testa-fuori-casa-1-famiglia-ogni-272/3348138/

Gruppo Intercultura CdB S. Paolo. (2011). Parliamo dei Rom solo se ne muore qualcuno tra le fiamme? [We talk about Romani people only when some of them die in a fire]. Retrieved from http://www.amicoqua.org/?p=3304

Hancock, I. (2009). Responses to the Porrajmos: The Romani Holocaust. In A. Rosenbaum (Ed.), *Is the Holocaust unique?* (3rd ed., pp. 39–64). Boulder: The Westview Press.

Hancock, I. (2010). *We are the Romani* [Ame Sam E Rromane Džene]. Hatfield: The University of Hertfordshire Press (Original work published 2002).

ISMU. (2011). Alunni con cittadinanza non italiana: Verso l'adolescenza. Rapporto nazionale A.s. 2010/2011 [Students with no Italian citizenship: Towards adolescence. National report academic year 2010/2011]. Quaderni ISMU, 4. Retrieved from http://www.ismu.org/index.php?page=85

Istituto per gli Studi sulla Pubblica Opinione. (2008). Italiani, Rom e Sinti a confronto: Una ricerca quali-quantitativa. [A comparison between Italians, Roma and Sinti: A quali-quantitative research]. European Conference on the Roma Population, Scuola Superiore dell'Amministrazione dell'Interno. Retrieved from http://www.interno.gov.it/mininterno/export/sites/default/it/sezioni/sala_stampa/documenti/minoranze/0999_2008_01_22_conferenza_rom.html_1411422173.html

Jones, A. (2011). *Genocide: A comprehensive introduction* (2nd ed.). New York: Routledge.

Kington, T. (2008, May 17). 68% of Italians want Roma expelled: Poll. The Guardian. Retrieved from http://www.guardian.co.uk/world/2008/may/17/italy

Kjaerum, M. (2012). Making a tangible difference to Roma people's lives. Retrieved from http://fra.europa.eu/en/speech/2012/making-tangible-difference-roma-peoples-lives

Klímová-Alexander, I. (2005). *The Romani voice in world politics: The United Nations and non-state actors*. Aldershot: Ashgate Publishing Limited.

Lee, R. (2002). Roma ande Kalisferia: Roma in limbo. In S. Montesi (Ed.), *Terre Sospese: Vite di un campo rom* [Suspended Worlds: Lives of a campo rom]. Roma: Prospettiva Edizioni Srl. Retrieved from http://kopachi.com/articles/

Lynch, M. (2005). Lives on hold: The human cost of statelessness. Retrieved from http://www.refintl.org/policy/in-depth-report/lives-hold-human-cost-statelessness

Maggian, R. (2011). *Guida al welfare italiano: Dalla pianificazione sociale alla gestione dei servizi* [A guide to Italian welfare: From social planning to service management]. Santarcangelo di Romagna, Rimini: Maggioli Editore.

Marcenaro, P. (2012b, May 15). Regolarizzazione dei Rom provenienti dalla ex Jugoslavia [Regularisation of the Romani peoples from former Yugoslavia]. Retrieved from http://www.pietromarcenaro.it/index.php?option=com_content&task=view&id=1325&Itemid=247

Marzoli, D. (Ed.). (2012). Rom, Sinti e Camminanti in Italia [Roma, Sinti and Travellers in Italy]. Retrieved from http://www.fedevangelica.it/documenti/2/17d6721180962c67446aec731479cde2.pd

Matras, Y. (2004). The role of language in mystifying and demystifying Gypsy identity. In N. Saul & S. Tebbutt (Eds.), *The role of the Romanies: Images and counter-images of 'Gypsies'/Romanies in European cultures* (pp. 53–78). Liverpool: The University Press.

Ministero del Lavoro e delle Politiche Sociali. (2010). Senza Dimora: Storie, vissuti, aspettative delle persone senza dimora in cinque aree metropolitane [Of no fixed abode: Stories, experiences and expectations of homeless people in five metropolitan areas]. Retrieved from http://www.lavoro.gov.it/NR/rdonlyres/CE06FD73-D361-4414-96D8-8EB7E5243058/0/QRS10_senzadimora.pdf

Ministero dell'Interno. (2006). La pubblicazione sulle minoranze senza territorio [The publication on stateless minorities]. Retrieved from http://www1.interno.gov.it/mininterno/export/sites /default/it/assets/files/13/La_pubblicazione_sulle_minoranze _senza_territorio.pdf

Ministero dell'Interno. (2009a). Censimento dei campi nomadi: Gli interventi adottati per superare lo stato di emergenza [Census of the nomad camps: Interventions implemented to overcome the state of emergency]. Retrieved from http://www1.interno.gov.it/mininterno/export/sites/default/it/sezioni/sala_stampa/speciali /censimento_nomadi/

Ministero dell'Interno. (2009b). Third report submitted by Italy pursuant to article 25, paragraph 2 of the framework Convention for the Protection of National Minorities. Retrieved from http://www.coe.int/t/dghl/monitoring/minorities/3_fcnmdocs/PDF_3rd_SR_Italy_en.pdf

Ministero dell'Interno. (2012). Le comunità sprovviste di territorio [Stateless communities]. Retrieved from http://www1.interno.gov.it/mininterno/export/sites/default/it/temi/minoranze/sottotema002.html

Ministero dell'Interno. (2014). IV rapporto dell'Italia sull'attuazione della convenzione quadro per la protezione delle minoranze nazionali [IV Report on the implementation of the Framework Convention for the Protection of National Minorities]. Retrieved from http://www.interno.gov.it/sites/default/files/allegati/2014_05_12_iv_rapporto_it.pdf

Ministero dell'Interno. (2016). Pubblicazione sfratti 2016 [The publication on the evictions in 2016). Retrieved from http://ucs.interno.gov.it/ucs/contenuti/Andamento_delle_procedure_di_rilascio_di_immobili_ad_uso_abitativo-168224.htm

Ministero dell'Interno. (2017). Minoranze [Minorities]. Retrieved from http://www.interno.gov.it/it/temi/cittadinanza-e-altri-diritti-civili/minoranze

Ministero dell'Istruzione. (2009). Firmato protocollo d'intesa tra Miur e Opera Nomadi [The agreement between MIUR and Opera Nomadi has been signed]. Retrieved from http://hubmiur.pubblica.istruzione.it/web/ministero/cs240409

Nessun luogo è lontano. (2008). Rom e Sinti, dalla legalità alla coesione sociale [Roma and Sinti, from legality to social cohesion]. Appunti Arancioni, 4. Retrieved from http://www.nessunluogoelontano.it/nuovosito/index.php?option=com_docman&task =searchresult&order=dmname&ascdesc=ASC& Itemid=48

Noi Consumatori. (2007). Diritto alla casa: Italia sotto accusa all'Onu [Housing rights: Italy is under UN indictment]. Retrieved from http://www.noiconsumatori.org/articoli/articolo.asp?ID=1138

OsservAzione. (2006). Political participation and media representation of Roma and Sinti in Italy: The case studies of Bolzano-Bozen, Mantua, Milan and Rome. Retrieved from http://www.osservazione.org/documenti/osce_italy.pdf

Paris, M. (2017, June 15). Ius soli, all'ultimo miglio in Senato. Ecco le regole negli altri Paesi Ue [Ius soli, last mile in the Italian Senate. Here are the rules in other EU countries]. Il Sole 24 Ore. Retrieved from http://www.ilsole24ore.com/art/notizie/2017-06-07/lo-ius-soli-tenta-l-ultimo-miglio-italia-come-francia-maguarda-modellotedesco--151755.shtml?uuid=AErfjLaB&refresh_ce=1

Parlamento Italiano. (2000). Legge 20 luglio 2000, n. 211: 'Istituzione del "Giorno della Memoria" in ricordo dello sterminio e delle persecuzioni del popolo ebraico e dei deportati militari e politici italiani nei campi nazisti' ['The institution of "Remembrance Day" for the commemoration of extermination and the persecutions of the Jewish people and the Italian soldiers and politicians deported to the Nazi camps']. Retrieved from http://www.camera.it/parlam/leggi/00211l.htm

Parra, J. (2011). Stateless Roma in the European Union: Reconciling the doctrine of sovereignty concerning nationality laws with international agreements to reduce and avoid statelessness. *Fordham International Law Journal, 34*(6), 1666–1694.

Per i Diritti Umani. (2017, March 27). Il percorso di superamento dei campi rom deciso dal Comune di Roma [The process for overcoming the Romani camps set by the Municipality of Rome]. Per i Diritti Umani. https://www.peridirittiumani.com/2017/03/27/il-percorso-di-superamento-dei-campi-rom-deciso-dal-comune-di-roma/

Piasere, L. (2004). *I Rom d'Europa: Una storia moderna* [The Roma of Europe: A modern history] Rome: Laterza.

Pittini, A., Ghekière, L., Dijol, J., & Kiss, I. (2015). The State of Housing in the EU 2015: A Housing Europe Review. Retrieved from http://www.housingeurope.eu/resource-468/the-state-of-housing-in-the-eu-2015

Pulzetti, A. M. (2010). I campi Rom: Le nuove sfide umanitarie [Romani camps: New humanitarian challenges]. Retrieved from http://www.crocerossachepassione.com/index.php?option=com_docman&task=cat_view&gid=12&Itemid=8

Quinto, V. (2017, February 28). Roma, ancora proteste contro i campi rom. Soluzione forse nel dialogo? [Rome, new protests against the Romani camps. Maybe dialogue is the solution?]. Aris Notiziari. Retrieved from http://www.arisnotiziari.it/wordpress/?p=5400

Rainews. (2017, May 31). Roma, cosa prevede il piano Raggi per il superamento dei campi rom [Rome, Raggi's plan to overcome the Romani camps]. *Rainews.* Retrieved from http://www.rainews.it/dl/rainews/articoli/roma-cosa-prevede-piano-raggi-per-superamento-campi-rom-ff1552ee-b1b5-424e-900d-05cb921c9f0e.html?refresh_ce

Riccardo, F., & Gruis, V. (2007, June). Social housing renovation in Italy: Which solutions can be found in the Dutch housing management model? Paper presented at the International Conference 'Sustainable Urban Areas', Rotterdam.

Ricordy, A., Trevisani, C., Motta, F., Casagrande, S., Geraci, S., & Baglio, G. (2012). La salute per i rom: Tra mediazione e partecipazione [The health of the Romanies: Between mediation and participation]. Bologna: Edizioni Pendragon. Retrieved from http://www.libertaciviliimmigrazione.interno.it/dipim/export/sites/default/it/assets/pubblicazioni/La_salute_per_i_rom_giugno2012.pdf

Rossi, M. (2010). The city and the slum: An action research on a Moroccan and a Roma Xoraxanè community in Rome. Doctoral dissertation. Retrieved from http://etheses.bham.ac.uk/1263/

Rövid, M. (2011). Cosmopolitanism and exclusion: On the limits transnational democracy in the light of the case of Roma. Doctoral dissertation. Retrieved from http://pds.ceu.hu/doctoral-school-phd-dissertations

Scutellà, A. (2016, January 27). Giornata della memoria, il Senato ricorda rom e i sinti deportati, confinati e sterminati [Remembrance Day, the Senate commemorates Roma and Sinti people deported, detained and exterminated]. *La Repubblica.* Retrieved from http://www.repubblica.it/solidarieta/diritti-umani/2016/01/27/news/giornata_della_memoria_il_senato_ricorda_rom_e_i_sinti_deportati_confinati_e_sterminati-132172210/

Senato della Repubblica. (2015). Atto Camera n. 2802 XVII Legislatura [Chamber Act No. 2802 XVII Legislature]. Retrieved http://www.senato.it/leg/17/BGT/Schede/Ddliter/45140.htm

Senato della Repubblica. (2016). Disposizioni concernenti la procedura per il riconoscimento dello status di apolidia in attuazione della Convenzione del 1954 sullo status delle persone apolidi [Provisions concerning the procedure for the recognition of stateless status in compliance with the 1954 Convention on the Status of Stateless Persons]. Retrieved from http://www.senato.it/japp/bgt/showdoc/17/DDLPRES/967066/index.html?stampa=si&spart=si&toc=no

Sigona, N. (2002). *Figli del ghetto: Gli italiani, i campi nomadi e l'invenzione degli zingari* [Sons of the ghetto: Italians, nomad camps and the invention of the Gypsies]. Civezzano: Nonluoghi.

Sigona, N. (2007). Lo scandalo dell'alterità: Rom e sinti in Italia [The scandal of otherness: Roma and Sinti in Italy]. In S. Bragato & L. Menetto (Eds.), *E per patria una lingua segreta: Rom e sinti in provincia di Venezia* (pp. 17–32). Portogruaro: Nuovadimensione.

Sigona, N. (2015). Campzenship: Reimagining the camp as a social and political space. *Citizenship Studies, 19*(1), 1–15.

Sigona, N., & Monasta, L. (2006). Imperfect citizenship: Research into patterns of racial discrimination against Roma and Sinti in Italy. Retrieved from http://www.osservazione.org/documenti/OA_imperfectcitizenship.pdf

Solopescara. (n.d.). Pescara citta' storia: Gli zingari. Retrieved from http://www.solopescara.com/content/knowledgebase/kb_view.asp?kbid=201

Spinelli, S. (2012). *Rom, genti libere: Storia, arte e cultura di un popolo misconosciuto* [Roma, free people: History, art and culture of an unrecognized people]. Milan: Dalai Editore.

Tomasone, M. (2012). Il genocidio nazista dei Rom [The Nazi Genocide of the Romanies]. Retrieved from www.istoreto.it/amis/micros/rom_micros.rtf

U Velto. (2008, March 7). Sucar Drom chiede misure urgenti al Ministero dell'Interno [Sucar Drom demands urgent measures from the Ministero dell'Interno]. *U Velto*. Retrieved from http://sucardrom.blogspot.com.au/2008/03/sucar-drom-chiede-misure-urgenti-al.html

Ufficio Nazionale Antidiscriminazioni Razziali. (2011a). Relazione al Parlamento sull'effettiva applicazione del principio di parità di trattamento e sull'efficacia dei meccanismi di tutela [Report to Parliament concerning enforcement of the principle of equal treatement and of the effectiveness of legal mechanism]. Retrieved from http://sbnlo2.cilea.it/bw5ne2/opac.aspx?WEB=ISFL&IDS=18688

Ufficio Nazionale Antidiscriminazioni Razziali. (2011b). Vai oltre i pregiudizi, scopri i Rom: Go beyond prejudice, discover the Roma. Retrieved from http://www.cominrom.it/wordpress/wp-content/uploads/2011/11/Volume_Campagna-Dosta_UNAR.pdf

Ufficio Nazionale Antidiscriminazioni Razziali. (2012). Brutte notizie: Come i media alimentano la discriminazione [Bad news: How media fuel discrimination]. LIL Quaderni di Informazione Rom. Roma: ISTSSS Editore

Ufficio Nazionale Antidiscriminazioni Razziali. (2014). Strategia Nazionale d'inclusione dei Rom, dei Sinti e dei Caminanti: Attuazione comunicazione commissione europea n.173/2011 [National Strategy for the inclusion of Roma, Sinti and Camminanti communities: European Commission communication no. 173/2011]. Retrieved from http://www.unar.it/unar/portal/wp-content/uploads/2014/02/Strategia-Rom-e-Sinti.pdf

United Nations. (2011). Guidance note of the secretary general: The United Nations and Statelessness. Retrieved from https://www.un.org/ruleoflaw/files/FINAL%20Guidance%20Note%20of%20the%20Secretary-General%20on%20the%20United%20Nations%20and%20Statelessness.pdf

United Nations High Commissioner for Refugees. (2017). Executive Committee of the High Commissioner's Programme Standing Committee 69th Meeting. Retrieved from http://www.refworld.org/pdfid/59a58d724.pdf

Vitale, T. (2010). Rom e sinti in Italia: Condizione sociale e linee di politica pubblica [Roma and Sinti in Italy: Social conditions and guidelines of public policies]. Osservatorio di Politica Internazionale, 21. Retrieved from http://www.parlamento.it/documenti/repository/affariinternazionali/osservatorio/approfondimenti/Approfondimento_21_ISPI_RomSinti.pdf

Volpi, F. (2017, April 7). The judicial statelessness determination procedure in Italy. LitigAction. Retrieved from http://www.litigaction.com/the-judicial-statelessness-determination-procedure-italy/

Warmisham, J. (2016). The situation of Roma and Travellers in the context of rising extremism, xenophobia and the refugee crisis in Europe. Retrieved from https://rm.coe.int/1680718bfd

Zema, A. (2012, April 3). In città, il prefetto: 'La casa è la vera emergenza' [In the city, according to the prefect: 'The house is the real emergency']. *Roma Sette*. Retrieved from http://www.romasette.it/modules/news/article.php?storyid=8363

Zincone, G. (Ed.). (2001). *Secondo rapporto sull'integrazione degli immigrati in Italia* [Second report on the integration of immigrants in Italy]. Bologna: Il Mulino.

3

The Paradoxes of the Italian Approach Towards the Romani People

The Enactment of the *Emergenza Nomadi*: National Level

At the end of 2007 and beginning of 2008 a number of 'high-profile crimes allegedly committed by individuals of Roma ethnicity from Romania [were] extensively reported in the news, exacerbating aggressive anti-Roma rhetoric by local and national politicians' (Amnesty International 2012: 6). As a consequence, the presence of Romani groups was associated with crime and treated as a security problem for the Italian population. In particular, the violent murder of Mrs Giovanna Reggiani, committed on October 30, 2007, supposedly by a Romanian Romani in the city of Rome, brought the 'Nomads/Gypsies' issue to national attention (Sigona 2008). At the beginning of 2007, the EU's enlargement during the centre-left Government led by Romano Prodi had also stimulated alarm among Italians with fear of an immigrant invasion from the newest entrants in the European bloc—Romania and Bulgaria (Sigona 2010). The political turmoil was exacerbated when the former centre-left mayor of Rome, Walter Veltroni, resigned to become the national leader of the Democratic Party (Sigona 2009). According to Sigona, this led to 'a transplant of "local" issues into the national arena' (287). Thanks to

© The Author(s) 2018
R. Armillei, *The 'Camps System' in Italy*, Mapping Global Racisms,
https://doi.org/10.1007/978-3-319-76318-7_3

79

Veltroni, who was in office at the time of the murder, an urgent meeting of the Italian Council of Ministers was called to tackle the alleged collective misconduct of Romani gangs. Eventually this resulted in the enactment and implementation of two governmental decrees, known as the 'anti-Roma Acts' (Lunaria 2011: 13).

Although these decrees were ostensibly designed to curb unspecified 'criminality', some of them made explicit reference to 'nomadi' (Office for Democratic Institutions and Human Rights [ODIHR] 2009). In October 2007, the Government adopted an emergency decree (No. 181/2007) which introduced a series of discriminatory measures 'aimed at facilitating the removal of EU citizens from Italy whenever they were deemed to represent a threat to public and national security' (Sigona 2008: 3). These measures authorised forced evictions from illegal camps, with no requirement to observe procedural safeguards or meet regional and international human rights standards. They also fuelled anti-Romani hysteria and violent attacks against them (ERRC et al. 2010). A year later, on May 21, 2008, the *Emergenza Nomadi* intervention was launched. Initially, it involved only the Lombardy, Campania and Lazio regions, but in May 2009 it was extended to Piedmont and Veneto. The choice to adopt such an extraordinary approach not only misused the terms 'nomads' and 'emergency' vis-à-vis the Romani people (Amnesty International 2010: 4), but also incited new efforts to disempower them. Romani voices were comprehensively ignored within the official operations of the 'Emergency'. They were further enmeshed in a system of 'welfare dependency' in which Government policies were directed at controlling and assimilating them.

Only amid the clamour of national and international criticism was the Government forced to re-frame the rationale for its intervention. New guidelines were issued, covering the manner in which the three crucial decrees—ordinances 3676, 3677 and 3678 signed by the President of the Council of Ministries on May 30, 2008—were to be acted upon. The Government reiterated that its extraordinary measures were not intended to target any particular ethnic group but were actually motivated by the official objective of improving Romanies' living conditions (Ministero dell'Interno 2008). The claim that this was an issue of urgent national significance was used to justify the enforcement by law of a 'state of exception'. As predicted by Agamben (1998), in fact, with every extension of the 'Emergency' its initial provisional character morphed into the new status quo, which slowly became the rule:

> On May 21, 2008, Prime Minister Silvio Berlusconi decreed a state of emergency until May 31, 2009. [...] On May 28, 2009 yet another decree was issued, extending the state of emergency to December 31, 2010. [...] On December 17, 2010, the Prime Minister issued yet another decree extending the state of emergency to December 31, 2011. (Associazione 21 Luglio 2012: 32)

Sigona (2002) also notes how the 'Emergency' became a 'new permanent political category', a measure designed to contain a problem rather than solve it once and for all.

In other words, this portrayal of an emergency allowed the Government to ignore the complexity of the Romani issue and its structural causes, while establishing a permanent policy of exclusion and marginalisation. Using a 1992 law, the Italian Government converted the very existence of Romani settlements into a threat to public order, requiring the adoption of extraordinary means and powers. According to the Article 5(1) of Law no. 225 of February 24, 1992, the President of the Council of Ministers is authorised to declare a state of emergency in a specified area for a specified period of time. This is to enable a swift response to natural disasters, catastrophes or other events requiring exceptional measures and powers. By decree of the Council of Ministers (DCPM May 21, 2008), special powers were conferred on prefects—permanent representatives of the national Government in a particular territory—allowing them to suspend existing laws (Amnesty International 2010). The presence of the Romani communities was compared to a sort of 'natural disaster' while, bizarrely, 'the Emergency did not relate to the shameful conditions that Romani people have been forced to endure, but rather to their presence itself' (Fiorucci 2010: 34).

Even though the Government denied it, the 'Nomad Emergency' was ethnically motivated. Under it were introduced:

> The monitoring of formal and informal camps, identification and census of the people (including minors) who are present there, and taking photos ('mug shots'); the expulsion and removal of persons with irregular status; measures aimed at clearing 'camps for nomads' and evicting their inhabitants; as well as the opening of new 'camps for nomads'. (ERRC et al. 2010: 18)

Since most 'camp-dwellers' were of Romani origin, this automatically made them the sole target of the measures adopted by the Government, thus replicating the assumptions underpinning the previous expulsion measure. As Favero (2010) argued, the authorities' main concern was to protect the 'good' local Italian population against the allegedly 'bad and dangerous' Romanies. The Italian Government, supported by an alarmed public, pushed for restrictive measures which reflected a widespread conception of the Romanies as an 'exogenous' threat, or even a 'degenerate' group, that had to be kept apart from the rest of society (Clough Marinaro 2009). Interestingly, legal action instituted in 2008, culminated in the Council of State, Italy's highest administrative court, declaring the 'Nomad Emergency' 'unfounded and unsubstantiated' on November 4, 2011, with its full judgement released 12 days later, on Berlusconi's last day in office (Amnesty International 2012; UNAR 2012).

However, despite this annulment, its legal and practical consequences persisted (Amnesty International 2012: 9). This left a legacy that continued to affect the way public policies specifically targeted Romanies. For instance, following Silvio Berlusconi's resignation, which took effect on November 16, 2011, new Prime Minister Mario Monti re-endorsed the 'Nomad Emergency' (Sina 2012). On February 15, 2012, the Monti Government appealed against the decision of the Council of State before the Court of Cassation. Three months later, on May 9, the Council of State suspended the operation of its previous ruling, pending the decision of the Court of Cassation (Associazione 21 Luglio et al. 2012). But the new prime minister's policy was unclear. On February 28, two weeks after lodging its appeal, the Monti Government endorsed UNAR's *National Strategy for the Inclusion of Roma, Sinti and Camminanti Communities*, which vowed 'to definitively overcome the emergency phase, which has characterised the past years' (UNAR 2014: 3). In July 2012, as CoE's Commissioner for Human Rights Nils Muižnieks noted after visiting Italy, the emergency approach was yet to be discontinued (Commissioner for Human Rights 2012). Despite Government avowals of a return to ordinary measures in meeting its official responsibilities, the suspension announced by the Council of State allowed the city of Rome to continue implementing its *Piano Nomadi* (Nomad Plan) unveiled in July 2009.

The *Piano Nomadi* in Rome

The *Piano Nomadi* was launched on July 31 of that year in Rome. The then former Interior Minister Roberto Maroni defined it as 'a model to be exported to the rest of Italy and elsewhere in Europe' (Clough Marinaro and Daniele 2011: 622). It was the first scheme developed under special powers provided by the presidential decree that had introduced the 'Nomad Emergency' in May 2008 (Amnesty International 2010). On October 22, 2008, months before the plan was even revealed, the Italian Government—together with the CRI and the police force—had conducted a special census to ascertain how many Romanies would be affected by the extraordinary measures. The census was carried out in the three major Italian cities of Rome, Milan and Naples, where the *Emergenza Nomadi* was consid ered most urgent. In these cities, the task of identification, prerogative of the CRI, revealed the existence of 167 encampments, of which 124 were *abusivi* (illegal) while 43 were *autorizzati* (recognised) (ODIHR 2009).[1] According to the census, 12,346 people were living in these camps, almost half of them (5436) children. It was also estimated that at least as many people had abandoned their dwellings since the state of emergency had been declared (Ministero dell'Interno 2009).

Prefects were authorised to 'carry out a census of individuals and families, children as well, and to collect and store personal information, including photos and fingerprints' (Amnesty International 2012: 9). This minority

---

[1] Today it is estimated that 18,000 Romanies live in 149 camps scattered throughout Italy that are run by public authorities. There are also 10,000 of them inhabiting informal settlements (Associazione 21 Luglio 2016b). This represents a clear increment since the end of the 'Nomad Emergency'.

group has always perceived the state as a threat. Afraid of being singled out and deported, many Romanies left the encampments before or during the census. The CoE (2012b: 8) noted,

> when required to register or to be fingerprinted they fear the worst. This is all the more understandable when they explain how they see similarities between much of today's anti-Roma rhetoric with the language used in the past in Europe by Nazis and fascists and other extremists.

The identification process was carried out with the aim of issuing a document known as a Document Authorising Temporary Stay (DAST). This paper would give the holder the right to reside for two years in a specified authorised camp (Amnesty International 2012). Ominously, DASTs were also 'granted' to 'Roma individuals with Italian citizenship who, according to the Constitution (art. 16, para. 1), have a full right to circulate freely throughout national territory' (Lunaria 2011: 47).

When the *Piano Nomadi* was about to be enacted by the right-wing administration of Mayor Gianni Alemanno, the city of Rome appeared to face the most drastic situation of all when it came to the living conditions of Romani communities. More than 80 *insediamenti abusivi* (illegal or unauthorised encampments), 14 *campi tollerati* (tolerated camps) and 7 *villaggi autorizzati* (authorised villages) were counted (Comune di Roma 2009). According to the census results released by the city council in 2009, some 2200 people lived in the first settlement type, 2736 in the second type and 2241 in the last-mentioned type. With an estimated (December 2008) population of 2,844,821 for Rome (Ferrazza and Menghi 2010), 'camp-dwellers' amounted to only 0.25 per cent of the capital city's entire population. Yet, despite these numbers, Rome, which 'has the highest number of Romani inhabitants' and is 'the main destination for rising numbers of Romanian Roma', was 'the focus of various media alarms referring to an "invasion" and "threats" posed by these groups' (Clough Marinaro 2009: 274).

Rome's *Piano Nomadi* envisaged the comprehensive re-organisation of existing camps (Cittalia 2011). The principal goals were the progressive closure of all the illegal and tolerated camps strewn across the city, the renovation of 'authorised' camps and the establishment of new ones.

The Municipality of Rome planned to settle 6000 camp inhabitants in 13 official 'authorised villages', all located on the urban fringe (Open Society Foundations and Open Society Justice Initiative 2010). One of the first critiques to emerge after the plan was sketched out concerned doubts over local authorities' capacity to carry it out. How could more than 12,000 people live in the 13 authorised encampments, which were already full and only had capacity for 6000? It seemed clear from the outset that not everyone could be accommodated. The mere creation of a transitional *Centro Emergenza Rom* (Romani Emergency Centre) with a capacity for only 600 people, as envisaged in the plan itself (Comune di Roma 2009), could not be considered a suitable solution. Interestingly, as Cosentino and Fico (2012) noted, Alemanno's administration built only one new camp (La Barbuta at an estimated cost of €10 million) out of the four initially envisaged.

As pointed out by Amnesty International (2010) in a recent report, significantly entitled 'The Wrong Answer', the eligibility criteria for a place in one of the 13 'villages' had also not been properly considered by the authorities:

> The criteria to determine who has access to the 'villages' would be based on good conduct – for instance, whether or not they had been involved in criminal activity. It is unclear whether this refers to a criminal conviction or whether mere criminal charges would be sufficient to deny a person a place in one of the new camps. Either way, the right to adequate housing is a basic human right, which cannot depend on past behaviour. (4–5)

Demolitions, forced evictions and other human rights violations were also major concerns. Lack of consultation with the individuals and communities affected by the plan, and the inadequacy of the housing solution offered, shed light on the rationale behind this official approach. According to Amnesty International (2010), many Romanies did not know how the administration's plan would affect them personally. Neither had Romani organisations and CSOs working in the camps been consulted. Most importantly and unsurprisingly, the Romanies interviewed by Amnesty International stated that they would prefer to live in ordinary accommodation, rather than being housed in metal containers within the confines of a camp. All these factors highlighted the limitations of the *Piano Nomadi* (Associazione 21 Luglio 2010; Lunaria 2011).

It is important to note that the implementation of the plan was in line with the policy adopted by Alemanno's immediate predecessor as mayor, left-winger Walter Veltroni. Veltroni had actually been the first to launch the idea of building *mega campi* (mega-camps) for Romani people. Although Veltroni managed in 2005 to complete only one of the four *villaggi della solidarità* (solidarity villages) he had planned, this type of accommodation would 'serve as the prototype for future ones' (Clough Marinaro 2009: 278). The approach of Veltroni's left-wing administration has been described by Clough Marinaro (2009) as deeply contradictory, oscillating between a vague sense of solidarity and a policy of exclusion. Veltroni's major concerns were the urban renewal of previously neglected working-class neighbourhoods and the fostering of a positive multicultural environment through the funding of intercultural projects and associations. However, his progressive project was stymied by the inhumane living conditions. His *strategia d'integrazione* (integration strategy) had two main features: the creation of four *mega campi* outside the city's ring road, and the portrayal of Romanies as a security risk.

The formal camp at Castel Romano, built after the dismantling of the more central camp of Vicolo Savini, illustrated Veltroni's approach to Romani issues, in that it was meant to be a 'model camp' under the *Patto per Roma Sicura* (Rome Security Pact) launched in May 2007. This camp had originally been established in 2005 alongside Pontina Road, a busy thoroughfare with the second highest rate of fatal car accidents in all of Italy. Built on a nature reserve named Decima Malafede, it is 30 km from the city centre and 5 km from the nearest town (EUropean ROma MApping 2008). Because of its extreme isolation, which forced residents to go to Rome or Pomezia for supplies and services, the 'equipped village' could hardly be considered fit to host 1000 or more people.[2] It was made up of

---

[2] This camp, which now hosts 1076 people, is experiencing a health emergency, with cockroaches, rats and contagious diseases such as scabies, proliferating (Di Toro 2017). The living conditions of its inhabitants have been worsening over time, to a degree that over the last five years 63 Romanies died of cancer in the Castel Romano camp (AffariItaliani.it 2017).

poorly insulated prefabricated metal huts, laid out in a grid and surrounded by high metal fencing, with no shade or greenery, or areas for socialising. Large parts of the plumbing and sewage system are defective and there is only one well that provides insufficient water for the needs of all the inhabitants, which they receive for a few hours a day. The water is undrinkable and there have been reports of residents contracting scabies and hepatitis. (Clough Marinaro 2009: 278–279)

The right-wing Alemanno administration continued its predecessor's strategy but also made a number of innovations. Among these was stricter attention to official supervision of the Romani residents in what were now called *villaggi attrezzati* (equipped villages). This particular aspect emerged from the 'Camp Regulations' adopted in February 2009 by local authorities in the Lazio region. These envisaged the presence of security officers in charge of controlling entry points to the camp and its residents; and video surveillance devices (Daniele 2011: 17). This severely limited the basic rights of access, residence and freedom of movement within this type of campsites (Open Society Foundations and Open Society Justice Initiative 2010: 4).

Political Bipartisanship on Romani Issues

Until 1994, as Chiarini (2011) argued, Italy was 'the only Western democracy in which a political force that unmistakably harks back to fascism can be observed in the institutions of the state'. More than a decade later, Berlusconi's last Government (May 2008–November 2011) was defined as 'the most right-wing cabinet since the Second World War' (Fekete 2008). He owns the largest private television company in Italy (Mediaset) and while serving as prime minister, he wielded 'considerable editorial influence over the three channels of public television, known collectively by the acronym RAI' (Human Rights Watch 2011: 10). A growing concern regarding the role of the Italian media in disseminating 'ideas of racial superiority or incitement to racial hatred' was especially stressed during his IV's Cabinet (CERD 2012: 5). In fact, after the 2008 national elections Berlusconi's right-wing coalition launched a massive campaign on security and immigration (Sciortino 2010). Nevertheless, manifestations of racism and xenophobia in Italy cannot be only ascribed to right-wing movements, Governments or parties. Contemporary discourses centred on some sort of racial superiority (CERD 2016) derive from a well-established 'tradition' of racism, in which the left-wing and liberal press find their place as well (Re 2010). For instance, the introduction of the so-called Emergenza Nomadi targeting Romani 'camp-dwellers' was the result of a bipartisan approach.

Broadly speaking, xenophobia is commonly understood as a hallmark of the right-wing. Certainly, the Right in Italy has the historical tendency to fuel racist tropes, particularly in relation to issues such as migration, crime and security (Vannucci and Della Porta 2011). As argued by Chiarini (2011: 141), for half a century (and more) the Right was 'synonymous with Fascism'. In the last two decades, the right-wing separatist *Lega Nord* (Northern League), one of Berlusconi's closest allies, regularly made the presence of immigrants' a political issue, while demonising 'aliens' in general as a security problem (Chiarini 2011). To the national ascendancy of this party, together with right-wing party *Alleanza Nazionale* (National Alliance)[3] and *Forza Italia* (Forward Italy) during the 1990s, must be added the emergence of assorted fascistic organisations such as Casa Pound, Forza Nuova, Militia and Contro Tempo (Berizzi 2012). As reported by Sigona (2008: 8), though, 'the old dichotomy which sees "security" as a prerogative of the right-wing and "solidarity" of the left-wing' was disrupted by the introduction of Emergency decree no. 181/2007 under a centre-left national administration.

This was one of a series of policy proposals labelled *Pacchetto Sicurezza* (Security Package), which former Prime Minister Romano Prodi had issued after the murder of Mrs Giovanna Reggiani. In particular it was the head of the left-wing Democratic Party, the then Mayor Veltroni, who was the first leader of a Left administration to co-opt the Right's approach to security (Sigona 2008: 8). The main feature of the decree was that it introduced certain residence conditions for non-citizens, which deepened the insecurity of undocumented migrants. Some of these

---

[3] AN, an evolution of the former neo-fascist party Italian Social Movement (MSI), 'never really renounced its fascist history' (Chiarini 2011: 150).

'emergency' measures explicitly targeted Romanies or 'nomads' (ECRI 2012: 8) but the decision to take a hard line against Romanies is not the result of a recent ideological shift. In many ways, it is an issue that always transcended political affiliations. For example, formalisation of the Romani presence by means of a 'camps strategy' in Rome was actually instigated by a left-wing administration in 1993 under Mayor Francesco Rutelli. It was during Rutelli's time that the first 'equipped camps' were built and projects to design separate schools for Romani children were reintroduced (Fiorucci 2010).

Clough Marinaro (2003, 2009) argues that Rutelli's approach to Romani issues back then should be considered the real precursor of the present politics of criminalisation. 'The ethnically discriminatory collection of personal data, the definition of Roma collectively as a "nomad emergency", and the alternative of living in approved camps or exposure to mass deportation' (Clough Marinaro 2009: 275) were all first introduced under Rutelli. Police raids, demolition of unauthorised camps and forced resettlement were also part of the then mayor's armoury. In 1995, Rutelli was responsible for the first ethnically based data collection on Romanies living in Rome (Clough Marinaro 2009), his aim being to corral them into specified and controlled zones, which only those with photo ID could access (Rondinelli 2008). As early as 1997, Rutelli had characterised the presence of Romanies in the capital as a 'nomad emergency' and a security issue, promoting the expulsion of 'irregulars' (Martirano 1997). Mayor Rutelli remained in office until 2001 when he decided to compete, unsuccessfully, against Berlusconi in the general election.

According to Clough Marinaro (2009: 275) as the actual election period neared, Rutelli

> bolstered his campaign by intensifying his criminalising discourse and repeatedly referring to an '*emergenza nomadi*' (Gypsy emergency) to justify increasing expulsions from the city. Within the context of a vocally anti-immigrant campaign by Berlusconi's centre-right coalition, Rutelli sought to demonstrate that he too could respond to security threats supposedly posed by groups like the Roma.

90   R. Armillei

Rutelli revisited this approach in 2008, when he announced his intention to re-contest the mayoralty, leading a local centre-left coalition. During the campaign, Rutelli used the *questione nomadi* (nomads issue) as one of the main planks of his political platform (Rondinelli 2008). He invoked the introduction of tougher measures against Romanies, especially those involved in criminal activities. In particular, the mayoral candidate focused on the Casilino 900 camp (Daniele 2011: 17). Notably, both candidates campaigned for its dismantlement. By the time the authorities began to 'clean up' the camp in January 2010—an operation that entailed the transfer of more than 600 Romani individuals—Casilino 900 was one of the largest camps in Europe and the oldest Romani settlement in Rome (EveryOne Group 2009).

For the new right-wing administration, closing this shanty town in the heart of the capital was a great symbolic victory. It demonstrated that it had succeeded where two previous left-wing Governments had failed. Romani intellectual Nazzareno Guarnieri (as cited in Associazione 21 Luglio 2011) differed. This was not 'a victory of the city over urban decay, but a humiliating defeat for civilisation' (7). Using the Romani issue as part of electioneering was nothing new. Already, in May 2006, it had played an important part in another mayoral campaign. At that poll, Veltroni—first elevated to office in 2001—won re-election as Mayor of Rome by defeating Alemanno. During the campaign, constant links were made between Romanies and the *campi nomadi*, as they were between irregular immigration and security concerns. That is why a recent study concluded it would be

> hypocritical to blame the Alemanno administration alone for Roma people's current standard of living in the capital. The 'Nomad Plan' approved by the centre-Right administration in 2009 [was basically] the logical extension of the 'Pact for a Safe Rome' agreed by Mayor Walter Veltroni and the Interior Ministry on May 18, 2007. (Lunaria 2011: 152)

In conclusion, neither left-wing nor right-wing coalitions showed the political will to innovate and initiate courageous reforms in respect of the Romani population. A 'tough' stance on Romani issues has so far been the common default position. Under Rutelli, Veltroni and Alemanno, this type of approach took precedence. No deliberations were ever held on what steps might have led to a more sustainable and humane policy in meeting the needs of one of the most deprived and marginalised populations in Europe. The history of these three civic leaders reveals a shared inability to find viable alternatives to the camps. Epitomising discrimination, segregation and exclusion, the camps fed, and continue to feed, the very insecurity that local authorities ostensibly oppose. A similar tendency continued during the left-wing Mayorships of Ignazio Marino (June 2013–October 2015). This was later reiterated by Virginia Raggi—the newly elected leader of the Five Star Movement (M5S) —a populist party founded as an alternative to establishment Italian politics. In both cases, they came to power on the promise that they would close down the camps while bringing back legality and transparency to the city's institutions (Bisbiglia 2017; Canettieri 2014). Their official declarations stood out in marked contrast to their politics which went in the opposite direction. In actuality, Marino and Raggi kept squandering public money on forced evictions and the infamous 'camps policy' (Associazione 21 Luglio 2014, 2016a).

A 'National Strategy'

Under pressure from EU agencies, the Italian Government has recently made an effort to develop a unified policy and guiding philosophy in prior consultation with Romani representatives. This approach is based on four pillars: access to housing, employment, education and health care (ODIHR 2009). It marks a major departure. Until 2008, notes Clough Marinaro (2009: 274), 'no explicit policy concerning Roma existed at the national level, and different practices and regulations were applied in different cities and regions'. If one could pinpoint when things began to change, it may have been February 2011, with the publication of a special report by the SCPPHR of the Senate of the Republic. This document, entitled the 'Final Report on the Condition of Roma, Sinti and Camminanti in Italy' and enjoying bipartisan support, was the very first example of research commissioned by the parliament on the circumstances of Italy's Romanies. The document explicitly criticised the Government's 'camps policy' and expressed concern about the parlous conditions of the 40,000 Romanies living in camps. As regards the city of Rome, the report judged the *Piano Nomadi* a failure, stating: 'To solve the Romani question efficiently, in terms of both national security and social integration, it would be useful to explore fresh solutions that go beyond *campizzazione* [campisation]' (SCPPHR 2011: 59).

The report also gave tacit endorsement to the conclusions drawn by the delegation from the Organisation for Security and Co-operation in Europe's (OSCE) agency ODIHR after its fact-finding mission to Milan, Naples and Rome in July 2008:

> The delegation considers the measures adopted by the government, starting with the declaration of a state of emergency, disproportionate in relation to the actual scale of the security threat related to irregular immigration and the situation the Roma and Sinti settlements. Moreover, the delegation is concerned that the measures taken, by in effect targeting one particular community, namely the Roma or Sinti (or 'nomads'), along with often alarmist and inflammatory reporting in the media and statements by well-known and influential political figures, fuelled anti-Roma bias in society at large and contributed to the stigmatisation of the Roma and Sinti community in Italy. (ODIHR 2009: 8)

Based on this document, the Italian Government drafted its own national plan for the social inclusion of this minority group (Marcenaro 2012a). The importance of UNAR's 'National Strategy'—with the title *European Commission Communication no. 173/2011*—is related to the fact that its launch signalled, as a member of the Senate's SCPPHR argued, the advent of a new 'counter-culture' in terms of Government attitude (Di Giovan Paolo 2012).

In line with the *Europe 2020 strategy*, the EU's agenda for growth and jobs for the current decade, this action was part of a larger initiative conceived on a Continental scale, to address Romani needs with a targeted approach directed at incorporating and adapting the national Romani integration strategies within the EU framework (European Commission 2011). This mounting interest in the condition of the Romani people marked 'an unprecedented commitment by EU member States to promote the inclusion of Roma on their territory' (European Commission

2012, para. 1). Despite the Italian Government's pledge to turn over a new leaf in its stance on social inclusion, the follow-up fell short. Several operative factors made it impossible to bridge the gaps between the theoretical framework of the 'National Strategy' and the practical possibility of real change. In particular, as recently observed by the Advisory Committee on the Framework Convention for the Protection of National Minorities of the CoE (2016a), its implementation has been slow as no dedicated funding has been earmarked for it. Most importantly, while recognising UNAR's extensive consultations with the key representative Romani organisations, the Advisory Committee reported that among Romanies themselves this was perceived as an act of politeness and political correctness rather than a genuine interest in hearing their views.

The strategy has been adopted as part of an inter-ministerial approach,[4] a systemic effort involving all the stakeholders along the four axes of intervention, as foreseen by the *EU Framework for National Roma Integration Strategies up to 2020*:

- Access to education: Ensure that all Roma children complete at least primary school; [...]
- Access to employment: Cut the employment gap between Roma and the rest of the population; [...]
- Access to healthcare: Reduce the gap in health status between the Roma and the rest of the population; [...]
- Access to housing and essential services: Close the gap between the share of Roma with access to housing and to public utilities (such as water, electricity and gas) and that of the rest of the population. (European Commission 2011: 4–7)

While declaring the adoption of a 'human rights-based approach', and linking it to the 'Fundamental Principles' (Articles 1–12) of the Italian Constitution, the Italian 'National Strategy' (UNAR 2014: 18–20) provides a number of examples of its application in a more 'consistent

---

[4] These included the Minister for International Cooperation and Integration; the Minister of Labor and Social Affairs; the Minister of Interior; the Minister on Health; the Minister on Education, University and Research and the Minister of Justice; representatives of regional and local authorities; and mayors of large urban areas (UNAR 2014: 5).

and effective manner'. For instance, it cites the pilot project launched in 2000 to teach the foreign languages and cultures of ethnic groups to State Police officers as a way to raise awareness and training in the field of human rights. The establishment in 2010, of the Observatory for Security against Acts of Discrimination (OSCAD) is another example.

At the same time, the document also recognises that all these initiatives are not sufficient to ensure the creation of a human rights culture. The need to move away from an emergency approach, the introduction of long- and medium-term actions (as part of an inter-ministerial endeavour) and the support of a comprehensive process of cultural growth, involving the society as whole, are some of the general objectives of the strategy repeatedly mentioned throughout the document. In order to achieve these goals, the governance system of the strategy is set up as follows: Inter-Ministerial Political Table/Control room; a control room with Regions and Local Authorities; a Roma, Sinti and Camminanti (RSC) Communities Forum; National Tables; and *ad hoc* Working Groups Regional/local Tables (UNAR 2014: 33). The document thus presents the core aspects of the 'National Strategy', which is made of systemic actions, cross-cutting axes of intervention and specific objectives.

The first systemic action, titled 'Increasing the institutional and civil society capacity-building for the social inclusion of the RSC people', refers to 'key-ideas' that can help to improve the 'capacity-building' expressed by institutions and CSOs dealing with Romani- and discrimination-related issues. As for the second action, which is entitled 'Promoting a permanent integrated system of networks and territorial centers against all forms of discrimination', this relates to the 'establishment of a national network of local antennae for detecting and taking charge of the phenomena of discrimination' (39). The third action instead is about 'Programming an integrated information, communication and mediation strategy aimed at eradicating prejudices and stereotypes against the RSC communities' (43). Finally, the fourth action aims at 'Developing and testing a participatory model of the RSC communities at the national and local decision-making levels' (47). Within each of these actions, a number of initiatives are generally only roughly sketched and it is never really possible to gauge their potential impact and feasibility. The vagueness of the document becomes even more evident when analysing the section of the strategy dedicated to the four axes of intervention and their specific objectives.

In the end, it is safe to say the 'National Strategy' has a complex structure which is often repetitive, wordy and hard to follow. It is mostly driven by good will, but there is neither clear evidence of new ways to create a real change nor enough information to understand how to achieve the objectives planned and to evaluate the expected results. The document looks more like a summary of suggestions around the main initiatives carried out across the nation in recent years, with a confirmation of the Romanies' situation and its causes, rather than a strategic plan to close the gap between mainstream society and these minority groups. As Pividori and de Perini (2016) recently observed, despite representing a clear break with the past, the implicit promise of planning in a more systemic and organic way did not lead to clear and significant follow-up. Most importantly, the role of the Romani people remains always marginal, an issue that has been extensively described in a recent volume edited by Di Noia (2016).

A Tokenistic Role

One of the major problems for the Romani people in Italy is their almost total absence from the political arena. Not only do these minorities continue to live in a condition of economic, social and cultural marginalisation, but the possibility of them expressing active citizenship through an informed participation remains an unresolved issue (Riniolo and Marcaletti 2013). A recent survey conducted by Sigona (2009) in the cities of Bolzano (Bozen), Mantua, Milan and Rome analysed the level of political involvement by these communities and emphasised their exclusion from political life. Sigona's analysis of the manifesto's and utterances of the main political contenders in the elections under investigation reveals how the Romani communities were mainly summed up in stereotypical tropes such as 'nomads', 'a threat to public security' and personifying a 'humanitarian emergency' and by references to 'urban decorum and [the] welfare system' (277). Despite their political invisibility, in all four locations, the 'Gypsy problem' came to play a key role in the local elections of 2006—the year before the issue became a national 'emergency' (287). Political engagement by the Romani people was further discouraged by the fact that neither public institutions nor CSOs working on

Romani-related issues were interested in promoting it. Both seemed unable to advance initiatives that might inspire Romani political participation, 'either as voters or candidates (for Italian Roma and Sinti) or in consultative bodies (for non-Italian Roma)' (288).

A couple of years later, during a fact-finding mission to Milan, Naples and Rome in the week of July 20–26, 2008, an ODIHR delegation (2009: 10) noted

> with concern the low level of involvement and representation of Roma and Sinti in direct dialogue and consultations with the authorities. In this regard, it has been also noted that the interests and concerns of the Roma and Sinti communities are often not voiced or represented directly by themselves but rather through intermediaries.

Dijana Pavlović (as cited in OsservAzione 2006: 32) came to the same conclusion. She said, 'some associations seem too much inclined to mediation with local authorities because of their funding dependency. [...] In other words, the Romani voice is always mediated by these associations'. This point was highlighted in later studies as well (CoE 2012a, b). By recognising the need to enhance the political participation of Romani people in Italy, UNAR (2017) has recently launched an open call for tenders to ensure the achievement of this goal as part of the National Operational Programme (PON) on inclusion for the 2014–2020 cycle. Co-financed by the European Social, the PON plays a crucial role in creating appropriate models of intervention for the most vulnerable of people (e.g. victims of trafficking or violence, Romani people, unaccompanied foreign minors, prisoners and former Prisoners; Ministero del Lavoro e delle Politiche Sociali 2014).

A number of international conventions have already stressed the importance of increasing the participation in politics of national minority groups. Article 2.2 of the UN General Assembly's 1992 *Declaration on the Rights of Persons Belonging to National or Ethnic, Religious and Linguistic Minorities* states that 'persons belonging to minorities have the right to participate effectively in cultural, religious, social, economic and public life' (CoE 2012b: 207). The 1995 *Framework Convention for the Protection of National Minorities* also points out (in art. 15) the importance of creating 'the conditions necessary for the effective participation of persons belonging to national minorities in cultural, social and economic life and in public affairs, in particular those affecting them' (207). Nonetheless, as observed by the European Committee of Social Rights in 2010, one of the main obstacles depriving the Romani people in Italy (particularly 'camp-dwellers') of the capacity to formally exercise their rights to take part in decision-making has been the 'lack of personal status or denial of citizenship or a residence permit' (CoE 2012b: 209). These people, in particular, while 'firmly located at the margins of post-Yugoslav citizenship regimes; caught between conflicting national and state projects', they also have to face the unwillingness of their diplomatic representatives in Italy to assist them (Sigona 2016: 269).

Surely, the most welcome new element of the Italian 'National Strategy' was that for the first time, it contemplated co-operating with the representatives of Romani communities in Italy. 'The aim of engaging in a participatory manner, not only men and children, but also women and girls' belonging to the different Romani groups was clearly stressed within the strategy framework (UNAR 2014: 24). Romani organisations were actually consulted during the design phase. However, very little scope was granted to them, and they ultimately had little influence on the decision-making process. UNAR was the official body designated by the Italian Government for developing and co-ordinating the entire strategy. Together with a series of initiatives directed at preventing episodes of racial hatred, one of the main goals of this body was to include the Romani people in the devising of the 'National Strategy'. As a matter of fact, UNAR produced a 100-page document as a first draft on February 17, 2012, and forwarded it to all Romani associations. Only a few days later, they were invited to a meeting at UNAR's head office, where they were given a chance to comment on the draft or suggest amendments to it (U Velto 2012). The tight time limit permitted for preparing a response spoke volumes about the type of involvement that was on offer.

This is how Federazione Rom e Sinti Insieme described the draft at that meeting arranged by UNAR for February 22:

> It is too weighty and illustrates a number of measures that are too hard to analyse in only a few hours. It is also difficult to express an opinion regarding its capacity to influence conditions for more than 100,000 Romani people living in Italy. If all the references to what was done, suggested or

written in the past could be removed, the strategy would be more original and less ponderous, and the positive proposals would be more readily appreciated. (U Velto 2012, para. 4)

On May 30 the President of *Fondazione Romani* (Romani Foundation), Nazzareno Guarnieri, organised a meeting to discuss the new 'National Strategy'. Representatives from several organisations working on Romani issues joined academics and politicians in contributing:

Some defined [the 'National Strategy'] as redundant, while others saw in it a new means of controlling Romani people. The proposed consultation with Romani organisations represents a mere advisory forum. The government sits the main Romani organisations around the same table, but they are given next to no time to work through their response in the planning stage. As for the future, we will remain in thrall to decisions dictated from the top. (Personal communication, May 30, 2012)

As Guarnieri further argued, Romani people need a 'governing' body rather than a 'consultative' one. Instead, they are still being relegated to a 'token' role, he noted. A few years later, in April 2016, the *European Platform for Roma Inclusion* was launched with the aim of contributing to national policies more sensitive to Romani needs. While dealing with topics particularly relevant to the *EU Framework of National Roma Integration Strategies up to 2020*, this new European initiative promotes 'the participatory interaction among all types of stakeholders of Roma integration (including national and local authorities of the EU Member States and enlargement countries, international organisations, European institutions, representatives of European and national Roma and pro-Roma civil society, media and academia)' (European Commission 2016: para. 1). However, as recently reported by Carbotti and Maffia (2017), the involvement of the Romani people in Rome still appeared to be limited. According to them, the city council has power to decide who can participate at the round tables organised to discuss inclusion policies towards this minority group. As Carbotti and Maffia further state, what is needed is a *Tavolo istituzionale* (institutional round table), rather than a mere consultative one; one in which public authorities, together with Romani people, can discuss about the most effective ways to overcome the politics of the camps.

'A Book of Dreams'

A number of Romani activists and intellectuals, as well as non-Romani advocates and CSO representatives, have criticised the 'National Strategy'. Their chief complaint is that the new approach still does not treat self-determination for Romani communities as a priority. Since the launch of the 'National Strategy' in 2012, they were never offered a genuine opportunity to be involved in designing and executing projects for the betterment of their lives. Other issues discussed during my research interviews included the following: the little time granted to Romani and non-Romani organisations for formulating their own proposals; insipid recommendations contained in the strategy; the small amount of executive power conceded to UNAR and testy relations among the different organisations working on Romani issues. This section provides an overview of the main criticisms of the 'National Strategy' that emerged during my fieldwork. The data which may seem to be dated, however after five years not much has changed and the comments recorded are still just as relevant today.

The following observation was made by Italian academic and expert Marco Brazzoduro on Romani issues during a private meeting in the presence of several official and Third Sector representatives:

> This is a book of dreams, of good intentions and nice words. 'No to the nomad camps' is repeated many times. In every section of the 'National Strategy' there are many redundancies. It is tiresome: the same things are repeated over and over using a *burocratese ampolloso e altisonante* (pompous and pretentious gobbledegook). They talk about holding regional and local round tables, but who should organise them? How would they work? Who could take part? In short, everything is still to be determined! But the most striking thing is that they decide to create this beautiful thing, with its noble architecture and splendid values, and then the mayors of Rome and Milan keep evicting Romanies as much as they like! So what power does UNAR have to influence political decisions? (Personal communication, July 21, 2012)

Nazzareno Guarnieri also expressed doubts about UNAR's capacity to shift the Government's Romani policy,

UNAR is a governmental body and it is supposed to 'control' the government? Do you really think UNAR can control the government that actually created it? This is a clear contradiction. Of course, there are limits at a European level too. In a European society that is increasingly multicultural, if there are no clear and rigid rules to combat discrimination and racism we will never be able to improve the situation of the Romani people. (Personal communication, June 26, 2012)

Marco Brazzoduro illustrated this point in more detail:

UNAR does not have funding independence at the moment. This issue undermines its autonomy and capacity to fulfil its official obligations. Hence the 'National Strategy' is just a *carta morta* [literally 'a dead sheet of paper'], it does not have its own funds and never will. So, I do not really know how the full-inclusion strategy will proceed. (Personal communication, July 11, 2012)

The CoE (2016a, b) also observed that, with no dedicated funding being earmarked for the implementation of the 'National Strategy', UNAR's mandate and status do not guarantee its independence. It is worth noting that 'the EU does not fund the functioning of national equality bodies, but their funding is ensured from the national budget of Member States' (European Parliament 2017). The European Commission can only monitor that all national equality bodies have the powers and resources to effectively carry out their tasks under EC law.

On the prospect of Romanies being given an opportunity to influence Government decisions, Graziano Halilovic, a representative of *Federazione Romani* (Romani Federation), had this to say:

We had scant time to develop our proposals. We had six days to write about a strategy for the coming eight years! [...] We are being invited to meet UNAR, then UNAR will meet the other authorities (provincial, regional, Italian Cabinet ministers, the CoE), but we will never really play a part in shaping decisions. At the very least we will only do what they have decided for us. [...] If you talk with UNAR they will tell you the Romani people were involved in defining a national strategy and that they are just doing what we requested. But it is not like that. As a Romani person and representing a Romani organisation, I want to be a part of all meetings where decisions are taken. They have to at least give us a chance to listen to what they are on about. Given that they are talking here about me and the destiny of my people, we should sit around the table together and have the power to oppose any decision of theirs if we believe it is not in our best interest. (Personal communication, April 28, 2012)

A 'partnership approach' (Cemlyn 2000) whereby officialdom would be ready to learn from and with the Romanies—and willing to share power—was nowhere to be seen. Guarnieri also cited the small scope for participation by Romani representatives as one of the National Strategy's weakest points.

UNAR said, 'Let's give Romani people a voice' but then they do not use it. […] The big problem today is the lack of participation, a 'qualified' participation! UNAR has created an inter-ministerial body, a *cabina di regia* [control room] as they called it, but without having any Romanies in it. Instead they've given us a small *contentino* [a sop]. They created an 'open forum' involving the Romani organisations. This is nonsense, it is a mere *carrozzone autoreferenziale* [self-referential bandwagon]. UNAR disliked this definition, but that's what it really is. In fact, if Romani people are not granted decision-making powers, what is the purpose of creating a 'forum'? (Personal communication, June 26, 2012)

The representatives of a number of non-Romani CSOs have also joined in criticism of the 'National Strategy'. The spokesperson for Casa dei Diritti Sociali (CDS), for instance, defined it as 'a mere consultative body, an observer with no decision-making authority. The forum of associations promoted by UNAR surely represents an opportunity to vent our opinions, but in the end these are not really used to make any real change' (personal communication, June 22, 2012).

The existence of divisions between the Romani people surely represented an obstacle to the creation of a cohesive movement, as pointed out by Fulvia Motta—a representative of the charity Caritas Diocesana di Roma. According to Motta, however, this problem is common among immigrant communities in general, especially in the city of Rome.

In Rome you will find people of more than 100 national origins. These foreign communities are not very strong and tend to be dispersed within the city. In other cities, where they are more cohesive, perhaps they have a better chance of communicating with public authorities. In Rome they are not only scattered across town, they are also constantly fighting one another. And public bodies have no time for them. In Rome we have the *consiglieri aggiunti* [additional councillors],[5] there to represent the interests of foreigners in our midst. There are only three of them, though, while there are 120 communities in the city. Who, really, do they represent? Only a fraction of the immigrant population. As for the Romani people, they are not well organised among themselves. There are strong disagreements between different groups. If they cannot agree with each other, no wonder public authorities are not going to listen to them. (Personal communication, June 11, 2012)

Because of the existence of internal rivalries, as Guarnieri argues, deciding which Romani individuals to work with should be approached with great care:

This is a historical landmark and we have to take advantage of it, even if this is all the result of pressure coming from European institutions. We should have the maturity to be united and to exchange views with one another. But if we want to achieve concrete progress we should work only with those who are willing to commit to this project. The 'National Strategy' must not become the *sfogatoio* [a place to let off steam] for all our problems. It is not possible to bring all Romani people around the same table, each with their own particular problem. […] I've taken part in many *tavoli* [round tables] with a number of Romani organisations, but their focus is usually more local than national. On top of that, they never set themselves practical objectives. We should follow the example of the Jewish community. They are also riven with internal divisions but in the end they manage to speak with one voice. We also have to learn to pull together in the common cause. (Personal communication, May 30, 2012)

---

[5] In December 2013, after seven years of its introduction, the experience of the 'consiglieri aggiunti' came to an end (Redattore Sociale 2014).

To conclude this section, it is useful to consider Nicolae Gheorghe's thought (a Romani intellectual from Romania but with a deep understanding of Italian circumstances). Gheorghe believed that, despite its limitations, the prospect of developing a 'National Strategy' together is a great opportunity that must not be squandered:

> The Romani issue is going to be very trendy for a few years – maybe for the next two to five years. We need to use all available resources to get supplementary assistance. Maybe I am a bit naïve, but an alliance between experts in the social sector and intellectuals can provide the Romani people with the know-how to act more strategically. They can aspire to become *funzionari* or *burocrati di progetto* [public servants or project managers]. The younger generations should get involved. If at this juncture we cannot create significant change, I am afraid we might be paving the way for extremist, nationalistic and racist discourses. This is because mainstream society will start thinking that, although bags of money were spent on improving the lives of the Romanies, they continued to live as criminals and tax evaders. (Personal communication, July 21, 2012)

Final Observations

Analysis of the Italian context during the *Emergenza Nomadi* emphasises the dichotomous approach adopted by the Italian Government concerning the Romanies. The application of extraordinary measures, disproportionate to the real degree of any threat, was used to justify the suspension of democratic rules, the curtailment of human rights and the disempowerment of the Romani people, leading to the broadening of socioeconomic gaps between them and mainstream society. True, the 'National Strategy' was launched, but an official commitment to accelerate the inclusion of Romanies was not supported by any apparent intention to introduce real change. Both these actions contributed to reproducing and reinforcing a well-established condition of welfare dependency. Fieldwork interviews, in particular, provided evidence of the Romani people's exclusion from access to genuine power. The gap between declarations of intent and actions to implement an innovative approach is there for all to see.

Six years after the April 2011 *European framework for Roma Integration Strategies*, much remained to be done. Already in 2012, European Commission Vice-President Viviane Reding, of Luxembourg, while welcoming the Member States' commitment to deliver Romani integration strategies, stressed the importance of securing the effective implementation as a priority objective. According to her,

> presenting national strategies is a first and important step, however, Member States now need to move up a gear and strengthen their efforts with more concrete measures, explicit targets, earmarked funding and sound monitoring and evaluation. We need more than strategies that exist on paper. We need tangible results in national politics that improve the lives of Europe's 10 to 12 million Roma. (As cited in Euractiv 2012, paras 2–3)

Today, Member States have addressed some of these challenges (institutional arrangements, stakeholder cooperation, monitoring and funding), but the national approaches to Romani inclusion vary considerably from country to country. In particular, the impact of their measures on the situation of Romanies in education, employment, health care and housing remains inadequate (European Commission 2017).

It is the Roma Education Fund (2012) which identified the EU's limited mandate for national projects as a weakness. The EU has basically no power over the way member states choose to implement their strategies. This aspect clearly emerged from analysis of the 'National Strategies' recently conducted by the Open Society European Policy Institute. In its 2017 report, it acknowledged the non-binding character of the EU Roma Framework as a 'soft' policy tool. This means a national mechanism for enforcing the 'National Strategies' is missing, and Member States can effectively avoid implementing specific inclusion measures (Open Society European Policy Institute 2017: 5–8). With regard to the Italian context, the EU platform can only support policy implementation and make recommendations; it has no control over UNAR. In turn, UNAR not only cannot guarantee, in both law and fact, the principles of independence and impartiality (ECRI 2016) but also has no power to impose penalties and punish certain types of racist behaviour by private or public institutions. In addition, UNAR has been criticised for duplicating OSCAD's field of activity (Mackinson 2017). There is a clear gap between the theoretical framework and the concrete possibility of effecting a real change. The effectiveness and impact of the Italian 'National Strategy' must depend on the political will at each level of Government. At neither level, though, have the powers-that-be, really welcomed the involvement of Romani representatives.

Bibliography

AffariItaliani.it. (2017). Rom scatenati denunciano Minniti e Raggi [Angry Romanies denounce Minniti and Raggi]. Retrieved from http://www.affaritaliani.it/roma/rom-scatenati-denunciano-minniti-raggi-a-castel-romano-cilasciano-morire-496176.html?refresh_ce

Agamben, G. (1998). *Homo Sacer: Sovereign power and bare life* (trans: Heller-Roazen, D.). Stanford: Stanford University Press. (Original work published 1995).

Amnesty International. (2010). The wrong answer. Italy: The 'Nomad Plan' violate the housing right of the Romani people in Rome. Retrieved from https://www.crin.org/en/docs/AI_the_wrong_answer_Italy_nomad%20plan.pdf

Amnesty International. (2012). Italy: Briefing to the UN Committee on the Elimination of Racial Discrimination 80th session February 2012. Retrieved from http://www2.ohchr.org/english /bodies/cerd/docs/ngos /AI_Italy_CERD80.pdf

Associazione 21 Luglio. (2010). Esclusi e ammassati: Rapporto di ricerca sulla condizione dei minori rom nel villaggio attrezzato di via di Salone a Roma [Excluded and massed: Report on the condition of under-age Romanies in the equipped village of Via Salone in Rome]. Retrieved from http://www.21luglio.org/index.php/report/12-esclusi-e-ammassati

Associazione 21 Luglio. (2011). Casilino 900, parole e immagini di una diaspora senza diritti [Casilino 900, words and images of a diaspora with no rights]. Retrieved from http://www.21luglio.org/index.php/report/13-casilino-900

Associazione 21 Luglio. (2012). Memorandum per il Comitato per l'Eliminazione della Discriminazione Razziale dell'ONU [Memorandum to the United Nations Organisation Committee for the Elimination of Racial Discrimination]. Retrieved from http://www.21luglio.org/images /Memorandum_richiesta_protezione_def.pdf

Associazione 21 Luglio. (2014). Roma e i rom, la politica "senza luce" della Giunta Marino [Rome and the Romanies, the 'no hope' politics of the

Marino Mayorship]. Retrieved from http://www.21luglio.org/21luglio/roma-i-rom-la-politica-senza-luce-della-giunta-marino/

Associazione 21 Luglio. (2016a). La Giunta Raggi e i rom: 12 milioni per un nuovo "sistema campi" [The Raggi's administration and the Romani people: €12 million for a new 'camps system']. Retrieved from http://www.21luglio.org/21luglio/la-giunta-raggi-e-i-rom-12-milioni-per-un-nuovo-sistema-campi/

Associazione 21 Luglio. (2016b). Rapporto annuale 2016 [Annual report 2016]. Retrieved from http://www.21luglio.org/21luglio/wp-content/uploads/2017/04/RAPPORTO-ANNUALE_2016_WEB.pdf

Associazione 21 Luglio, Associazione per gli Studi Giuridici sull'Immigrazione, Amnesty International, Human Rights Watch, & Open Society Justice. (2012). Italy: Leave 'Nomad Emergency' in the past. Retrieved from http://www.statewatch.org/news/2012/may/italy-nomad-emergency-press-release.pdf

Berizzi, P. (2012, June 5). Fascisti del terzo millennio è la Cosa Nera in cerca d'autore [Fascists of the third millennium are the Black thing in search of an author]. *La Repubblica.* Retrieved from http://inchieste.repubblica.it/it/repubblica/rep-it/2012/06/05/news/fascisti_e_post-fascisti_del_terzo_millenino-36171750/

Bisbiglia, V. (2017, May 31). Campi rom, Raggi presenta "piano di superamento" [Romani camps, Raggi launches her plan]. *Il Fatto Quotidiano.* http://www.ilfattoquotidiano.it/2017/05/31/campi-rom-raggi-presenta-piano-per-il-superamento-patto-di-responsabilita-su-servizi-e-casa-prime-chiusure-in-24-mesi/3627998/

Canettieri, S. (2014, November 22). Marino: "Chiudere i campi e dare una casa alle famiglie rom" [Marino: 'Closing the camps while giving a house to the Romani families']. *Il Messaggero.* Retrieved from http://www.ilmessaggero.it/roma/cronaca/comune_roma_marino_chiusura_campi_rom_case-709842.html#

Carbotti, G., & Maffia, C. (2017, January 2). 'Campi nomadi a Roma, la montagna ha partorito un topolino [Nomad camps in Roma, so much promise, so little delivery]. Agenzia Radicale. Retrieved from http://www.agenziaradicale.com/index.php/diritti-e-liberta/4370-campi-nomadi-a-roma-la-montagna-ha-partorito-un-topolino

Cemlyn, S. (2000). From neglect to partnership? Challenges for social services in promoting the welfare of traveller children. *Child Abuse Review, 9,* 349–363.

Chiarini, R. (2011). The extreme right in Italy. In N. Langenbacher & B. Schellenberg (Eds.), *Is Europe on the 'right' path? Right-wing extremism and right-wing populism in Europe* (pp. 141–157). Berlin: Friedrich-Ebert-Stiftung.

Cittalia. (2011). Le politiche di integrazione urbana e la marginalità: Il caso dei Rom e Sinti in Italia [Integrating urban planning and marginality: The case of the Roma and Sinti in Italy]. Retrieved from http://www.lavoro.gov.it/ NR/rdonlyres/67FB0B61-D7A8-4923-9E7C-1DB0DD9C2934/0/ INTEGRAZIONE_URBANA.pdf

Clough Marinaro, I. (2003). Integration or marginalization? The failures of social policy for the Roma in Rome. *Modern Italy, 8*(2), 203–218.

Clough Marinaro, I. (2009). Between surveillance and exile: Biopolitics and the Roma in Italy. *Bulletin of Italian Politics, 1*(2), 265–287.

Clough Marinaro, I., & Daniele, U. (2011). Roma and humanitarianism in the Eternal City. *Journal of Modern Italian Studies, 16*(5), 621–636.

Commissione straordinaria per la tutela e la promozione dei diritti umani. (2011). Rapporto conclusivo dell'indagine sulla condizione di Rom, Sinti e Camminanti in Italia [Final report of the survey on the status of Roma, Sinti and Travellers in Italy]. Retrieved from http://www.senato.it/service/PDF/ PDFServer/DF/233751.pdf

Commissioner for Human Rights. (2012). Report by Nils Muižnieks Commissioner for Human Rights of the Council of Europe following his visit to Italy from 3 to 6 July 2012. Retrieved from https://wcd.coe.int/com. instranet.InstraServlet?command=com.instranet.CmdBlobGet&InstranetIm age=2143096&SecMode=1&DocId=1926434&Usage=2

Committee on the Elimination of Racial Discrimination. (2012, March). Eightieth session. Consideration of reports submitted by States parties under article 9 of the convention. Concluding observations of the Committee on the Elimination of Racial Discrimination: Italy. Retrieved from http://www2. ohchr.org/english/bodies/cerd/docs/CERD.C.ITA.CO.16-18.pdf

Committee on the Elimination of Racial Discrimination (2016). Concluding observations on the nineteenth and twentieth periodic reports of Italy http:// www.cidu.esteri.it/resource/2016/12/49098_f_CERD_C_ITA_ CO_1920_26015_E.pdf

Comune di Roma. (2009). Il piano nomadi [The nomad plan]. Retrieved from http://briguglio.asgi.it/immigrazione-e-asilo/2009/agosto/slides-piano-nomadi-rm.pdf

Cosentino, R., & Fico, A. (2012, November 2). Deportazioni, sprechi e illegittimità: Così è fallito il piano nomadi di Roma [Expulsions, inefficiencies and illegitimacy: This is how the Nomad Plan has failed]. La Repubblica. Retrieved from http://inchieste.repubblica.it/it/repubblica/rep-it/2012/11/ 02/news/il_fallimento_del_piano_nomadi-45769127/

Council of Europe. (2012a). Descriptive glossary of terms relating to Roma issues. Retrieved from http://a.cs.coe.int/team20/cahrom/documents/Glossary%20Roma%20EN%20version%2018%20May%202012.pdf

Council of Europe. (2012b). Human rights of Roma and Travellers in Europe. Retrieved from https://www.coe.int/t/commissioner/source/prems/prems79611_GBR_CouvHumanRightsOfRoma_WEB.pdf

Council of Europe. (2016a). Fourth opinion on Italy adopted on 19 November 2015. Retrieved from https://rm.coe.int/16806959b9

Council of Europe. (2016b). Stop evictions of Roma and Travellers. Retrieved from https://www.coe.int/en/web/portal/roma-latest-news/-/asset_publisher/Wf2OtrKpyHUY/content/stop-evictions-of-roma-and-travelle-3?_101_INSTANCE_Wf2OtrKpyHUY_languageId=en_GB

Daniele, U. (2011). 'Nomads' in the eternal city. *Géocarrefour, 86*(1), 15–24. Retrieved from http://geocarrefour.revues.org/8230

Di Giovan Paolo, R. (2012, April). Presentazione del volume 'La condizione giuridica di Rom e Sinti in Italia' [Book launch 'The legal status of Roma and Sinti in Italy']. Speech presented at the Fondazione Adriano Olivetti, Rome.

Di Noia, L. (Ed.). (2016). *La condizione dei Rom in Italia*. Venezia: Edizioni Ca'Foscari.

Di Toro, M. (2017). Castel Romano, rom denunciano emergenza sanitaria [Castel Romano, the Romani people denounce the health emergency]. Retrieved from http://www.ilcorrieredellacitta.com/primo-piano/castel-romano-rom-denunciano-emergenza-sanitaria.html

Euractiv. (2012, May 24). 'Brussels urges EU countries to act on Roma integration'. Euractiv. Retrieved from http://www.euractiv.com/socialeurope/brussels-urges-eu-countries-act-news-512944

European Commission. (2011). An EU framework for national Roma integration strategies up to 2020. Retrieved from http://ec.europa.eu/justice/policies/discrimination/docs/com_2011_173_en.pdf

European Commission. (2012). National strategies. Retrieved from http://ec.europa.eu/justice/discrimination/roma/national-strategies/index_en.htm

European Commission. (2016). 10th Meeting of the European Platform for Roma Inclusion: "Mutual accountability of all". Retrieved from http://ec.europa.eu/newsroom/just/item-detail.cfm?item_id=36992

European Commission. (2017). Communication from the Commission to the European Parliament and the Council: Midterm review of the EU framework for national Roma integration strategies. Retrieved from http://eur-lex.europa.eu/legal-content/EN/TXT/PDF/?uri=CELEX:52017DC0458&from=EN

European Commission Against Racism and Intolerance. (2012). ECRI report on Italy (fourth monitoring cycle). Retrieved from http://www.coe.int/t/dghl/monitoring/ecri/country-by-country/italy/ITA-CbC-IV-2012-002-ENG.pdf

European Commission Against Racism and Intolerance. (2016). ECRI report on Italy (fifth monitoring cycle) Adopted on 18 March 2016. Retrieved from https://www.coe.int/t/dghl/monitoring/ecri/Country-by-country/Italy/ITA-CbC-V-2016-019-ENG.pdf

European Parliament. (2017). Parliamentary questions 30 May 2017 E-001180/2017: Answer given by Ms Jourová on behalf of the Commission. Retrieved from http://www.europarl.europa.eu/sides/getAllAnswers.do?reference=E-2017-001180&language=EN

EUropean ROma MApping. (2008). Castel Romano Report. Retrieved from http://www.eu-roma.net/dblog/data.asp?s=Castelromano

European Roma Rights Centre, osservAzione, & Amalipé Romanò. (2010). Submission of the European Roma Rights Centre, osservAzione and Amalipé Romanò concerning Italy for consideration under the universal review by the United Nations Human Rights Council at its 7th session February 2010. Retrieved from http://www.errc.org/cms/upload/media/04/29/m00000429.pdf

EveryOne Group. (2009). Imminent camp clearance of 700 Roma citizens. Retrieved from http://www.everyonegroup.com/EveryOne/MainPage/Entries/2009/12/16_Imminent_camp_clearance_of_700_Roma_citizens.html

Favero, P. (2010). Italians, the 'good people': Reflections on national self-representation in contemporary Italian debates on xenophobia and war. *Outlines – Critical Practice Studies, 2*, 138–153.

Fekete, L. (2008). The Italian general election and its aftermath. *European Race Bulletin, 64*, 2–15.

Ferrazza, D., & Menghi, B. (2010). La popolazione di Roma [Rome's population]. Retrieved from http://www.comune.roma.it/PCR/resources/cms/documents/Doc_Dati_demografici.pdf

Fiorucci, M. (2010). Un'altra città è possibile. Percorsi di integrazione delle famiglie Rom e Sinte a Roma: Problemi, limiti e prospettive delle politiche di inclusione sociale. [Another city is possible. Integration trajectories of Roma and Sinti families in Rome: Problems, limitations and perspectives of social inclusion policies]. Roma, Italia: Geordie onlus.

Human Rights Watch. (2011). Everyday intolerance: Racist and xenophobic violence in Italy, Human Rights Watch. Retrieved from http://www.hrw.org/sites/default/files/reports/italy0311WebRevised.pdf

Lunaria. (2011). *Chronicles of ordinary racism: Second white paper on racism in Italy* (trans: Di Pietro, D. & Marshall, C.). Rome: Edizioni dell'Asino.

Mackinson, T. (2017, July 25). UNAR, il numero antidiscriminazioni costa 800 euro a chiamata [UNAR, the anti-discrimination number costs €800 per call]. *Il Fatto Quotidiano*. Retrieved from http://www.ilfattoquotidiano.it/2017/07/25/unar-il-numero-antidiscriminazioni-costa-800-euro-a-chiamata-ed-e-un-doppione/3750752/

Marcenaro, P. (2012a, February 08). Rapporto conclusivo dell'indagine sulla condizione di Rom, Sinti e Camminanti in Italia [Final report of the survey on the status of Roma, Sinti and Travellers in Italy]. Retrieved from http://www.pietromarcenaro.it/index.php?option=com_content&task=view&id=1029&Itemid=247

Martirano, D. (1997, February 14). Criminalità: Il sindaco chiede aiuto allo Stato per l'emergenza nomadi [Criminality: The mayor asks the government for help in relation to the Romani emergency]. *Corriere della Sera*. Retrieved from http://archiviostorico.corriere.it/1997/febbraio/14/Rutelli_Roma_molto_piu_sicura_co_10_9702144012.shtml

Ministero del Lavoro e delle Politiche Sociali. (2014). Italy's Operational Programme (OP) For Social Inclusion ESF – European Social Fund 2014–2020. Retrieved from http://www.lavoro.gov.it/temi-e-priorita/europa-e-fondi-europei/focus-on/pon-Inclusione/Documents/Sintesi-Pon-Inclusione-inglese.pdf

Ministero dell'Interno. (2008). Linee guida per l'attuazione delle ordinanze del presidente del consiglio dei ministri del 30 maggio 2008, n. 3676, 3677 e 3678, concernenti insediamenti di comunità nomadi nelle regioni Campania, Lazio e Lombardia [Guidelines for the implementation of the ordinances issued by the President of the Council of Ministries of 30 May 2008, nos. 3676, 3677 and 3678]. Retrieved from http://www.statewatch.org/news/2008/jul/italy-roma-ministry-guidelines-italian.pdf

Ministero dell'Interno. (2009). Censimento dei campi nomadi: Gli interventi adottati per superare lo stato di emergenza [Census of the nomad camps: Interventions implemented to overcome the state of emergency]. Retrieved from http://www1.interno.gov.it/mininterno/export/sites/default/it/sezioni/sala_stampa/speciali /censimento_nomadi/

Office for Democratic Institutions and Human Rights. (2009). Assessment of the human rights situation of Roma and Sinti in Italy: Report of a fact-finding mission to Milan, Naples and Rome on 20–26 July 2008. Retrieved from http://www.osce.org/odihr/36374

Open Society European Policy Institute. (2017). Revisiting the EU Roma framework: Assessing the European dimension for the post-2020 future. Retrieved from https://www.opensocietyfoundations.org/sites/default/files/revisiting-eu-roma-framework-20170607.pdf

Open Society Foundations & Open Society Justice Initiative. (2010). Roma in Italy: Briefing to the European Commission October 2010. Retrieved from http://www.soros.org/sites/default/files/memorandum-italy-ec-20101018.pdf

OsservAzione. (2006). Political participation and media representation of Roma and Sinti in Italy: The case studies of Bolzano-Bozen, Mantua, Milan and Rome. Retrieved from http://www.osservazione.org/documenti/osce_italy.pdf

Pividori, C., & de Perini, P. (2016). Tendenze e prospettive per il «sistema diritti umani» in Italia: a che punto siamo? *SUDEUROPA, 1*, 17–40.

Re, L. (2010). Italians and the invention of race: The poetics and politics of difference in the struggle over Libya, 1890–1913. *California Italian Studies, 1*(1), 1–58.

Redattore Sociale. (2014, February 7). Immigrati, a Roma finisce l'avventura dei consiglieri comunali aggiunti [Immigrants, end of the road for the added councilors in Rome]. Redattore Sociale. Retrieved from http://www.redattoresociale.it/Notiziario/Articolo/454202/Immigrati-a-Roma-finisce-l-avventura-dei-consiglieri-comunali-aggiunti

Riniolo, V., & Marcaletti, F. (2013). Active participation of Roma: An experience of participatory planning towards labour integration. Retrieved from http://www.errc.org/article/roma-rights-2012-challenges-of-representation-voice-on-roma-politics-power-and-participation/4174/6

Roma Education Fund. (2012, July 20). A good start: An upcoming revolution in Roma education in Eastern Europe? TOL Chalkboard. Retrieved http://chalkboard.tol.org/a-good-start-an-upcoming-revolution-in-roma-education-in-eastern-europe

Rondinelli, G. (2008, March 12). Rutelli riscopre l'emergenza-rom [Rutelli retrieves the Romani emergency]. *Il Giornale.* Retrieved from http://www.ilgiornale.it/news/rutelli-riscopre-l-emergenza-rom.html

Sciortino, G. (2010). Diversity and the European public sphere: The case of Italy, Eurosphere Country Reports, Online Country Report No. 13. Retrieved from http://eurospheres.org/files/2010/06/Italy.pdf

Sigona, N. (2002). *Figli del ghetto: Gli italiani, i campi nomadi e l'invenzione degli zingari* [Sons of the ghetto: Italians, nomad camps and the invention of the Gypsies]. Civezzano: Nonluoghi.

Sigona, N. (Ed.). (2008). The 'latest' public enemy: Romanian Roma in Italy. The case studies of Milan, Bologna, Rome and Naples. Retrieved from http://www.osservazione.org/documenti/OSCE_publicenemy.pdf

Sigona, N. (2009). The 'Problema Nomadi' vis-à-vis the political participation of Roma and Sinti at the local level in Italy. In N. Sigona & N. Trehan (Eds.), *Romani politics in contemporary Europe: Poverty, ethnic mobilization, and the neoliberal order* (pp. viii–xiii). New York: Palgrave Macmillan.

Sigona, N. (2010). 'Gypsies out of Italy!': Social exclusion and racial discrimination of Roma and Sinti in Italy. In A. Mammone & G. Veltri (Eds.), *Italy today: The sick man of Europe* (pp. 143–157). London: Routledge.

Sigona, N. (2016). Everyday statelessness in Italy: Status, rights, and camps. *Ethnic and Racial Studies, 39*(2), 263–279.

Sina, Y. (2012, April 3). Rom: Il governo ci riprova [Roma: The government tries again]. *Il Manifesto*. Retrieved from http://www.giustizia-amministrativa.it/rassegna_web/120403/1d3exz.pdf

U Velto. (2012, February 28). L'Italia presenta la 'Strategia nazionale d'inclusione dei Rom, Sinti e Camminanti' [Italy presents the 'National Strategy for the Inclusion of the Roma, Sinti and Camminanti']. *U Velto*. Retrieved from http://sucardrom.blogspot.it/2012/02/litalia-presenta-la-strategia-nazionale.html

Ufficio Nazionale Antidiscriminazioni Razziali. (2012). Brutte notizie: Come i media alimentano la discriminazione [Bad news: How media fuel discrimination]. LIL Quaderni di Informazione Rom. Roma: ISTSSS Editore.

Ufficio Nazionale Antidiscriminazioni Razziali. (2014). Strategia Nazionale d'inclusione dei Rom, dei Sinti e dei Caminanti: Attuazione comunicazione commissione europea n.173/2011 [National Strategy for the inclusion of Roma, Sinti and Camminanti communities: European Commission communication no. 173/2011]. Retrieved from http://www.unar.it/unar/portal/wp-content/uploads/2014/02/Strategia-Rom-e-Sinti.pdf

Ufficio Nazionale Antidiscriminazioni Razziali. (2017). Bando di gara per l'affidamento di servizio 'Interventi pilota per la creazione di tavoli e network di stakeholder coinvolti con le comunità RSC' [Call for tenders for the assignment of the service 'Pilot actions for the creation of stakeholders' networks involved with RSC communities]. Retrieved from http://www.unar.it/unar/portal/?p=8519

Vannucci, A., & Della Porta, D. (2011). Countries at the crossroads 2011: Italy. Retrieved from http://www.freedomhouse.org/sites/default/files/inline_images/ITALYfinal.pdf

4

The Business of the Camps During the 'Nomad Emergency'

From Left to Right: The Introduction of the CRI in Camps' Management

In April 2008, after defeating Francesco Rutelli, Gianni Alemanno became the first right-wing mayor of Rome since the end of the Second World War. Until then, the political scene in the city had been dominated by centre-left or left-wing coalitions. A couple of years later, in May 2010, Alemanno's administration tried to eliminate all left-wing associations from the 'Romani platform' in Italy's capital, and more specifically, from management of the camps. At that time, the Municipality of Rome appointed the *Gruppo di Coordinamento e Garanzia del Piano Nomadi* (Group for the Co-ordination and Protection of the Nomad Plan)—an advisory body composed exclusively of religious organisations—with the sensitive task of mediating between Romani representatives and local authorities (Associazione 21 Luglio 2010). Seven months later, on December 15, 2010, an agreement signed by Mayor Alemanno and CRI Special Commissioner Francesco Rocca (CRI 2010) seemed to crown the

© The Author(s) 2018
R. Armillei, *The 'Camps System' in Italy*, Mapping Global Racisms,
https://doi.org/10.1007/978-3-319-76318-7_4

113

shift from Left to Right in the business of camp management.[1] Clough Marinaro and Daniele (2011: 621) argued that the CRI's involvement redefined the Romani issue as a 'humanitarian problem'. An early manifestation of this paradigm shift had previously appeared with the founding of Castel Romano camp. Back in 2005, during the Veltroni administration, *Protezione Civile* (Civil Protection)—the national agency tasked with managing exceptional events—had been given responsibility for dealing with the Romanies in what was termed then as a sort of 'humanitarian emergency' (Gruppo Attivo WWF Roma XI 2005).

What distinguished Alemanno's approach, and that of his right-wing civic administration, was a willingness to strike direct agreements, with no publicity or tendering process, such considerations having been abandoned with enactment of the 'state of emergency'. Under these circumstances, Mayor Alemanno and the then prefect of Rome, Giuseppe Pecoraro, were made joint special commissioners for the Romani 'crisis'—appointments that came with far-reaching extraordinary powers (Lunaria 2011: 45). They tried to forge a new management model that involved only those organisations deemed controllable and compliant. Bodies that had devoted decades to working on Romani issues now found themselves suddenly on the outer (La Repubblica 2011). Particularly over the previous decade and a half, centre-left administrations under Francesco Rutelli and Walter Veltroni had governed the city of Rome employing organisations that were politically aligned with them to work inside the *campi nomadi*. This reversal of the political leanings of those on the ground should be considered part of a broader power struggle between rival political coalitions waged by the incoming right-wing administration. The idea of transferring management of the camps to the CRI and a number of religious agencies was no accident. Just before becoming the CRI special commissioner, for instance, Francesco Rocca

---

[1] As stated by Daniele (2011), the activities implemented for the social inclusion of the Romani people represented one of the biggest items of expenditure for the municipality. Since 1991 Italian CSOs have been contracted to run a number of projects within the camps (chiefly the cleaning/maintenance of the camp areas and the schooling of Roma children). The fact that hundreds of workers are employed each year for the camp management and that the amount of the grant provided to the CSOs is about €3 million per year (only for the schooling activities) transformed the inclusion of the Romani people into a lucrative business. According to a recent study, the city council spent around €200 million over the last 12 years for running the camps (Mariani 2017).

The Business of the Camps During the 'Nomad Emergency'   115

had headed up Mayor Alemanno's social policy department (CRI 2013). Rocca and Alemanno came from the same political alliance, the right-wing Alleanza Nazionale party. Furthermore, Rocca had a lengthy personal history of activism and managerial responsibility with a range of religious bodies, including Caritas Diocesana di Roma and Associazione Centro Astalli, both members of the Group for the Co-ordination and Protection of the Nomad Plan (Falcioni 2010).

There was one reason in particular, why the CRI was induced to join the 'camps system'. Over the years, the CRI had incurred an enormous debt of some €90 million (Falcioni 2010). A TV documentary screened by the channel Rai 3 in 2010 uncovered CRI's scandalous track record in management (Giannini and Gabanelli 2010). The ups and downs of the CRI were also extensively documented by Alberto Puliafito (2011) in a book entitled *Croce Rossa: Il Lato Oscuro della Virtù* (*Red Cross: The Dark Side of Virtue*). In it, the author defined this once revered institution as a 'monster with a noble visage' (16). Puliafito stressed the CRI's anomalous use of concepts such as 'impartiality', 'neutrality' and 'independence'—three of the movement's seven guiding principles. At best it interpreted these principles inconsistently. Poor management led to the CRI first being placed under the supervision of a 'special commissioner' in 1980. Such an extraordinary step is taken only in an emergency. Of all the Red Cross societies around the globe, Italy's was unique in having to endure this radical intervention. The movement's Geneva HQ issued strongly worded criticism of the Italian society (Forti 2008). Even though the CRI has been under Government control ever since, its executive management and staff (see reports of fieldwork interviews below) have continued protest on their neutrality and independence. Only just recently, with Legislative Decree no. 178 (September 28, 2012), has it been envisaged that by 2018, the structure of the CRI will be transformed, giving it the juridical status of a private entity under the law. As Martin (2017) observes, though, it is highly unlikely that the CRI's privatisation will occur within this time frame, due to its ongoing debt and the difficulty of rebalancing the organisation's budget.

Other circumstances have also placed the CRI in the spotlight. For many years, it was the only organisation contracted by the Government, to work inside the detention and deportation centres, while, as one report noted, 'other rights-based groups were frequently denied access to the facilities' (Global Detention Project 2012: 8). A series of rights violations, arising from the treatment of detainees and the standard of living inside the detention centres, has heaped repeated criticism on the heads of the Italian Government and CRI, from 'human rights organisations, the media and the CoE's Committee for the Prevention of Torture' (ibid.). Associazione 21 Luglio President Carlo Stasolla (as cited in Falcioni 2010) contends that the announcement of the *Piano Nomadi*, which brought private security officers inside the camp walls, along with CRI workers, instantly reminded inmates of how *campi nomadi* resembled 'deportation centres'. In regard to the *Emergenza Nomadi* itself, the CRI steadfastly backed the objectives of the Municipality of Rome, even before its role was made official. The CRI played various key roles in implementing the Government's strategy: using its own vehicles to forcibly remove Romanies from unauthorised camps to 'equipped villages' (Associazione 21 Luglio 2010) and even carrying out the deeply controversial census that mapped the Romani presence in the camps network (Open Society Foundations and Open Society Justice Initiative 2010).

Change of Plan: The Emergence of Inefficiencies, Overlaps and Conflict

Reaction against the Municipality of Rome's policy was swift and unexpected. Rolling protests by Third Sector organisations and groups of Romani activists forced a change of tack. Alemanno's Third Sector critics attacked his new strategy for putting 200 social workers' jobs at risk (La Repubblica 2011; Roma Soc!al Pr!de 2010). The Romanies accused him of 'racialising' policies affecting them and opposed the Mayor's unilateral nomination of Romani Najo Adzovic as his authorised liaison.[2] Condemnation also came from some of the religious entities Alemanno had tried to involve in his strategy, with Caritas Roma being one of the strongest opponents (Fico 2012). According to one of its representatives,

---

[2] One of the novelties introduced by Alemanno was the establishment of a direct communication channel with the Romani 'leaders' in the camps. However, Adzovic was not elected by the Romanies to represent them; he was chosen for reasons of political expediency.

The Business of the Camps During the 'Nomad Emergency'   117

we have always kept our distance from the government's 'camps policy' and so we decided to reject the offer to be part of the co-ordinating committee created by Alemanno. [...] The idea of using the Italian Red Cross to reorganise the camps system was unnecessary, especially considering his organisation had no previous experience in managing nomad camps. (Personal communication, June 11, 2012)

Faced with this crescendo of opposition, the municipality could not accomplish what Alemanno had defined in a fit of hyperbole back in 2008 as a 'Copernican Revolution' (Cosentino and Fico 2012, para. 2). Overhauling the 'camps system' was no longer possible, and the mayor was forced to negotiate and seek compromises with his critics (Daniele 2011).

Eventually, both the CRI and Third Sector organisations co-operated in restructuring the *campi nomadi*. The former was granted a supervisory role, which authorised it to co-ordinate and monitor the other organisations involved. The latter were contracted by the municipality to run an assortment of short-term (month-long) projects, which excluded them from any part in long-term strategic planning and left with almost no authority to make decisions. In such circumstances, arguments and conflicts began to break out between the different organisations working in the camps and in the field. Disputes on how to handle Romani issues flared up between the religious and secular associationists (Castri and Aversano 2011). At the same time, different stakeholders in the field grew confused as to the expectations of their roles and responsibilities. One concrete example of this confusion should be explanatory enough; since the CRI had no prior experience in running camps, many of the personnel it hired to co-ordinate activities in the camps were from the very same Third Sector organisations that had been managing the camps before. Several social workers were simultaneously employed in the camps by the CRI and other non-profit organisations. Hence, these social workers were both supervising the lower ranks, while they themselves were in the lower ranks being supervised—and earning double pay, a situation replete with conflicts of interest.

To recapitulate: under this new dispensation the Alemanno administration was contracting an external organisation (the CRI) to co-ordinate and monitor activities carried out by the Third Sector within the camps, thus delegating to a third party its own official duty to be in control. This inevitably created inefficiencies. Since the very beginning of his mandate, Alemanno had blamed leftist associationism for the disastrous results of the operations it had been running in the camps. This alleged failure of the non-profit sector should, rather, be perceived as a failure of the organs of state. In truth, they were never able to manage a smooth and efficient relationship with the organisations to which they outsourced their work. On top of this, it should be noted that these municipal authorities have often found themselves struggling with issues beyond their control or responsibility. According to Cefisi (2011), it is the failure of policies regarding education, housing and employment that causes criminal behaviour within Romani communities, not a failure to carry out operations in situations that are already fraught. A report released by the *VII Commissione Cultura, Scienza e Istruzione della Camera dei Deputati* (VII Commission for Culture, Science and Education of the Chamber of Deputies[3] 2011) concluded that the campaign for educational integration of the Romanies had been a failure. As reported in this document, in the last 15 years the Municipality of Rome 'has allocated €2.5 million every year for the schooling of approximately 2000 children. But until now the results have been unfortunately almost nil' (ibid.: 23–24).

An argument could be made that one of the main reasons for the unsuccessful outcome of educational projects carried out by the Government in partnership with the Third Sector lies in the existence of the camp itself and the policy of sending Romani people to these enclosures. This conclusion also emerged from a study conducted by Associazione 21 Luglio (2011). This focused on one of seven school bus lines used by the city council, who contracted CSOs to transport Romani children to school and back to the camp where they live. The analysis of this specific case study places a particular emphasis on a raft of discomforts Romani children had to face, as a consequence of their being part of this educational project. These are some of the common problems Romani children encounter in most of the 'equipped villages' around Rome: delayed start and distracting anticipation of exit from classes; the application of differ-

---

[3] The Chamber of Deputies and the Senate of the Republic are the two houses of the Italian bicameral system.

ent standards for the evaluation of learning abilities; the existence of didactic gaps (often leading to episodes of marginalisation from the class) and the school's inability to give adequate back-up to teachers who are often untrained or unsuited to the management of Romani children. All this produces psychological side effects as well, and inevitably affects how Romani students perceive schooling. Fast forward a few years, and the situation remained unchanged, as emerged from the latest research published by Associazione 21 Luglio (2016). Despite an investment over €10 million for the schooling programme in the period between 2009 and 2015, nine out of ten Romani minors do not attend school on a regular basis, and one out of two is behind with schooling and is attending classes non-compliant with his/her age.

Interview with CRI Representatives in Rome

On May 4, 2012, I conducted a focus-group session with the local committee of the CRI in Rome. The meeting was attended by the official spokesperson, six intercultural mediators and the project co-ordinators in charge of the *villaggi attrezzati* where the CRI was operating. Our meeting canvassed several issues concerning the *Piano Nomadi*, with four major themes being identified: lack of transparency and an attitude of concealment; strong belief in the neutrality and independence of the CRI; an over-optimistic view of CRI's intervention; and conflict between CRI and other CSOs. The following subsections will outline each in turn.

Lack of Transparency and an Attitude of Concealment

One of the main issues to emerge from the meeting concerned the CRI's duty of confidentiality to its contracting party, the Municipality of Rome. This point was particularly emphasised by one of the participants. Every time 'confidential' information was about to be disclosed, either intentionally or unintentionally, the first interviewee (denoted as INT. 1 for our purposes) would stop the other participants from completing their statements, and remind them of their legally defined duties. This attitude prevented me from reaching a closer understanding of the rationale behind the CRI's involvement in the 'camps system' and of its relationship with the city council. At the same time INT. 1 was monopolising information that ought to be treated as a matter of public interest.

Questions such as the following went unanswered:

1. 'What is the City Council's response to your suggestions, as the [authorised] monitoring and co-ordinating body, regarding the problems inside the camps that need resolving?';
2. 'Do you think the camps are run efficiently?';
3. 'What is your opinion of the policies, in particular the "Nomad Emergency", announced by the City Council with regard to the aim of including Romani people?'

Surprisingly, though, INT. 1 seemed willing to reformulate the questions:

> There is probably a misunderstanding. If you are asking my opinion regarding the policies of the Municipality of Rome, this is something the CRI cannot and does not want to reply to. But if you ask me whether, since the *'Piano Nomadi'* was introduced, conditions for the Romani people living in the camps have improved or worsened, this is another way of formulating the question. We can answer the latter, by saying that they have actually worsened, especially because the number of 'camp-dwellers' has increased.

It felt like being part of a strategic game in which things could be said but only in very subtle and indirect ways. The plight of Romani communities in Italy constituted a matter of extreme importance, involving human rights abuses. Criticism was raised by European and international bodies against Italian officials. The focus-group participants all had extensive previous experience working for CSOs dealing with these self-same issues. So it came as a surprise to see so much defensiveness. The situation appeared even more paradoxical when I reflected that the civic administration itself withheld detailed information on these issues. Its website does not include any reports or such information that might have allowed a better understanding of the 'camps system'. In addition, most of the departments contacted did not reply to formal interview requests.

Strong Belief in the Neutrality and Independence of the CRI

As part of the International Red Cross and Red Crescent Movement, the CRI is dedicated to performing its duties according to seven fundamental principles which were adopted in 1965: humanity, impartiality, neutrality, independence, voluntary service, unity and universality (CRI 2017). Some of the questions raised at the meeting were deliberately formulated with the aim of acquiring a clearer understanding of how those principles—in particular neutrality and independence—were translated into practice in the camps.

As stated in its constitution, in order to continue to enjoy the confidence of all, the Movement is independent and may not take sides in hostilities or engage at any time in controversies of a political, racial, religious or ideological nature. The 190 member National Societies, while auxiliaries in the humanitarian services of their Governments and subject to the laws of their respective countries, must always maintain their autonomy so that they may be able at all times to act in accordance with the principles of the Movement (International Federation of Red Cross and Red Crescent Societies [IFRC] n.d.).

All participants expressed their acceptance of these values. They constantly referred to the fact that the CRI was a neutral and independent body whose main goal was to serve those in need, without distinction as to nationality, race or religious creed. INT. 2 repeatedly questioned my research focus on those two principles, as if his National Society's adherence to them was beyond question. My particular interest was driven by consideration of the following data, which seem to undermine CRI's commitment:

1. Between 2005 and 2013, the Italian Red Cross received €180 million in State funding each year to support its operating budget;
2. CRI is a voluntary relief movement, but it had around 5000 public employees in its workforce, before Rocca's extraordinary intervention (Pavesi 2013);

3. Since 1980 the CRI has been managed by a special commissioner appointed by the Government;
4. IFRC headquarters in Geneva has repeatedly requested the Italian arm of the society to address these anomalies (Forti 2008).

Despite these facts, all the participants in the meeting asserted that their organisation was performing genuine and impartial service, especially when compared with the other CSOs working in the camps.

According to INT. 3, for instance,

> the main difference between CRI and the other organisations is that, before our intervention, camps were a big business. CRI does not do it for money, since we are a voluntary organisation. CRI is actually taking a loss out of this. The fact that the other CSOs protested at being excluded shows that they were enjoying a hefty profit.

INT. 2 uttered a very similar remark: 'we are neutral because we are independent both of politics and the Municipality of Rome: this is impossible for the CSOs since they are economically dependent on it'. INT. 4 also reinforced this point: 'we are not subject to any type of conditioning. We get paid, but that's another thing, because we provide a service to the city council'. These statements were later contested by Carlo Stasolla, of Associazione 21 Luglio. Stasolla pointed to the CRI's strong interest in the operation of the 'camps system'. According to him,

> the CRI has debts amounting to €50 million and is keen on calling for tenders. At the end of 2010, CRI signed an agreement with the Municipality of Rome aimed at securing a deal worth €4 million a year, to cover the management of all the camps. (Personal communication, May 6, 2012)

The impression received was that CRI employees interpreted 'neutrality' as requiring them to operate within the framework of the 'Nomad Emergency', just like other CSOs, but with the difference that they must avoid explicitly criticising the municipal administration. After all, Stasolla continued, 'How could the CRI, which is *de facto* a Government body, criticise the Government?' (personal communication, May 6, 2012). The elasticity of the concept of 'neutrality' is even more evident when considering the position of

The Business of the Camps During the 'Nomad Emergency' 123

particular CRI members. INT. 1, for instance, was working concurrently for CRI and one of the CSOs that CRI was supposed to co-ordinate and monitor. This was a matter the interviewee did not question, even if a conflict of interest became apparent.

An Over-Optimistic View of CRI's Intervention

In the course of the meeting, all participants appeared strongly aligned with the idea that replacing the other CSOs was essential. They all blamed these organisations for the Romanies' parlous state. According to INT. 4, for instance, 'the camp management carried out by the [other] CSOs had been a failure, especially with regard to the schooling of the Romani children'. That the CRI's intervention had also failed to deliver the predicted results mattered not, because the CRI's efforts had been obstructed by the simultaneous presence of other CSOs within the camps. INT. 4 said that the agreement signed with the city council had not been completely respected:

> the plan was that CRI would have been the only one in charge of co-ordinating all the camps. It is not possible that at any given time two organisations [the CRI and any CSO] can jointly co-ordinate. The [other] CSOs are obstructing the CRI's work. According to our agreement with the city council, these organisations had to leave.

The CRI participants appeared to feel they were permitted to criticise CSOs, regardless of their obligation to neutrality, but they did want to mention the city council's obligations. In addition, it can be charged also; the municipal authority had an official duty to monitor the performance of the organisations whose services it had contracted and to ensure they met certain benchmarks. Therefore, the CSOs' failure necessarily implicates City Hall, calling into question the effectiveness of its supervision.

A number of other institutional 'roadblocks' have also lessened the possibility of these organisations bringing about real change: among others, the lack of comprehensive national legislation covering Romani issues, the lack of cultural recognition, a tendency to classify Romani people as 'nomads', the constant sinking of public funds into the construction and operation of 'ghetto camps' rather than permanent housing and a determination to deny Romanies all opportunity of making decisions for themselves. One is being asked to assent to the rather dubious proposition that merely replacing the CSOs would have yielded valid and lasting solutions for the encamped Romani population. If the Italian Government does not first address the specific limits of its legislative and cultural framework, all other measures are doomed to fail, and an emergency stance will be the only option.

All members of the focus group took pride in what they regarded as the positive impact their organisation had on the Romani issue. This was justified on the basis that the CRI was a substantial servant of the public with more than a century of experience in aiding the victims in all manner of emergencies and calamities. They saw this new CRI mission as an advancement in their professional careers. They also felt that their job assignments were much easier to fulfil, as part of the CRI, than with CSOs' they had worked for previously.

INT. 1 emphasised that obtaining a *permesso di soggiorno* (residency permit) for a Romani under his management was a much more rapid process when the request was presented by the CRI. There was general agreement this was mainly due to the fact that the CRI and 'Questura di Roma'—the State Police Department in charge of such applications—were both public bodies and could communicate via an internal channel. This sounded quite shocking, since both the CRI and other CSOs were working for the Municipality of Rome (and therefore in the public domain and offering a useful service to the public). Why, then, should an administrative request presented by the CRI be considered more urgent or important than the one submitted by a CSO?

And yet, despite a generally favourable assessment of the CRI's involvement in the 'Nomad Emergency', self-criticism did surface. INT. 4 confessed that things were not as good as he had expected:

> I am sorry for those Romani people who thought things would have been different with the CRI in the driver's seat. Things, as we know, turned out otherwise. The situation of this minority group is something that can be solved only on a political level.

INT. 1 also admitted that 'the failure of the [other] CSOs was not completely their fault. That was mainly owing to a "systemic issue"'. Some of the interviewees even disagreed with using the term 'emergency' for the authorities' new policy. This was no trifling matter: it basically implied a repudiation of the main plank in the Government's ideologically driven scheme. It queried both the case for emergency action and the decision to replace CSOs already in the camps. If this was not an emergency, why was the CRI called out?

Conflict Between CRI and Other CSOs

Immediately after the CRI had signed up to the Alemanno administration's scheme to manage the *campi nomadi*, relations between CRI and the other CSOs became strained. In 2011, after a series of public demonstrations by Third Sector organisations and Romanies (La Repubblica 2011), the municipality was forced to revisit its decision to replace all pre-existent CSOs with the CRI. Instead of taking their place, the CRI was now asked to assume oversight, a duty that by rights should have been within the city council's remit. The situation in the camps became extremely confused. If Alemanno was seeking an improved model for camps management, this change of direction only ended up increasing inefficiencies more.

The first obstacle the CRI had to face was the unwillingness of other CSOs to co-operate. Despite the CRI's newly defined charter to monitor and co-ordinate them, these organisations refused to share the field data they had been collecting and accumulating for a decade. According to INT. 2, 'theoretically we should have taken possession of that information, but in practice the CSOs wouldn't let us [have it]'. Since the CRI was without prior experience in managing 'equipped villages', this lack of collaboration and inaccessibility of data made it very difficult for its employees to attain their objectives. A second obstacle for the CRI related to the coexistence of multiple organisations in the field and resultant confusion over the roles and responsibilities of each. This led to overlaps and mutual obstruction. It should be noted that the CRI itself has sometimes provided the ammunition for conflict with the organisations it has been given the job of monitoring.

The 'residency permit' issue offers another pertinent example of a dysfunctional process. Since the CRI's role was merely supervisory, the other CSOs should have taken responsibility for handling permit applications. CRI members, however, had also been forwarding these requests in an effort to expedite responses from the authorities. The CRI virtually supplanted these CSOs instead of merely overseeing how they conducted activities they had officially been contracted to perform. In fact, one of the CRI's job specifications was to make sure everyone knew the limits of each other's role. The following statement by INT. 1 ignored this point:

> I am not interested in who is in charge of what; I am only interested in the living conditions of these people. Even if the Third Sector was responsible for that, we felt we had a right to intervene as the CRI to improve the situation of those living in camps and we were successful. [...] It is of secondary importance why the State Police accept our applications instead of those forwarded by the Third Sector.

Instead of seeking to minimise confusion by clarifying roles and responsibilities, the CRI's intervention produced less dialogue and more uncertainty.

CSOs' Involvement Within the 'Camps System'

This section analyses the role of Third Sector organisations in Rome's 'camps system'. The fieldwork conducted in 2011–2012 revealed a fragmented and internally disparate not-for-profit constellation of organisations. Some were involved in running camps; some denounced the 'camps system' and the authorities and other organisations administering it; yet others preferred to remain officially neutral, though they were not necessarily inactive or entirely impartial. Within this context, it was not always easy to understand what strategic alliances had been formed between various 'players'. Interestingly, while advocating for the Romanies' rights, these organisations often had very little time for Romani voices. That the Romanies as a whole were disorganised and internally riven was used to justify the importance of their role as mediators between Romani communities and authorities.

Although Romani intellectuals have often recognised these problematics, many of these organisations have slowly become self-referential, turning their own interests and survival into their main priorities. Competition also triggered mutual rivalries between those in the field.

Carlo Stasolla's 2012 book examined Romani 'inclusion' under the right-wing Alemanno mayoralty. In his work, Stasolla described the municipality's strategy as a 'business' and quantified its market worth (at least €60 million) as well as its workforce (450). Also noted was what University of Verona professor of anthropology Leonardo Piasere had defined as 'late modern anti-Gypsism', a sentiment that manifested itself beneath the 'noble visage' of associationism. Vital to this policy is the segregation of Romanies in camps, on the pretext that it is for their own good. Piasere described associationism as 'machinery' that, to preserve its own members' jobs, was coerced into supporting the Government's treatment of the Romani communities (ibid.: 7–8). It is undeniable that the camps had become a huge business in which it was really hard to know exactly how funds were used (Cecchini 2012). Rossi's (2010: 219) term *mercato della solidarietà* (solidarity market), when referring to Third Sector activity in Italy, aptly conveys the notion that the social sector's stock is quite literally on the rise. As one Romani intellectual pointed out, 'nobody is really interested in improving the conditions of these minority groups. Everyone considers us as a mere commodity' (Nazzareno Guarnieri, personal communication, April 12, 2012). Meanwhile, conditions continued to deteriorate.

On the municipality's 'camps policy', a division into three distinct attitudes can be discerned among Third Sector organisations:

1. Non-Romani CSOs involved in running authorised camps are in favour of them ('pro-camps'[4]);
2. Non-Romani lobby groups reject the camps outright ('no-camps');
3. Catholic organisations display an ambivalence hovering between endorsement and rejection of the *Piano Nomadi*.

---

[4] This grouping can be defined 'pro-camps' because, even if they all declare to be against the existence of 'ghetto camps' for Romani people, they also define them as part of a necessary transitory stage. They do not reject the camp as strategy and embrace it as an 'emergency' tool.

The view of Romani individuals themselves (activists, intellectuals and ethnic-group representatives) will be discussed in the next chapter.

Non-Romani CSOs Working Within the Camps ('Pro-camps')

Together with the CRI, which was singled out by the Alemanno administration during the 'Nomad Emergency', other organisations were eventually contracted by the city council to work in the 'solidarity villages': Arci Solidarietà Lazio, Ermes Cooperativa Sociale, Eureka I Onlus and CDS. Of these, the last mentioned was alone in refusing to be involved in running the camps, but it did agree to manage schooling projects for Romani children. The other organisations were generally required to take on several extra responsibilities connected with supervision of the camps. Running the authorised camps entailed the following socio-educational tasks: transporting children to and from school; liaising between the children's families and educational institutions; support activities within the schools (i.e. intercultural workshops, supplying teachers of Italian as a second language); encouraging the pupils' parents to take responsibility for their attendance; and staffing help desks dispensing advice to the Romani inhabitants on health, legal and employment issues.

During interviews, representatives from the above-mentioned CSO quartet revealed their clear opposition to the Government's 'camps policy' and the enactment of emergency measures for dealing with the Romani issue. Their criticism of Mayor Alemanno's right-wing administration was so pronounced that two of these CSOs had even joined a protest movement, 'Soc!al Pr!de', in November 2010. They had, in total, three main complaints: first, the unclear role played by the CRI in the camps and the Government's attempt to replace all established CSOs; second, the municipality's reduction of funds for social purposes while boosting expenditure on security surveillance; and, third, the introduction of short-term (month-long) contracts for CSO hirings, which made long-term planning impossible for them.

All the informants agreed that before Alemanno became mayor, there was a better dialogue between CSOs and local administrations, but some things, they said, had not changed, despite the recent political shifts. Previous administrations had ignored their proposed alternatives to the camps' regime, as did the current one. (They had wanted the exercise of ethnic politics replaced with inclusive programmes tailored in broad terms for 'disadvantaged people', and argued that derelict urban spaces should be converted into new permanent housing plots.)

The interviewees evidently shared a philosophy which had three underlying assumptions:

1. They recognised the camps were a fact of life—albeit part of a municipal strategy, not a CSO initiative—and dealing with them was unavoidable. They were all against the recommendation of some organisations that they should boycott the 'camps policy' and refuse to bid for management tenders. The interviewees reasoned that even if every one of them refused to have anything to do with the council's politically driven plans, another individual or entity would have been found to fill the gap. The agreement Alemanno had reached with the CRI was cited as proof of the futility of boycotts.
2. They expressed willingness to hand control of the camps over to Romani organisations. Yet they also argued that Romanies lacked the requisite competencies and political maturity to take on this responsibility.
3. They did not reject *a priori* the notional usefulness of camps—provided they were temporary (the first step in a wider process of inclusion for disadvantaged Romanies and non-Romanies alike). Left-wing ex-mayor Veltroni has postulated a three-step process of 'hospitality' for Romanies, in which camps have their place as a transitional home. In the first two stages new arrivals would be lodged in a camp and, after some time, helped by a multidisciplinary team to acclimatise to Italian society, including orientation exercises in accessing public services such as health care, employment assistance and education. The final stage would see Romanies occupying proper homes.

Although the 'pro-camps' bodies were working to predetermined guidelines and fixed job specifications, they all considered themselves completely independent from the city council. According to them, being contracted and paid by the authorities to roll out social inclusion projects for Romanies living in camps did not curb their freedom of action. The city council could not tell them what to do or what not to do; they said they had ample scope to explore best practices for improving conditions in the camps. Even so, they recognised that they could not have a big impact on Romanies' lives in general.

Their shortcomings were blamed on the backwardness of Italy's social sector and the Government's politics. The schooling project, for instance— one of the most controversial initiatives (VII Commissione Cultura, Scienza e Istruzione della Camera dei Deputati 2011)—earned their tick of approval. The following comment, by one of the interviewees, acknowledges the CSOs' achievements as well as their daily challenges:

We have been engaged in schooling Romanies and in advocacy for many years. When I started in 1995 only 30 [Romani] children were attending school in the city of Rome; today, more than 2,000 do.[5] There is certainly a host of problems but the main one is that the Italian school system is imploding and incapable of serving everybody well. Our workers are not teachers, their role is not to replace them – and schools should have the resources to deal with the individual children. The question to be answered for us is not whether our work has been helpful or unhelpful, but whether things would have been the same without us. I doubt it. I think the education of Romani children is not as disastrous as it seems. Before we became involved, Romani kids did not go to school at all. Unfortunately, the city council's department of educational policy obstructs our work. They have this rule that we may enrol only one Romani kid per class.[6] The message is that, above all, the school is short of resources, and second, the Romani children are considered to be a problem *a priori*. This is very discriminatory. […] In this context, the decision to replace us with the Italian Red Cross in the camps was illegal according to Law 328/2000[7] and pointless.

---

[5] By November 2016, a slight decline could be recorded with 1679 pupils of Romani background enrolled across 182 educational institutes (Comune di Roma 2016b).

[6] According to the most recent school regulation, it is acceptable to have two Romani students per class (Comune di Roma 2016b).

[7] With the introduction of this law, which is entitled *Framework legislation for the realisation of an integrated system of interventions and social services*, voluntary organisations were recognised as official partners of local authorities for programming and implementing social assistance programmes. According to this law, the voluntary organisations registered in the regional registries can participate in calls for tenders issued by local authorities, becoming equal partners in case their applica-

Besides, there was never a productive dialogue with them. The municipality should be duty-bound to support a useful exchange of views with everyone involved in the Romani issue, rather than being divisive towards them and ignoring their suggestions. (Personal communication, June 12, 2012)

Given these conditions, one could be pardoned for doubting whether CSOs could ever be completely independent, free to implement their own programmes for the betterment of Romani life. Any project they may initiate would have been undermined from the start. In fact, although they sponsored a fresh attempt to overcome the politics of the camps, in the end they came up against the intractable facts of the camps' existence. These CSO representatives argued that their principal challenge for the future would be to unify the Third Sector so that it could counter the Government's decisions on an equal footing. But they also admitted that each organisation had a different agenda, with its own goals and interests. Disunity acted as a brake on progress. One of the interviewees concluded:

We all agree on certain issues but then it is hard to create a network capable of devising and applying a common long-term strategy. In the end, we find ourselves co-operating with only those bodies whose ideas are similar to ours. (Personal communication, June 22, 2012)

Non-Romani Advocacy Organisations Rejecting the Camps ('No-Camps')

On June 19, 2012, three of the four CSOs involved in the management of 'authorised villages' (Arci Solidarietà Lazio, Ermes Cooperativa Sociale and Eureka I Onlus) organised a public meeting under the banner of *Oltre il Campo* (Beyond the Camp). Together with other speakers, they presented their reflections and experiences on the condition of Romanies living in Rome. On that occasion, Associazione 21 Luglio, Controcampo, Cooperativa Berenice, Fondazione Romanì[8] and Popica Onlus also made

---

tion is successful. Consequently, they also receive funds to implement projects that will benefit their communities (European Commission n.d.).

[8] *Fondazione Romanì* is a non-profit organisation founded by a Romani intellectual, Nazzareno Guarnieri, with the goal of enhancing the condition of Romanies in Italy. Although the main goal

a contribution to the meeting: they sent an open letter to the event's organisers, asking them to boycott La Barbuta 'equipped village', which was about to be inaugurated by the Alemanno administration (Associazione 21 Luglio 2012a). Their letter stated that all 'equipped villages' should be considered ghettos and 'the product of ethnic bias, the result of institutionalising segregation and discrimination' (para. 4). They argued that social work projects could achieve nothing while all the things people valued—human rights, above all—were 'suspended'. In their view 'camps' offered no scope for personal improvement and no hope of assimilation into the wider community.

No mention of this letter was made during the entire conference, and the existence of alternatives to the 'camps policy' was also disregarded. What had been advertised as a *Tavola Rotonda* (round table)—a setting in which one would normally expect some interaction between participants and the audience—in the end looked more like a press conference. There were no questions and no answers, certainly no question-and-answer session. Throughout the meeting the 'pro-camps' bodies spoke of their 'best-practice' work in encouraging Romanies to become self-sufficient. Their main goal was to chart a reliable career path for the camp's inhabitants. The granting of *borse lavoro* (paid traineeships) was held out as the passport to reach this destination, and one of the organisations' biggest achievements. Their 'no-camps' opponents, however, disputed that claim, dismissing the traineeships as a huge failure. A study published by Associazione 21 Luglio (2012b) entitled *Lavoro Sporco* (Dirty Job) purported to demonstrate how the *borse lavoro* programme was merely a scam, because it provided no genuine employment for Romani trainees who completed their apprenticeships.

One of the participants defined the scheme's lure as 'fake jobs' (personal communication, April 4, 2012). This research found evidence of ineptitude and corruption on the Government's part. But it also revealed a level of collusion by some of the delegates from Romani camps. Here follows a brief extract from the report:

---

of the foundation has to do with Romani issues, Guarnieri has intentionally decided to open it to Romani and non-Romani membership. He proudly defined his foundation as a multicultural organisation.

The Business of the Camps During the 'Nomad Emergency'

> '*sedicenti rappresentanti rom*' (alleged Romani leaders) have apparently facilitated the closing and the relocation of formal and informal encampments, in exchange for a number of promises that local authorities gave them, mainly employment opportunities for members of their own communities. An important aspect of this system is the way funding was allocated: The available money, which had to be used to recruit, [within 'camp cleaning projects'], the Romanies living in the camps, were not subjected to any form of control enacted by the local administration. No criteria were requested regarding the employment of the Romani people or the results to be achieved. (Associazione 21 Luglio 2012b: 54)

In other words, deciding who could work and who could not was left to these 'alleged' Romani leaders' own discretion (ibid.: 46).

The screening of a documentary by Ermes Cooperativa Sociale showing conditions in Salone camp confirmed that the traineeships led jobseekers down a cul-de-sac. One video told the story of eight Romani individuals who had trained as tree surgeons. At the end of this project not one was hired by the company that had offered the training. Some were put to work on makeshift jobs inside the camp itself—cleaning the common areas or acting as 'teacher's aides' in the camp's crèche. In a later interview, a representative of Ermes Cooperativa Sociale stressed the importance of restricting partnerships to companies that could hire Romani participants at the end of their four-month traineeships (personal communication, May 3, 2012). Traineeships did not mean real jobs for Romani people. The 'no-camps' lobby identified AMA Roma S.p.A.—a council-owned waste-management company—as one of these 'fake jobs' merchants, saying it had not employed anyone in the past ten years. After this challenge to their approach, the representative of a 'no-camps' organisation wondered aloud: Was it really possible to think of the camp as a 'starting point' for social inclusion? Nevertheless, to this day, the city council continues to use *borse lavoro* and other policy measures for the social inclusion of Romani 'camp-dwellers', as foreseen by the recent call for bids announced by the city council (Comune di Roma 2016a).

According to 'no-camps' advocates, although camps were always being 'sold' as a temporary necessity, they had gradually become a permanent institution, with increasing amounts of public money being devoted to a number of services associated with the camps' operation. During the introductory phase of the *Piano Nomadi,* the entire cost of running the 'camps system' almost doubled as compared with the Veltroni administration's expenditure on camps in 2006. Associazione 21 Luglio talked about the frustration of having its alternatives to forcing Romanies to live in camps ignored:

> We calculate that a 'camp-dweller' costs the council €450 to €500 a month. This means that €2,000 is spent on a family of four every month. With this much money, any social worker could help a Romani family find a better solution than a camp. The problem is not a lack of resources: on the contrary, there are funds available. But there is no political will to make a real change. (Personal communication, April 4, 2012)

Associazione 21 Luglio added that each camp should be treated on its own merits, with solutions customised to the needs of the family involved, subject to available resources. For instance, you might have a Sinto with a small merry-go-round and funfair business who would prefer to live on a plot of land with his caravan, while other Romanies would choose to live in an apartment blocks.

Ultimately, while the 'pro-camps' lobby campaigns for more support, this is propping up a system that furthers marginalisation. Together with the public instrument, in fact, Third Sector organisations are responsible for turning the 'camps policy' into reality. According to Guarnieri,

> these organisations manage the camps, though it should be clear by now that they can only ever be a graveyard for Romani culture. Nomad camps could be dismantled tomorrow if everyone stopped working in them. [...] Many organisations would rather keep the Romani people on the margins of society. This way they can get funds for all their 'social inclusion' projects, even though they do not really improve the lot of the Romanies. [...] These organisations deal with Romani immigrants for only one reason: such interaction makes it easier to blackmail them. The fact there are still so many Romanies from the former Yugoslavia without documents amounts to extortion. Without documents, not only can these people do nothing legally, but all the projects these 'pro-camps' bodies come up with are useless and meaningless. (Personal communication, April 21, 2012)

A representative of Associazione 21 Luglio reinforced what Guarneri had said:

The Business of the Camps During the 'Nomad Emergency'   135

All Third Sector organisations are very vulnerable and open to blackmail by the government: they have no clout, which explains why they've been unable to pressure the local authorities. You have to think of the *Piano Nomadi* as a medium- to large-scale enterprise with 450 employees and €60 million in annual turnover. Business logic counts for more than human rights. 'If you do not like it, I [the city council] can easily find somebody to replace you.' That's one of the reasons we are against camps. In a camp, even the best and most efficient organisation is powerless. (Personal communication, April 4, 2012)

In conclusion, the 'no-camps' organisations looked on the 'camps policy' as a harmful strategy that ultimately worked against the 'social inclusion' of Romanies, even if that goal can only be defined in vague terms.

The Catholic Organisations

In May 2010, Mayor Alemanno established a co-ordinating committee, the *Gruppo di Coordinamento e Garanzia* and tasked it with mediating between public institutions and Romani communities during implementation of the *Piano Nomadi*. As reported in the *Piano Regolatore Sociale 2011–2015* (Social Town Plan 2011–2015), this group planned to assemble all the voluntary organisations that had been dealing with Romani issues (Comune di Roma 2011a). Only Catholic organisations took part,[9] and none of them had previously been involved in managing *campi nomadi* (Bonaccorsi and Vazzana 2011). During the preliminary stage of the *Piano Nomadi* another large Catholic organisation, Comunità di S. Egidio, had joined the committee. But after a few months it abandoned its support for the council plan for two main reasons: first, the closure of Casilino 900 camp; and, then, the forced removal of Romani families from Salone 'equipped camp' to the Asylum Seekers Centre in Castelnuovo di Porto. Comunità S. Egidio complained that

---

[9]The committee was composed of the following 11 Catholic organisations: Acli di Roma, Arciconfraternita del SS. Sacramento e San Trifone, Camminare Insieme, Caritas Diocesana di Roma, Centro Astalli, Centro Socio Educativo Interculturale San Giovanni Bosco, Compagnia delle Opere di Roma, Comunità della Riconciliazione, Gruppi del Volontariato Vincenziano, Gruppo Ercolini di Don Orione and Istituto di Medicina Solidale Onlus.

not only were most of the transferees Italian-born but also this action was being taken without obtaining the concerned individuals' consent. Of the 128 people forcibly transferred, 74 were minors, who were or had been enrolled in Salone schools. While S. Egidio was taking a strong position against Alemanno's *Piano Nomadi*, fellow Catholic agencies reaffirmed their support. This bolstered co-operation between those organisations represented on the committee (Frignani 2012).

One of the main consequences of including only Catholic organisations in the *Gruppo di Coordinamento e Garanzia* was the creation of a certain tension between secular and religious varieties of associationism (Castri and Aversano 2011). As argued by a representative of Arci Solidarietà Lazio, the existence of this committee itself constituted an act of discrimination. 'The Government should collaborate with everyone, instead of setting up selective networks', he noted (personal communication, June 12, 2012). In December 2010, a few months after the committee's inception, the municipality and the CRI signed an agreement. As Stasolla observed, the democratic void created by the 'Nomad Emergency' had permitted the local administration to hand-pick only those organisations that would have applauded its politics. It basically eliminated any point in calling for tenders and the CRI was given full authority to hire the selected Catholic participants directly. After all, as Stasolla added, 'in Rome it is possible to govern only with the Church's blessing' (Stasolla, as cited in Castri and Aversano 2011: 32). Significantly, though, neither the CRI nor the Catholic committee members had prior experience of *campi nomadi*.

By analysing the interviews with some of the religious representatives (from Comunità di S. Egidio, Caritas Diocesana di Roma, Seminario Romano Maggiore and Fondazione Migrantes), a better understanding of perspectives on Romani issues in the Italian capital is attainable. First of all, these interviews showed how the Alemanno administration took advantage of the rivalry between religious and secular entities to revolutionise the city's social work sector. Secondly, they shined a light on divisions within the Catholic movement. In the end, the opposition of left-wing organisations, combined with existing disunity in the ranks of religious associationism, has prevented the city council from fully implementing its political project. Ever since becoming mayor, Alemanno had accused his left-wing predecessors, together with their Third Sector allies, of wasting public funds (Di Blasi 2010). In order to emphasise the lucrative approach carried out by the left-wing organisations, Alemanno strategically used the 'noble visage' of the Catholic bodies and the CRI, arguing that they based their work predominantly on voluntarism, charity and spirituality, rather than politics and profit.

Indeed, what emerged from these interviews with religious representatives was a strong sense of their spiritual mission and their non-partisanship. This constituted a marked difference from the attitudes of the left-wing associations. The Comunità di S. Egidio stressed that it had always adamantly refused to be formally contracted to work in the *campi nomadi* on behalf of the city council:

> Our commitment towards the Romani communities is based on voluntarism. We do not want to be paid for that. We want to have a unselfish relationship with them. [...] Unlike us, so-called pro-Romani organisations have agreed to work for the municipality so they have become pro-government and lost their claim to be independent parties. (Personal communication, June 5, 2012)

A representative of Rome's Caritas Diocesana voiced a similar view:

> The problem for the Third Sector is that, once it started working for the government, it sacrificed its independence. When the authorities pay you, you have to obey their rules. Besides, these private organisations' only aim is to keep functioning rather than supporting true emancipation for Romani people. (Personal communication, June 11, 2012)

Even though the religious organisations liked to think of themselves as non-political, they did support the newly elected right-wing administration and its *Piano Nomadi*. Their presence in the *Gruppo di Coordinamento e Garanzia* is a reminder of this support. 'Pro-camps' organisations responded by talking up the value of their professional skills, as opposed to the charity-based voluntarism typical of the religious bodies. As the spokesperson for Ermes Cooperativa Sociale pointed out, 'the increasing need to offer new services to people in a number of "disadvantaged" categories required a more professionalised approach. Particularly in the past decade, the Third Sector has raised service standards substantially' (personal communication, May 3, 2012). The Arci Solidarietà Lazio representative agreed: 'The Third Sector is made up of people who have chosen a specific profession. Voluntarism and charity are both worthy things, but they have nothing to do with social work' (personal communication, June 12, 2012). The ostensibly non-political approach of the religious bodies made them perfect partners for a right-wing administration out to transform the Third Sector's involvement in its 'camps policy'.

Two Catholic organisations maintained their independence within the framework of religious associationism—Comunità di S. Egidio and Caritas Diocesana di Roma. They jealously guarded their right to dissent from, and even openly criticise, the city council and its strategy. Eventually, they quit the committee. The Comunità di S. Egidio representative recalled:

> We started meeting Romani people in the 1980s. Over the years we were publicly outspoken against Italian politicians' contempt for this minority. We deplored all emergency-style interventions by the government. We stressed the importance of introducing long-term policies, particularly in education and housing, while the logic of the camp creates a perverse mechanism of exclusion. (Personal communication, June 5, 2012)

The interviewee from Caritas Diocesana di Roma echoed this sentiment:

> The attitude of Campidoglio [City Hall] has always been appalling: stubborn, reeking of cronyism and characterised by an emergency mindset. A bureaucracy has never been able to lead Third Sector work. Then again, the Third Sector never had a Gandhian figure who would say, 'No, this is not the right thing to do! We are going to do things our way and we will pay the price if we are wrong'. (Personal communication, June 11, 2012)

An insight into the *Piano Nomadi* and the role of the *Gruppo di Coordinamento e Garanzia* was offered by a representative of Caritas Diocesana di Roma. She began by revealing why, eight months after the committee had been formed, the council at last decided to sign an agreement with the CRI on responsibility for managing the camps:

At first the administration wanted to transfer management of the camps to the Catholic world – to S. Edigio and us, basically. We said we would not take responsibility for something we completely disagreed with. Instead, we asked the administration to promote real dialogue between all the parties involved. But, since the *Gruppo di Coordinamento e Garanzia* would not accept that, we refused to be part of it. And that is why, in the end, the city council had to use the Italian Red Cross to execute its *Piano Nomadi*. Saying their left-wing predecessors were guilty of having done nothing in 20 years was just an excuse. (Personal communication, June 11, 2012)

In conclusion, Caritas Diocesana di Roma and the Comunità di S. Egidio's disagreement forced the city council to modify its action plan. These two entities also stood out against the other religious associations' connivance with the municipal administration. It is difficult to understand where the boundary between the spiritual and temporal realms lies for those who collaborated.

The Role Played by Public Institutions

This section analyses interviews conducted with a number of bureaucrats directly involved in activating the *Piano Nomadi*. Administrators from these offices were interviewed: V Department, 'Nomads Office'[10]; XI Department, Education and Schooling Policy Office; and XII Municipal Hall, Culture Office. The mayoral delegate with responsibility for Romani relations also agreed to an interview: his statements will be scrutinised in the next chapter. A formal interview request was also sent to the then representatives of other city council departments: Deputy Mayor Sveva Belviso (in charge of the overall plan); Deputy Commander Antonio Di Maggio of the Municipal Police (responsible for public security and emergency actions); Angelo Scozzafava (director of the V Department for Health and Social Services); Marcello Menichini (director of the Department of Economic Development, Training and Employment); and Giovanni Williams (the director of the Department of Schooling and Education). None of these officials replied.

---

[10] With the ordinance 102 signed by the current Mayor Virginia Raggi on July 4, 2017, this office has been named *Ufficio Speciale Rom, Sinti e Caminanti* (Special Office Rom, Sinti and Caminanti; Comune di Roma 2017).

The information I gathered afforded me an insight into the functioning of the municipal administration, with a particular focus on Romani issues. This insight includes the relation between public authority and contracted CSOs. Although each of the interviewees dealt with different aspects of the *Piano Nomadi*, their professional experiences were linked by a common thread. All rejected the approach that councils governed by left- and right-wing coalitions had adopted. At the same time, a sense of frustration and helplessness pervaded their statements and attitudes. Cognisant of the realisation that they were powerless to reform the system, they told of feeling obliged to do things they did not agree with. They also felt constrained from freely expressing their views. In fact, the Alemanno administration had prohibited them from releasing information about their activities on this very issue. Each informant spoke forthrightly on the Romani issue: the administrative aspect of the *Piano Nomadi*; educational policy; the administration's approach to the 'equipped village' of Tor de' Cenci, situated in XII Municipal Hall. The overall message coming out of these interviews was of disconnection between administrative and political levels, with directions from one level routinely being ignored by staff at another level.

V Department: Nomads Office

Until recently the website of city council's V Department carried the following summary of the *Ufficio Nomadi* (Nomads Office) activities:

> The Nomads Office manages and co-ordinates activities at all the Solidarity Villages and Nomad Camps situated in the city of Rome. In particular, this office deals with the entry and release of individuals into and from the Solidarity Villages, while furnishing social assistance and administrative structures for the improvement of living conditions for the nomad population. The Nomads Office is also in charge of guaranteeing and maintaining basic hygiene in the camps and averting public health or security risks. (Lunaria 2013: 23)

An interview with a representative of this office highlighted the gap between official commitments and outcomes. He argued that even if in the past, under administrations of the Left, the effectiveness of this office had been blunted by an authoritarian resort to forced evictions and 'campisation', implementing the *Piano Nomadi* would only accentuate this tendency.

One of the major problems to emerge after the state of emergency had been declared, he confided, was that the Nomads Office was immediately deprived of some of its already truncated authority. In effect, the new Government policy approach added a parallel administrative channel and multiplied the workload of those individuals and organisations involved. Two parallel and non-communicating lines of authority had been created: the Nomads Office going off in one direction, with more or less the same functions as before, chiefly the ordinary camp management; and a new, more senior administrative division, the *soggetto attuatore*, or plan implementation unit, in charge of all extraordinary decisions and moving in the opposite direction. Apart from the deployment of multiple agencies working on Romani issues, this Nomads Office staff member confirmed that bringing in the CRI had produced administrative indecision. It was no longer clear who was responsible for what: 'The security delegate would head off in one direction, the Municipal Police in another, the State Police in a third – and the city council, possessing two distinct and mutually annihilating souls, charged off in opposite directions at once. Everyone just went their own way' (personal communication, May 29, 2012).

As regards the contract agreed with the CSOs to work inside the camps, the role of the Nomads Office has always been marginal. All it was asked to provide were routine administrative services like accounting, invoicing and scheduling meetings. Proclamation of a 'Nomad Emergency' reduced that role even further, since most of the *Piano Nomadi* was now being directly administered by the *soggetto attuatore*. Henceforth, the implementation unit would decide whether, where and under what terms to conduct a new camp (i.e. La Barbuta, the only one established during Alemanno's tenure), the number of 'shipping' containers to be built and who would be entitled to occupy them—all this and more they could decide without consulting the Nomads Office in advance. As a result, the Nomads Office would often be ignorant of what policy was being visited on Romani communities in the council's name. The municipality's agreement, giving the CRI a role inside the camps, hacked away at the Nomads Office's residual decision-making power.

Indeed, the CRI was asked to control and co-ordinate the CSOs, a task the Nomads Office had performed.

The interview emphasised the continuities between left- and right-wing local administrations. Politicised councils of both persuasions were lukewarm about going beyond the 'camps policy', which had always blocked the door to real change. The interviewee argued that both administrations had been careless about the following: people living in illegal encampments being evicted without having anywhere else to go; camps being built despite mounting evidence that they soon became ghettos rather than paving the way for social inclusion; camps being built despite mounting evidence that they were ghettos in the making rather than conducive to social inclusion; the absence of any dialogue with the camps' residents; and the persistent problem of statelessness. At the same time, the informant, who had worked in both the Veltroni and Alemanno administrations, pointed out one important difference between the two. According to him, the Left could well have been described as more 'proactive', in the sense of less talk and more action. Although the Left of the political spectrum has historically stood up for human rights, it was a left-wing mayor of Rome who actually ordered more evictions and built more camps than his right-wing replacement in office. The Right banged the drum more loudly, but it was the Left that mastered the snares, helping to divert the attention of the media.

Probably the most astonishing aspect of this representative's comments were his appreciation that the concepts 'emergency' and 'nomad' were central to the theory and practice of the *Piano Nomadi*:

> In my opinion, at the very moment the city council decided to declare the state of emergency it basically created the emergency. I do not think there was a real emergency or any need for extraordinary measures before. I have never believed that. [...] The fact that Romanies are still defined as 'nomads' is just an old habit. They are called 'nomads' even if they are actually better settled than many other people. One consequence of this caricature is that the moment you adopt the category 'nomad' you are ticking the box for social service needs as well. [...] Besides, I just wish that one day I will be able to say I work for the 'Citizens Office', rather than the Nomads Office. But in my experience I can tell you this will never happen. It is pure Utopia. (Personal communication, May 29, 2012)

In conclusion, the drive for better living conditions for Romanies did not appear to be of any real concern for the power brokers of the city council. There were always other agendas, and here he cited a couple of examples.

The first concerned the 'equipped camp' of Tor de' Cenci. According to him, Sveva Belviso, before being appointed deputy mayor, had used this camp for political purposes. In 2008, she won the elections in XII City Hall district, after basing most of her campaign on the demands for it to be shut down. Relocation of the Romani inhabitants was completed in September 2012 (Brogi 2012), probably out of a desire to have it completed before June 2013s council elections: 'It was just a symbolic action so they could show their program produced concrete results. In reality, though, the closure of that camp caused the opening of another and the overpopulation of yet others' (personal communication, May 29, 2012).

The second example detailed the creation of a municipal anti-discrimination body. On October 22, 2009, the council's watchdog against prejudice-based actions—the *Osservatorio Cittadino Contro le Discriminazioni*—was officially launched (Comune di Roma 2009a). On this occasion, an agreement was signed between Alemanno and Equal Opportunities Minister Mara Carfagna. Despite the publicity, this watchdog never became operational. The informant argued that this was all driven by a well-tuned political judgement: 'Various initiatives, not confined to the Romani issue, were initially advertised by Alemanno's mayoral team but they were never realised. They should all be interpreted as nothing more than campaign tactics' (personal communication, May 29, 2012).

These two cases were not isolated. This informant contrasted the administration's ratification of several national and international conventions and treaties, such as the *Convention on the Rights of the Child* and the *International Convention on the Elimination of All Forms of Discrimination*, and its passivity in leaving what he termed its discriminatory policy against Romani communities untouched. At the same time, reports containing practical proposals to improve the lot of this minority group—reports that the contracted CSOs regularly forwarded to the Nomads Office—were never taken into serious consideration. In this interlocutor's view, it was a question of a small ruling class with the power to influence decision-making overshadowing all those below. It was a top-down relationship; there was no bottom-up exchange, he concluded.

XI Department: Education and Schooling Policies

Interestingly, former executive director of the 'Ufficio Nomadi', Emanuela Salvatori, was sentenced to four years in prison for corruption as part of the process of *Mafia capitale* (Portanova 2016).

XI Department: Education and Schooling Policies

The city council's website offers scant information on the schooling of Romani children and adolescents in Rome. The available documents (e.g. Comune di Roma 2008, 2011b, 2014)—calls to tender, contractual terms and internal bulletins—are generally difficult to find, often out of date and contain mainly technical information. None of these documents deal with teaching methods, class assessments, meeting specific Romanies' needs or cost-benefit analysis. The available material is mostly an assemblage of general aims, with no information about the achievement of planned objectives or the evaluation of expected results. The only material the city council was willing to offer up (after a formal request) amounted to a basic study of the extent of school integration among Romani children and a document on the monitoring of school attendance (personal communication, July 20, 2012). In other words, a request for evidence that would have allowed a reasonable evaluation of the education of Romani children by the city council drew a response that narrowly focused on only two parameters: the number of children enrolled and attendance statistics collected monthly. This made it impossible to gauge with any accuracy the outcomes of various schooling projects initiated by the city council and carried out by its contracted CSOs.

On several occasions, the documents featured a foreword in which the administration would perfunctorily acknowledge its commitment to the promotion of cultural diversity and social inclusion for people of Romani heritage. This point was underscored by reference to council's adoption of the principles proclaimed in the 1989 UN *Convention on the Rights of the Child*. The following is an excerpt from a document released by the council's XI Department on schooling activities between 2008 and 2011. It briefly summarises what objectives the council has set for Romani children of school age and how it envisages these objectives will be achieved:

The city council, by adopting the *Convention on the Rights of the Child*, confers special attention on the implementation of a program aimed at safeguarding the rights of children and adolescents. The cornerstone of this program is an assurance that all children and adolescents will have the chance to attend school within the [municipal] territory. At the same time, careful cultural planning will be carried out to guarantee that the highest standard of academic inclusion is provided, rather than merely temporary aid. […]. The goal of facilitating their regular attendance and school inclusion will be attained while avoiding congested situations where too many Romani children and adolescents are channelled into just a few institutions. In this way any risk of ghettoising them will be averted. (Comune di Roma 2008: 3)

A similar tone was used in more recent policy documents highlighting the city council's commitment towards the education of marginalised Romanies: avoiding actions which can create welfare dependency, initiating measures to empower Romani communities and dismiss segregational or ghettoisating practices (Comune di Roma 2014, 2016b).

Despite these fine sounding words, the city council appeared to chart a political course that took it in a different direction altogether. The fact that the official imperative is largely centred on housing the Romanies in camps—beyond the city ring road and far from regular schools—creates a number of obstacles that clearly make it less likely that children and teenagers could ever attain the above-mentioned goals. It is the presence of these impediments that prompted the establishment of 'Romani-specific services' (such as 'solidarity villages', schooling projects and transport services). During the interview with a representative of the Education and Schooling Policies Office, an awareness of the issues clearly emerged. But, just as with the Nomads Office informant, so a rather passive tone seemed to inform the planned activities. When I asked the interviewee whether she felt the creation and location of camp structures outside the city ring would push the Romanies into dependency on State aid, a feeling of impotence emerged:

Of course! [She replied]. This is one of the main consequences of that political choice. But we cannot do anything about it because we are just an administrative office. We can only execute the programs we are required to carry out. The current administration made choices, very similar to those of the previous mayors' offices, which will worsen the situation of the Romani people. For instance, in a camp like Castel Romano, remote from the city and attended by more than 300 children,[11] you will never eliminate the need for a school bus service. What is more, the city council has even abandoned the public bus stop near the camp. (Personal communication, May 19, 2012)

These are not the only impediments that have deprived Romani children of the possibility of normally attending school. The one major deprivation probably stemmed from the decision to divide and disperse them into as many different schools as there were in the capital, permitting a maximum of two Romani enrolments per class, preferably one. The data contained in the *Social Town Plan 2011–2015* gives an idea of what results can be expected from this approach. According to this document, the CSOs Arci Solidarietà Lazio, Ermes Cooperativa Sociale, Eureka I Onlus and CDS undertook to manage 16 encampments, including 'solidarity villages' and authorised camps. These sites were located in 11 different municipal halls. The council contracted the transporting of Romani children to ATAC S.p.A., the municipality's tramways and bus operator. This required the services of 33 bus lines. By April 2011, 1788 children were enrolled in 300 schools. On average, there were 5.96 Romani kids per school (Comune di Roma 2011b: 6–9). And 70 per cent of these children absolutely depend on these transport arrangements to get to school (personal communication, July 20, 2012). Five years later, the situation remained unchanged with 30 bus lines (Comune di Roma 2016b). Despite assisting all those who live in peripheral and isolated areas, it was seemingly unable to counter their low level of school attendance (19 per cent), as shown in a recent study conducted by Associazione 21 Luglio (2016).

According to the interviewees' argument, although the initial purpose of the schooling project was to fight discrimination by providing equal opportunity to everyone, it actually created the basis for a 'racialising' intervention. Because of the 'de-localisation' of the camp areas, 'of the €2

---

[11] During the academic year 2016–2017 these were 321 (Comune di Roma 2016b).

The Business of the Camps During the 'Nomad Emergency'   147

million per year that the city council invests for the schooling projects, more than half of that goes on transport instead of activities to promote school attendance, learning opportunities, extracurricular activities and individual educational projects' (personal communication, May 19, 2012). Another issue that emerged during the interview concerned the difficulty this department had in assessing students' work for the purpose of long-term planning. The informant admitted that even the monitoring of school attendance was poorly executed. According to the available data,

> approximately half of all the children enrolled have a mediocre attendance record; one-quarter of them have low attendance and another quarter do not go to school at all. [...] The Romani children were surely the worst-prepared students. [...] All the available information is the result of a mere quantitative assessment carried out by an unpaid intern as a one-off exercise. At the moment, frankly, we lack the necessary resources for a more analytical inquiry. (Personal communication, May 19, 2012)

A qualitative analysis of the educational project was completely lacking. According to a study conducted by Fiorucci (2010), neither the assessment criteria nor the assignment tasks were made clear. How can one press for socially inclusive practices without the possibility of evaluation?

More recently, a number of high-profile members of the Alemanno administration were arrested as part of the *Mafia Capitale* operation. Some of them had been part of the previous Veltroni administration as well (Angeli et al. 2014). Thanks to this investigation, 'the tendering process that led to some CSOs working within the solidarity villages was declared illegal. These organisations have thus been excluded from the management of the camps' (Carlo Stasolla, personal communication, December, 22, 2016). The only service that has been retained is the school bus service. A new private cooperative, Multiservizi, is now in charge of it. Interestingly, an internal memo produced by the Department of Educational Services of the city defined the personnel of this company as 'unsuitable for this clientele [Romani children]' (personal communication, December 16, 2016). As stated by a representative of this division, 'nowadays we have either small camps, where CSOs provide a number of services on a voluntary basis, or we simply have chaos' (personal communication, December 21, 2016).

XII Municipal Hall: Cultural Office

My interview with the official from XII Municipal Hall provides an illuminating perspective on the city council's attitude to a specific case study, the former 'tolerated camp' Tor de' Cenci. In the city district where this site is located, the first Romanies settled there as far back as the 1950s. For a long time, this encampment was characterised by illegal dwellings and it only became an 'equipped camp' in the first half of the 1990s, under left-wing Mayor Rutelli's administration. A prolonged state of institutional neglect, though, has slowly turned the camp into a 'garbage dump', posing enormous health and safety hazards to residents of the camp. International human rights organisations and Italian civil society spokespersons had repeatedly raised concerns over the state of this camp (Grilli 2011). Due to its deplorable conditions, it was downgraded to its old 'tolerated camp' status during rightist Mayor Alemanno's time at City Hall.[12] This meant that according to the *Piano Nomadi,* Tor de' Cenci camp had to be shut down and the land assigned for other purposes. So, all of its 400 inhabitants had to be moved to some of the 13 'authorised villages' the city council had planned. These villages were either old camps that would have been renovated or ones just newly built (Comune di Roma 2009b).

The recovery of this area was one of the major goals set by former Deputy Mayor Belviso during her 2008 election campaign. According to the president of the local *Comitato di Quartiere* (Neighbourhood Committee) Guido Basso, Belviso actually won her seat in this municipal election by pledging to close the camp (Grilli 2012). Despite her using this goal as a rallying cry on the campaign trail, the camp was closed only four years later, in September 2012 (Brogi 2012). In the meantime, though, since Alemanno's election, most of the services essential to running the camp were disrupted. The informant from XII Municipal Hall confirmed this account:

---

[12] In 2008, according to the 'Terms of Contract Regarding the Schooling Project for Romani Children and Adolescents in the 3-Year Period 2008–2011', this area was still classified as an 'equipped camp' (Comune di Roma 2008). Then, in 2011, the *Social Town Plan 2011–2015* defined it as 'non-equipped settlement' (Comune di Roma 2011a).

There has been a widespread lack of interest in the 'Romani Question' over the last four years. The only activity that has consistently received steady support from the city council is the educational project. That was carried out in this particular camp by the CSO Arci Solidarietà Lazio. Other initiatives have been also in place but, broadly speaking, they are run either by grassroots organisations or the individuals (be they social assistants, from CSOs or activists) who took the plight of this or that person or family to heart. In other words, these were not part of an all-encompassing social inclusion policy enacted by the local administration. Basically, what the government did on a national level with the launch of the *Emergenza Nomadi* did nothing to improve the condition of the Romani people. Quite the contrary. (Personal communication, April 24, 2012)

The informant did not simply criticise the types of actions implemented by the Government to overcome a situation of social emergency. He also challenged the rationale behind the extraordinary intervention itself. This measure was mainly based on the assumption that this population was 'nomadic' and that they represented a threat to national security. He pointed out a major anomaly:

The launch of the schooling project for the Romani children was quite paradoxical. Its compulsoriness, in fact, implied that Romanies were basically required to reside in order to fulfil this duty, somehow disregarding their supposed nomadism. Over the years the *campi nomadi* became permanent ghetto-like spaces where Romanies have totally lost their own identity. Today these people live in a sort of social limbo. They lost their own traditions and they did not develop new ones that could replace the old. They just internalised the worst aspects of mainstream Italian society. Besides, because there is no proper management of these camp areas and no dialogue with the Romani communities, these places have slowly turned into a hive of illegality, where certain Italian people are involved as well. Most of the Romanies in this camp (70 percent) are drug dealers. Many want to stay there because there are no controls and they are free to carry on their illicit business. But it is the existence of the camp itself, the institutional neglect, the lack of real inclusion policies, which caused the development of these behaviours. (Personal communication, April 24, 2012)

An important feature revealed by the informant during the interview was the existence of an operational gap between the central authority and local administrative levels. In this case, although the site of Tor de' Cenci camp fell under the jurisdiction of XII Municipal Hall, the local administrative office lacked the power to influence the management of this issue: 'I cannot do anything to find the right solutions to the problems of those living in this place. This camp is a law unto itself. There are political reasons for that, and they are out of my control' (personal communication, April 24, 2012). Particularly during the *Emergenza Nomadi* period, everything was managed from the centre and no municipality could influence decision-making processes. For instance, the interviewee confessed that in four years he had never been invited to a meeting with anyone from the department his office depended on. He was at pains to point out that things were the same under the previous left-wing mayor: 'Politicians were never interested in long-term strategies. It wouldn't be profitable for them to invest in something that might bring positive results only in 20 years' time. Their every action is focused on garnering as many votes as possible' (personal communication, April 24, 2012). He added,

> all the residents of this camp are very skilled in recycling materials. They go around the city and look for recyclable items in garbage bins, on the streets. If the local administration were sincere about working with them to find the best solutions to this problem, their recycling activity would have been legalised. Instead of introducing legislation that would create a whole new market, the city council keeps neglecting this issue because there are obviously no votes in it. (Personal communication, April 24, 2012)

The following issues, the informant noted, are some of the main barriers to the Romani people becoming fully accepted by, and integrated into, this host society: their sense of collective strength and opposition to mainstream values; lack of respect for their culture by the host culture; and widespread corruption—as the host society regards it—among their own. This is the informant's comment on Romanies' cultural distance from Italians:

The Business of the Camps During the 'Nomad Emergency' **151**

On the one hand the Romanies represent a 'problem' because they refuse to integrate. On the other, they were never offered a real opportunity to integrate. Rather, they have always been the object of attempts to force them to assimilate. For instance, their culture and language are still not officially recognised by the Italian legislative system. It is thus predictable that they will refuse to have a dialogue with a society that is violently hostile towards them. [...] Millions of Euros have been spent on Romani issues. Unfortunately, this was mainly used either to keep the 'camps policy' alive or to carry out forced evictions. This approach is not intended to solve the problem but to move it somewhere else for a time. Two of the main projects supported by the government in Tor de' Cenci – the *borse lavoro* (paid traineeships) and *pulizia del campo* ('clean up the camp') – were not designed to promote inclusion. Rather, they were bribes doled out to persuade the alleged *portavoce* (spokesperson) for the camp to move from one place to another. (Personal communication, April 24, 2012)

In conclusion, the testimony provided by this informant highlighted the corrupt management of the Tor de' Cenci camp. The lack of interest in its inhabitants' living conditions, together with a disastrous and unaccountable use of available resources, puts the blame squarely on the administration at various levels. Without a clear change of attitude from senior echelons, who are more interested in harvesting a crop of electoral returns than in democratic accountability, it is unlikely the Romani residents are going to respond positively.

Final Observations

Even though the 'camps system' was already in place when leftists Rutelli and Veltroni occupied the mayoral seat, its operation became even less transparent under their right-wing successor, Alemanno. The interviews conducted for this study have revealed the existence of a pyramidal hierarchy with top-down relationships connecting upper-level positions to lower-level positions at several points, but with no bottom-up exchange. In this context, the upper levels never received feedback from the lower ones. One important difference between the right-wing civic administration and its left-wing predecessors was the communication channel that

Alemanno established with the Romani 'leaders' in the camps. Using Najo Adzovic as his special liaison with the 'camp-dwellers', the mayor ostensibly endeavoured to establish direct dialogue with the Romani communities. As the CDS representative said,

> paradoxically, Alemanno was better than Veltroni with regard to the Romani issue. For all its contradictions [Najo did not speak for the community, as many Romanies repeatedly pointed out: he would just say what the mayor wanted him to say], this was the very first time the public authorities in Rome had talked directly to Romani people, without the filter of associations or a cooperative. (Personal communication, April 2, 2012)

This chapter has exposed a democratic deficit in the way local authorities have operated during the past decade. A lack of transparency and accountability are the main issues. No independent bodies exist that can analyse the performance of tasks and functions within the Romani camps, let alone ones that can provide all the relevant information or arguments for projects involving the Romanies. We can tell, though, that the administrative structures are ineffective and unable to deliver the services they are mandated to provide. The decision-making system about resource allocations and expenditures remains opaque. A formal process of both internal and external evaluation represents a lacuna in our understanding of the system, and corruption is evidently widespread. Impartial and expert decision-making and policy implementation are out of reach. A report released in 2012 by Transparency International linked Italy's current economic crisis with administrative mismanagement. According to this study, Italy was

> ranked 69th out of 183 countries, one of the worst-performing EU countries on Transparency International's Corruption Perceptions Index, which measures perceptions of public sector corruption. [...] Italy's public sector is weakest, with problems both in law and in practice including nepotism, lack of access to information and lack of oversight. (ibid.: 1)

Public-sector inefficiency inevitably affects the Third Sector, especially the organisations that are most dependent on state funds. In fact, as Romani activist Pavlovic (cited in OsservAzione 2006: 32) once argued,

The Business of the Camps During the 'Nomad Emergency'   **153**

'some associations seem much too inclined to conciliate local authorities because of their funding dependency'. In 2013, there were 35 organisations (mostly CSOs but also joint-stock company controlled by the city council) orbiting around the 'camps system' and 80 per cent of their services were subcontracted by the city council through the procedure called *affidamento diretto* (direct endorsement; Ponziano 2014). This is part of a broader trend in Italy, where 60 per cent of public investments take place without a tendering process, as shown in a recent study conducted by the National Anticorruption Authority. However, this figure goes up to 86.51 per cent in the capital (Il Fatto Quotidiano 2015). The *Mafia Capitale* investigation was therefore important for unveiling the existence of a lobby group which was living off the marginalised condition of the Romani people. Among the CSOs involved, the first was the founder of Cooperativa 29 Giugno, Salvatore Buzzi (Bechis 2014). Later came the president of the Ermes Cooperativa Sociale, Salvatore Di Maggio (Teolato 2016). Both were arrested for their racket which controlled key municipal services, including the management of the 'nomad camps'. However, the city council have continued to manipulate public contracts as a way to favour certain CSOs, as recently denounced by Associazione 21 Luglio (cited in Drogo 2017).

Bibliography

Angeli, F., Forgnone, V., & Giannoli, V. (2014, December 2). 'Mafia a Roma, 37 arresti per appalti del Comune. Indagato Alemanno'. [Mafia in Rome, 37 people arrested for the subcontracting inquiry. Alemanno investigated.] *La Repubblica*. Retrieved from http://roma.repubblica.it/cronaca/2014/12/02/news/perquisizioni_alla_pisana_e_in_campidoglio-101923254/

Associazione 21 Luglio. (2010). Esclusi e ammassati: Rapporto di ricerca sulla condizione dei minori rom nel villaggio attrezzato di via di Salone a Roma [Excluded and massed: Report on the condition of under-age Romanies in the equipped village of Via Salone in Rome]. Retrieved from http://www.21luglio.org/index.php/report/12-esclusi-e-ammassati

Associazione 21 Luglio. (2011). Linea 40: Lo scuolabus per soli bambini rom [Line 40: The school bus for Romani children only]. Retrieved from http://www.21luglio.org/index.php/notizie/9-lassociazione-21-luglio-presenta-la-ricerca-qlinea-40q

Associazione 21 Luglio. (2012a). Cinque associazioni chiedono pubblicamente l'obiezione di coscienza alle organizzazioni romane che lavorano dentro i 'campi nomadi' [Five organisations publicly ask the organisations that work in the 'nomad camps' in Rome to opt for conscientious objection]. Retrieved from http://www.21luglio.org/index.php/comunicati-stampa/107-19-giugno-2012-cinque-associazioni-chiedono-pubblicamente-lobiezione-di-coscienza-alle-organizzazioni-romane-che-lavorano-dentro-i-qcampi-nomadiq

Associazione 21 Luglio. (2012b). Lavoro Sporco: Il Comune di Roma, i rom e le 'borse-lavoro' [Dirty job: The Municipality of Rome, the Romani people and the 'paid traineeships']. Retrieved from http://www.21luglio.org/images/Report/lavorosporco.pdf

Associazione 21 Luglio (2016). Ultimo Banco [Last school desk]. Retrieved from http://www.21luglio.org/21luglio/wp-content/uploads/2017/03/abstract-Last-Desk.pdf

Bechis, F. (2014, December 3). Roma, inchiesta Mafia Capitale [Rome, 'Capital Mafia' inquiry]. *Libero Quotidiano*. Retrieved from http://www.liberoquotidiano.it/news/roma/11729234/Roma--inchiesta-Mafia-Capitale-.html

Bonaccorsi, M., & Vazzana, R. (2011, February 18). Sui rom si fanno i milioni [Making millions out of Romanies]. Left. Retrieved from http://www.arcisolidarietaonlus.eu/content/sui-rom-si-fanno-i-milioni

Brogi, P. (2012, September 28). Nomadi, raso al suolo Tor de' Cenci: Scontro Campidoglio-governo [Nomads, razed Tor de' Cenci: Clash between local and national governments]. *Corriere della Sera*. Retrieved from http://roma.corriere.it/roma/notizie/cronaca/12_settembre_28/tor-de-cenci-cancellato-campo-nomadi-2112023098792.shtml

Castri, C., & Aversano, L. (2011). Piano Nomadi: Questione di integrazione o di ordine pubblico? [Nomad Plan: A matter of integration or rather public order?]. *Reti solidali*, *1*, 21–35. Retrieved from http://it.calameo.com/read/0 00605228b53276e869f6

Cecchini, C. (2012). Oltre il campo: Tavola rotonda con testimonianze sulla condizione dei Rom a Roma [Beyond the camp: Round-table on the condition of the Romanies in Rome]. Speech presented at Palazzo Valentini, Rome.

Cefisi, L. (2011). Bambini ladri: Tutta la verità sulla vita dei piccoli rom, tra degrado e indifferenza [Children thieves: All the truth about the life of the Romani children, between decay and indifference]. Rome: Newton Compton Editori.

Clough Marinaro, I., & Daniele, U. (2011). Roma and humanitarianism in the Eternal City. *Journal of Modern Italian Studies, 16*(5), 621–636.

Comune di Roma. (2008). Capitolato per l'affidamento della realizzazione del progetto di scolarizzazione per i bambini e gli adolescenti rom per il triennio scolastico 2008–2011 [Terms of contract regarding the schooling project for Romani children and adolescents in the 3-year period 2008–2011]. Retrieved from http://62.77.53.204/repository/ContentManagement/information/P1914591917/CAPITOLATO_ROM.pdf

Comune di Roma. (2009a, October 22). 'Contro ogni discriminazione', protocollo Comune-Dipartimento Pari Opportunità [Against any discrimination: Agreement between City Council and the Department of Equal Opportunity]. Retrieved from http://www.comune.roma.it/wps/portal/pcr?contentId=NEW110254&jp_pagecode =newsview.wp&ahew= contentId:jp_pagecode

Comune di Roma. (2009b). Il piano nomadi [The nomad plan]. Retrieved from http://briguglio.asgi.it/immigrazione-e-asilo/2009/agosto/slides-piano-nomadi-rm.pdf

Comune di Roma. (2011a). Allegato 7 allo schema del Piano Regolatore Sociale 2011–2015: Interventi per le popolazioni rom [Social Town Plan 2011–2015 of the city of Rome: Interventions on behalf of the Romani people]. Retrieved from http://www.oasisociale.it/myDesk/_temp/All%207%20PRS-Popolazioni%20Rom.pdf

Comune di Roma. (2011b). Capitolato per l'affidamento della realizzazione del progetto di scolarizzazione per i minori appartenenti alle comunita' rom dei campi non attrezzati di Roma Capitale 1 Gennaio 2011–31 dicembre 2011 [Terms of contract regarding the schooling project for Romani children inside non-equipped camps between 1 January 2011 and 31 December 2011]. Retrieved from https://www.comune.roma.it/PCR/resources/cms/documents/CAPITOLATO.pdf

Comune di Roma. (2014). Capitolato Speciale di Appalto per l'affidamento del Servizio di scolarizzazione dei minori appartenenti alle comunità rom, sinti e caminanti dei Villaggi attrezzati e dei Campi non attrezzati di Roma Capitale periodo 1 settembre 2014–31 agosto 2015 [Terms of contract regarding the schooling project for Romani children inside non-equipped camps and equipped villages between 1 September 2014 and 31 August 2015]. Retrieved from https://www.comune.roma.it/PCR/resources/cms/documents/bando_rom_2014_capitolato.pdf

Comune di Roma. (2016a). Procedura aperta per l'affidamento del servizio di gestione sociale, formazione lavoro, di interventi di piccola manutenzione e del servizio di vigilanza dei villaggi di Roma capitale [Open procedure for the assignment of the services of social management, work and training, small-scale maintenance and surveillance inside the capital's villages]. Retrieved from https://www.comune.roma.it/resources/cms/documents/Procedura_aperta_affidamento_servizio_gestione_villaggi_di_Roma_Capitale_BANDO_DI_GARA.pdf

Comune di Roma. (2016b). Scolarizzazione dei minori rom, sinti e caminanti residenti nel territorio di Roma Capitale: Anno Educativo 2016–2017 [Terms of contract regarding the schooling project for Romani Children in the 2016–2017 Period]. Retrieved from http://www.comune.roma.it/pcr/do/jpsite/Site/home

Comune di Roma. (2017). Ordinanza Sindacale n. 102 del 4 luglio 2017 [Mayoral Law no. 102 of July 4, 2017]. Retrieved from https://www.comune.roma.it/pcr/it/dip_sss_ufficio_nomadi.page

Cosentino, R., & Fico, A. (2012, November 2). Deportazioni, sprechi e illegittimità: Così è fallito il piano nomadi di Roma [Expulsions, inefficiencies and illegitimacy: This is how the Nomad Plan has failed]. La Repubblica. Retrieved from http://inchieste.repubblica.it/it/repubblica/rep-it/2012/11/02/news/il_fallimento_del_piano_nomadi-45769127/

Croce Rossa Italiana. (2010). Rom: CRI – Campidoglio, protocollo su presidi nei campi nomadi [Romani people: CRI – City Council, protocol agreement regarding the nomad camps]. Retrieved from https://www.cri.it/flex/cm/pages/ServeBLOB.php/L/IT/IDPagina/5773

Croce Rossa Italiana. (2013). Croce Rossa, i volontari eleggono Francesco Rocca nuovo presidente Nazionale [Red Cross, the volunteers elect Francesco Rocca new national president]. Retrieved from https://www.cri.it/flex/cm/pages/ServeBLOB.php/L/IT/IDPagina/15706

Croce Rossa Italiana. (2017). Chi siamo [Who we are]. Retrieved from https://www.cri.it/chisiamo

Daniele, U. (2011). 'Nomads' in the eternal city. *Géocarrefour, 86*(1), 15–24. Retrieved from http://geocarrefour.revues.org/8230

Di Blasi, F. (2010, July 28). Campi rom, Opera Nomadi lancia l'allarme su Castel Romano [Romani camps, Opera Nomadi sounds the alarm regarding Castel Romano]. Retrieved from http://www.suglizingari.it/rassegna-stampa/campi-rom-opera-nomadi-lancia-lallarme-su-castel-romano

Drogo, G. (2017, April 04). 'Il fantastico piano di Virginia Raggi per (fingere di) superare i Campi Rom'. NeXt Quotidiano. Retrieved from https://www.nextquotidiano.it/virginia-raggi-campi-rom/

European Commission. (n.d.). Study on volunteering in the European Union: Country report Italy. Retrieved from http://ec.europa.eu/citizenship/about-the-europe-for-citizens-programme/studies/index_en.htm

Falcioni, D. (2010, December 16). Roma: Il 'Piano Nomadi' in mano alla Croce Rossa. Anzi, ad Alemanno [Rome: The 'Nomad Plan' in the hands of the Red Cross, or rather of Alemanno]. Inviato Speciale. Retrieved from http://www.inviatospeciale.com/giornale/2010/12/il-piano-nomadi-in-mano-alla-croce-rossa-anzi-ad-alemanno/

Fico, A. (2012, November 2). Dopo lo sgombero di Tor de Cenci é rottura tra Alemanno e mondo cattolico [The forced eviction of Tor de Cenci lead to a breakup between Alemanno and the Catholic world]. La Repubblica. Retrieved from http://inchieste.repubblica.it/it/repubblica/rep-it/2012/11/02/news/alemanno_isolato-45768915/

Fiorucci, M. (2010). Un'altra città è possibile. Percorsi di integrazione delle famiglie Rom e Sinte a Roma: Problemi, limiti e prospettive delle politiche di inclusione sociale. [Another city is possible. Integration trajectories of Roma and Sinti families in Rome: Problems, limitations and perspectives of social inclusion policies]. Roma, Italia: Geordie onlus.

Forti, M. (2008, October 25). Una Croce Rossa sotto controllo di stato [A Red Cross under state control]. Il Manifesto. Retrieved from http://www.lettera22.it/showart.php?id=9818&rubrica=193

Frignani, R. (2012, January 20). Piano nomadi: 'No' di Sant'Egidio [Nomad Plan: S. Egidio says 'no']. Retrieved from http://www.santegidio.org/pageID/64/langID/cs/itemID/7234/Piano_nomadi_no_di_Sant_Egidio.html

Giannini, S. (Writer), & Gabanelli, M. (Director). (2010). La croce in rosso [The cross in red] [Television series episode]. In Bisogni, P. (Producer), Report. Rome: Rai 3.

Global Detention Project. (2012). Italy Detention Profile. Retrieved from http://www.refworld.org/pdfid/545b31704.pdf

Grilli, F. (2011, August 4). Tor de' Cenci: Da Campo Nomadi 'modello' a Campo 'tollerato'. Ecco cos'è cambiato [Tor de' Cenci: From being an 'ideal' nomad camp to a 'tolerated' camp. This is what has changed]. Roma Today. Retrieved from http://eur.romatoday.it/campo-nomadi-modello-campo-tollerato.html

Grilli, F. (2012, July10). Tor de' Cenci: 'Mantenete le promesse sul campo nomadi' [Tor de' Cenci: 'Keep the promises you have made regarding the nomad camp']. Roma Today. Retrieved from http://eur.romatoday.it/tor-de-cenci-residenti-chiedono-sindaco-mantieni-promesse.html

Gruppo Attivo WWF Roma XI. (2005). Sgombero di Vicolo Savini: Fu vera gloria? [The evacuation of Vicolo Savini: Was it really something to be proud of?]. Retrieved from http://www.wwfroma11.it/documenti/decima/intervista%20antonini%20nomadi%20decima.htm

Il Fatto Quotidiano. (2015, February 26). Appalti pubblici, il 60% dei contratti viene affidato senza gara. A Roma l'80% [Public contracts, 60% of them are entrusted without competition. In Rome 80%]. *Il Fatto Quotidiano*. Retrieved from http://www.ilfattoquotidiano.it/2015/02/26/corruzione-60-dei-contratti-pubblici-viene-affidato-gara-roma-l80/1458396/

International Federation of Red Cross and Red Crescent Societies. (n.d.). Our vision and mission. Retrieved from http://www.ifrc.org/en/who-we-are/vision-and-mission/

La Repubblica. (2011, March 3). Protesta del terzo settore. [The protest of the Third Sector]. *La Repubblica*. Retrieved from http://roma.repubblica.it/cronaca/2011/03/03/news/nomadi-13135597/?refresh_ce

Lunaria. (2011). *Chronicles of ordinary racism: Second white paper on racism in Italy* (trans: Di Pietro, D. & Marshall, C.). Rome: Edizioni dell'Asino.

Lunaria. (2013). Segregare costa: La spesa per i 'campi nomadi' a Napoli, Roma e Milano [Segregating is costly: The expenditure for 'nomad camps' in Naples, Rome and Milan]. Retrieved from http://www.lunaria.org/wp-content/uploads/2013/09/segregare.costa_.pdf

Mariani, F. (2017). I nomadi ci costano duecento milioni [Nomads cost €200 million]. Retrieved from http://www.iltempo.it/roma-capitale/2017/05/11/news/i-nomadi-ci-costano-duecento-milioni-1028298/

Martin, L. (2017, January 25). La Corte dei Conti "spara" sulla Croce Rossa [The Court of auditors "shoots" at the Red Cross]. Business Insider Italia. Retrieved from https://it.businessinsider.com/la-corte-dei-conti-spara-sulla-crocerossa/

Open Society Foundations & Open Society Justice Initiative. (2010). Roma in Italy: Briefing to the European Commission October 2010. Retrieved from http://www.soros.org/sites/default/files/memorandum-italy-ec-20101018.pdf

OsservAzione. (2006). Political participation and media representation of Roma and Sinti in Italy: The case studies of Bolzano-Bozen, Mantua, Milan and Rome. Retrieved from http://www.osservazione.org/documenti/osce_italy.pdf

Pavesi, F. (2013). Tutti gli sprechi della Croce Rossa italiana [All the CRI's squandering]. http://www.ilsole24ore.com/art/notizie/2013-02-04/conti-rosso-croce-rossa-190429.shtml?uuid=AbHUbBRH

Ponziano, G. (2014, December 9). Avevo denunciato il malaffare a danno dei rom [I reported the bad management of the Romani issue, but nobody listened]. *Italia Oggi*. Retrieved from http://www.italiaoggi.it/giornali/dettaglio_giornali.asp?preview=false&accessMode=FA&id=1945077&co

The Business of the Camps During the 'Nomad Emergency'   159

Portanova, M. (2016, June 22). Roma, le tangenti in diretta nell'ufficio del Comune [Rome, bribes live inside the office of the city council]. *Il Fatto Quotidiano*. Retrieved from http://www.ilfattoquotidiano.it/2016/06/22/roma-le-tangenti-in-diretta-nellufficio-del-comune-scusate-se-ho-interrotto-qualcosa/2849711/

Puliafito, A. (2011). *Croce Rossa: Il lato oscuro della virtù* [Red Cross: The dark side of virtue]. Rome: Alberti Editore.

Roma Soc!al Pr!de. (2010). Perché è nato il Roma Soc!al Pr!de? [Why was the Roma Soc!al Pr!de born?]. Retrieved from http://romasocialpride.wordpress.com/perche/

Rossi, M. (2010). The city and the slum: An action research on a Moroccan and a Roma Xoraxanè community in Rome. Doctoral dissertation. Retrieved from http://etheses.bham.ac.uk/1263/

Stasolla, C. (2012). *Sulla pelle dei Rom: Il Piano Nomadi della giunta Alemanno* [On the skin of the Romani People: The Nomad Plan of the Alemanno administration]. Rome: Edizioni Alegre.

Teolato, L. (2016, June 24). Roma, arrestato per corruzione su appalti gestione campi nomadi [Rome, arrested for bribery in relation to tender procurement contracts for the management of nomad camps]. *Il Fatto Quotidiano*. Retrieved from http://www.ilfattoquotidiano.it/2016/06/24/roma-arrestato-per-corruzione-su-appalti-campi-nomadi-aveva-affidato-bene-sequestrato-alla-mafia/2857090/

VII Commissione Cultura, Scienza e Istruzione della Camera dei Deputati. (2011). Indagine conoscitiva sulle problematiche connesse all'accoglienza degli alunni con cittadinanza non italiana nel sistema scolastico italiano [Cognitive study on issues related to the reception of foreign pupils in the Italian school system]. Retrieved from http://documenti.camera.it/_dati/leg16/lavori/stencomm/07/indag/alunni/2011/0112/INTERO.pdf

5

Between Self-Determination and 'Collective-Identity Closure'

Paternalistic Approaches and Romani Voicelessness

In a globalised world the existence of multicultural societies has become an indisputable fact, even when a 'politics of recognition' is not in place. According to Nye (2007), multiculturality can be understood as a complex range of issues associated with cultural and religious diversity, rather than merely as an ideology or as a social programme. Modern societies, though, tend to base their inclusion policy framework more in terms of the adaptation/assimilation of newly arrived immigrants rather than a belief in the development and contributions of every individual to the general societal good. According to Musgrave and Bradshaw's (2014: 202), for instance, social inclusion is sometimes conceptualised merely 'as a process of bridging a simple insider/outsider divide, where immigrants are seen as included to the extent that they gain access to the mainstream community'. It is therefore crucial to place more emphasis on facilitating active social and economic engagement. Tonkens and Hurenkamp (2011: 3) use the term 'culturalisation of citizenship' to describe 'the process by which culture (emotions, feelings, cultural norms and values, and cultural symbols and traditions, including religion)' come to play a central role in the

© The Author(s) 2018
R. Armillei, *The 'Camps System' in Italy*, Mapping Global Racisms,
https://doi.org/10.1007/978-3-319-76318-7_5

161

debate on social integration. One of the major issues in Italy, however, is that there is no 'organic' policy of inclusion in all fields of society. The prevailing trend is rather to devise policies that promote a balance between the safeguarding of the national identity and a vaguely defined idea of integration (Armillei 2016).

The need to empower groups and communities in danger of being 'left behind' is particularly relevant with regard to Romanies. This difficult task is complicated by the fact that the Romanies constitute an internally diverse ethnic group, characterised by cultural fragmentation as well as factional rivalries. Over the years, this became an obstacle to the creation of a movement that could unite around common social, cultural and political goals. This condition was often used by public authorities to justify adopting a paternalistic approach. A policy of education in community capacity-building, which would have enabled them to manage their own affairs and co-operate to foster and sustain positive changes (Howe and Cleary 2001), was never seriously considered, let alone instituted. Non-Romani CSOs should also be held to account for not upholding the Romani communities' aspirations. The lack of internal cohesion is still often misperceived as a 'lack of maturity' in politics and in the collective self-image they portrayed to the world, rather than as the natural consequence of national, cultural or socio-economic diversity (Sigona 2009). Disunity among Romanies was used as a justification by Third Sector organisations for claiming the right to represent them (see Chap. 4 for the attitudes of 'pro-camps' organisations). In turn, 'ventriloquism'—stemming from a lack of political self-representation—instead of real empowerment strategies can partly explain the political disengagement of the Romani people.

According to Romani actress and activist Dijana Pavlovic (as cited in Cugusi 2011),

> no Romani individuals are enabled to speak up for their interests before the authorities. Civil administrations keep delegating Romani issues to the Third Sector and Catholic organisations, instead of Romani representatives. [...] Social workers have their own reasons for using a charitable approach to dealing with the Romanies. Many of them would be without jobs if there were no 'Gypsies' to take care of – not to mention that the

Between Self-Determination and 'Collective-Identity Closure'   163

European Union provides plenty of money for this purpose. Many Romani generations have been 'managed' (and damaged) by a charitable approach and welfare dependency. (Para. 5)

As a consequence, interactions between the Romanies and the authorities or the Third Sector (chiefly the organisations working within the camps) are more like a monologue than a dialogue. A similar claim is made by Professor of Romani Language and Culture at Chieti University and internationally renowned musician Santino Spinelli:

Millions of Euros were wasted over the last 30 years, in the name and on behalf of Romani people. This created welfare dependency and segregation inside the camps, with inevitable consequences that are there for all the world to see today. (As cited in Associazione Thèm Romanó 2010, para. 4)

Even the execution of potentially ground-breaking initiatives, such as the then Mayor Alemanno's nomination of Najo Adzovic, a Romani, as his personal liaison with Rome's Romani communities, actually disempowered them and reduced their participation in politics.

Adzovic's nomination, in fact, had no democratic legitimacy. He was not elected by the Romanies to represent them but was chosen for reasons of political expediency. Addressing a rally in Rome on racial discrimination against Romanies in Europe in 2010, Spinelli noted:

The Mayor's delegate, Najo Adzovic, a semi-literate foreign Romani with no work qualifications, was chosen by Alemanno as his spokesman. Alemanno chose a puppet as his special mouthpiece, a person who is easy to blackmail. Not only that: Najo has no global view on the situation of the Romani people, which transcends the context of this capital city. [...] Most of the Romani people live in houses and are Italian citizens: they are honest workers but they have no representatives in the corridors of power. We asked Najo many times to consider how it is necessary to have a Permanent National Romani Council, made up of qualified experts, Romani intellectuals and delegates from Romani organisations and federations, to solve the problems besetting all Romani communities and not promote just the interests of a given group. But our request was ignored. (Associazione Thèm Romanó 2010, para. 1)

In turn, the political disengagement of the Romanies residing in Rome diverted attention from the authorities' and Third Sector's inability to hold a constructive dialogue with them.

A problem that emerged while fostering Romani political representation was that Romanies are often actively discouraged from speaking up and saying what they think. In fact, it was not uncommon for them to be expelled from organisations they were working for if they dared to oppose those bodies' activities and strategies. This happened to Pavlovic herself. She was fired by Casa della Carità—a Milan-based religious foundation contracted by the local municipality to manage the *campo nomade* at Via Triboniano—after spurning the *Patto di legalità e socialità* (Pact for Legality and Sociality) adopted by the CSO as a 'tool for cultural mediation and coexistence' (Officina Genitori 2008, para. 1). This 'pact' required Romani individuals to sign a pledge that they would be well behaved, and not steal or beg, in exchange for hospitality and a tailored inclusion project. Pavlovic rejected the pact on the basis that it was really a kind of discriminatory 'Gypsy law' (*legge speciale per gli Zingari*), a unilateral imposition rather than (as the word 'pact' would suggest) a voluntary agreement between two or more parties. As the ODIHR reported in 2009, there were even 'cases where a breach of the applicable rules in the camp by one Roma individual led to the expulsion of his or her whole family' (ibid.: 20). Pavlovic was fired when she joined a movement called *No Patto* (No Pact) (Cugusi 2011).

Similar cases of disempowerment were focused on the *campi nomadi*. These became the nub of a dispute involving two well-known Romani intellectuals, Spinelli and Guarnieri. The falling-out began back in September 2007, when Spinelli blamed supposedly 'pro-Romani' organisations for the discrimination against Romanies in Italy. His criticism was directed mainly at Opera Nomadi which, according to him, had actually supported the *campi nomadi* as a way to make money out of the Romani people. Guarnieri, who was the then president of Opera Nomadi in the Abruzzo region, not only defended Spinelli but railed at the organisation's national leadership, arguing for Romani self-determination: 'You should all resign and hand over the reins of this organisation to Romanies', he concluded (Osservatorio Sociale Regionale 2007, heading). In response, Opera Nomadi accused them of having produced misleading information about the organisation. On their blog they were called *quacquaraquà* (windbags; Romano Lil 2007). A recent corruption scandal involving its President Massimo Converso (Fiano and Sacchettoni 2016) would seem to confirm Spinelli and Guarnieri's concerns about Opera Nomadi. Although Romani individuals and communities were never given the chance to be fully included in Italian society, a certain social and political awareness evolved within their ranks until some Romanies finally decided to act and to be more visible on the political scene. For example, the above-mentioned rally in the capital was attended by 1800 people, belonging to about 120 Romani and non-Romani organisations (Associazione Thèm Romanó 2010).

The Proliferation of Romani Organisations

Italy's Romani communities have now been wracked by a decade of cultural and political turmoil. These convulsions have produced a veritable 'explosion' of Romani groupings all across the peninsula. In 2004, as Guarneri observed, there were only three or four Romani organisations in all of Italy (personal communication, April 21, 2012). More recently, as estimated by Graziano Halilovic, president of *Federazione Romani* (one of three Romani federations), there are around 87 so organisations in number (the precise figure is unknown because there is no dedicated register). Most were concentrated in the Lazio region and, more generally, in the biggest cities. The city of Rome alone could count 19 Romani organisations (U Velto 2012a). This number decreased drastically by the time this book was written. Only five Romani organisations are still active (Associazione Romà onlus, Associazione Romnì onlus, Coop. Antica sartoria rom, Centro studi e ricerche CILICLO, Associazione 21 Luglio). At least initially, the Romani movement appeared to be the product of a political schism. Since the 1960s, Romani affairs have been dominated by Opera Nomadi and the *Associazione Italiana Zingari Oggi* (Italian Association of Today Gypsies or AIZO), both pioneering Romani organisations. But, over time, internal dissent grew. This was principally stoked by influential Romanies such as Guarnieri and Spinelli, who increasingly questioned the value of the 'pro-Romani' groups.

What spurred this development, according to Yuri Del Bar, president of the *Federazione Rom e Sinti Insieme* (Federation of Roma and Sinti Together), was the Romanies' realisation that as the most affected of all the parties, they needed to speak with their own voice, unmediated by 'non-Romanies'. This was the only way to improve their situation and combat discrimination. Del Bar underscored the fact that all the federation's constituent groups were made up of Romani individuals. To quote him, they were not there just '*a fare il palo*' (to act as lookouts) (U Velto 2012b, para. 2). This was a clear allusion to the systematic exploitation of Romani representatives by many CSOs. He had a point: a mere fraction of these CSOs' staff are of Romani descent. Romanies typically hold lowly office in their hierarchies, the likes of 'cultural liaison' or 'teacher's aide'. Of the CSOs working on Romani issues, none were ever chaired or run by a Romani CEO. According to Spinelli, the prospect of Romanies creating their own organisations and giving voice to their own needs was one of the CSOs' worst nightmares. Using Guarnieri's own words, this was '*una "rivoluzione" che fa paura*' ('a threatening revolution'; Associazione Thèm Romanó 2010, heading). But the proliferation of Romani organisations in Italy had a dark side as well.

In an interview, Guarnieri recounted some of the twists and turns of that process:

> It was around 2003 that we started to get together and discuss what we could do to increase Romani self-representation. 2008 was the bumper year for new Romani groups in Italy. At that time, I was one of the promoters of the 'Federazione Rom e Sinti Insieme', which comprised around 20 Roma and Sinti organisations. Our main goal was recognition of the Romani people as a 'linguistic minority'. Yet, we also wanted to move from using intermediaries to this minority getting itself really actively involved. A year later, though, came the first big disagreement within the federation. Some of us believed that Romanies should be involved [as activists] regardless of how experienced they were, while others thought you should be more qualified to play a role. I was in the latter group. This situation gave rise to an internal split and a number of us dissenters formed the 'Federazione Romani'. I was elected president. Three years after it was created, the federation had not attained its two main goals – getting Romani

people actively participating in matters affecting them, and establishing a promising dialogue with the authorities based on equal respect. Some Romani associations and individuals had not fully grasped the importance of personal training, cultural growth, a professionalised approach and education. So, after this experience, I decided to quit and go looking for new platforms from which to apply the values that had summed up my thinking. (Personal communication, April 21, 2012)

As Guarnieri further explained, the evolution of the Romani movement after 2007 resulted from lone ambition and a determination to replace all the *Gadje* bodies rather than from a clearly thought-out political and cultural strategy. These bodies were completely self-obsessed and lacking any internal democracy. Since all member organisations were 'ego trips' (each family having its own organisation), the federation reflected the self-centredness of each family. To put it another way, 'the federation did some good because it gave everyone a "slice of the cake", but it did nothing to improve the Romanies' lot overall' (personal communication, April 21, 2012). In May 2012, after quitting as president of the *Federazione Romani*, Guarnieri founded the *Fondazione Romani*. Guarnieri's decision to leave 'on his own' spoke volumes about the current state of the Romani movement in Italy. Guarnieri is well aware of this, declaring: 'Romani associationism is in great crisis at the moment' (U Velto 2012a, para. 8). Guarnieri was particularly critical of 'certain Romani fringe groups' who he said were basically milking the 'system':

The problem is not just the 'pro-Romani' organisations that devote themselves to Romani business with the solitary aim of acquiring state funds. But it is time to say loud and clearly that there also exist Romani organisations that exploit Romanies. We need to battle all these organisations. If we have been as one in criticising the *Gadje* up till now, why should not we treat ourselves any differently? (Personal communication, June 26, 2012)

Romanian Romani intellectual Nicolae Gheorghe supports Guarnieri's stance. Recalling his visit to the authorised camp Tor de' Cenci in June 2012, he remarked:

Combating prejudice must be a concern not only for mainstream society – through the DOSTA campaign,[1] for example – but also for the Romani people. In my opinion, Romanies who exploit women and children are just as racist as other people. […] We in the Romani communities have to club together and strike back against attitudes like that. And at the same time, of course, we need to fight those who discriminate against Romanies. (Personal communication, July 21, 2012)

Stances such as those taken by Guarnieri or Gheorghe were important in understanding this key issue. Their contributions provide a privileged insight into the strategy adopted by the 'Romanies of the camps'. Their views represent a clear break with the past, when Romanies were often depicted merely as victims. Guarnieri and Gheorghe are members of a nationally and internationally recognised avant-garde. They also remain fairly controversial, however, and are not widely accepted within their own communities, particularly among those involved in the 'camps system'. Moreover, their deeds and words bring them into conflict with both the authorities and Third Sector organisations.

The Weakness of Romani Associationism in the City of Rome

The aim of this section is to describe the role played by the municipality in regard to strengthening the Romani movement within the context of the *Piano Nomadi* in Rome. As emerged from the book *Sulla Pelle dei Rom* (On the Skin of the Romani People) by Carlo Stasolla (2012), two key Romani figures during the implementation of Alemanno's inclusion project were Najo Adzovic and Graziano Halilovic. At the end of 2009, Halilovic willed into being a committee entitled *Coordinamento Rom a Roma* (Co-ordination of the Romani People in Rome) that included delegates from seven 'authorised villages' in Rome. The main task of this body

---

[1] 'Dosta' in Romani language means 'enough'. Started in 2006 as part of a wider Council of Europe/European Commission Joint Programme ('Equal Rights and Treatment for Roma in South Easter Europe'), the Dosta Campaign aimed at bringing 'non-Roma closer to Roma citizens by breaking down the barriers caused by prejudices and stereotypes' (CoE 2008: 2).

Between Self-Determination and 'Collective-Identity Closure'

was to function as special interlocutor to the Alemanno administration. However, only a few months after the committee's inception that it became inoperative due to internal conflicts between different factions, as well as a shortage of organisational skills (ibid.: 54).

On July 27, 2010, Mayor Alemanno named Adzovic as his special liaison on Romani issues. Adzovic was tasked to develop studies, undertake research and devise projects for Romani socio-cultural inclusion, with particular reference to education, employment and intercultural mediation. On the very day Adzovic's appointment was announced, a cooperative was founded in the name of *Cooperativa Rom a Roma* (Romani Cooperative in Rome), which, in Adzovic's own words, aspired to 'offer jobs not only to the Romani people in Rome but, more broadly, to people from "disadvantaged" social categories' ('Un rom delegato di Alemanno' 2010, para. 5). The president of this new organisation was none other than one—Graziano Halilovic. Stasolla (2012) argued that, despite the fanfare surrounding this event, the cooperative made no real difference. According to him, it was just one more cooperative among many, battening on to the public purse while supposedly claiming to provide assistance to Romanies in the city (ibid.: 56).

The 'explosion' of Romani associationism during the past decade, especially in the city of Rome, did not result in a strong and united movement. Its leadership was not able to enunciate a long-term strategy to influence Government policy on the Romani issue. On the contrary, the Romani 'big tent' appeared divided, disorganised and devoid of real political vision. The representative of CDS, a CSO working in the *campi nomadi*, surmised that this might also be due the fact that for years 'we have been teaching them only the worse things about us, rather than the best' (personal communication, June 22, 2012). A Caritas representative added that, as the 'Italian associationism aimed merely to survive, rather than to liberate the Romani communities' (personal communication, June 11, 2012), the Romanies had adopted the same philosophical approach. They were never offered the option of a genuine process of social inclusion. They basically extracted whatever good they could find in adversity.

What they put into practice was the 'art of survival', as Najo Adzovic defined it (personal communication, April 16, 2012). According to him, when you live in a camp, without documentation and the real possibility to get out of there and to find a regular job, of course you have no other option than to learn to survive. And in such a context the strongest ones have a better chance to survive. They stop being preys and turn into predators. This is all a consequence of the existence of these camps, and politics is responsible for that. Inevitably, they also became an emergency issue. (Personal communication, May 14, 2012)

Unfortunately, though, most of the Romani organisations that were mapped during the fieldwork conducted for this book had either ceased operating or were experiencing financial difficulties. This was the case, for instance, with *Cooperativa Romanò Pijats* and *Cooperativa Baxtalò Drom Stireria Romanì*. The main activity of the first cooperative was managing flea markets, scattered across several parts of the city's territory, where handmade products were traded, together with recycled items scavenged from rubbish bins. As for the second one, this was a dry-cleaning cooperative founded in 2006 and staffed exclusively by Romani women. Gauging the success of these and other cooperatives was really not possible: as pointed out by Associazione 21 Luglio (2012b), there were no available studies done at that time. Today, this issue remains unexplored but it seems likely to infer that all the co-ops have collapsed over time.

The Interview with Najo Adzovic

Before assuming the status of mayoral liaison, Adzovic had been a resident of camp Casilino 900 and played a key role in the process that brought about its closure in 2010 in the context of the *Piano Nomadi*. In 2008 he was cultural liaison officer in the schooling project undertaken by CDS inside this informal encampment, but later became one of the staunchest opponents of the CSOs that had been dealing with Romani issues. Adzovic had shown great political acumen during the process leading to the organised evacuation of his community from Casilino 900. It was this experience that made him a close acquaintance of Mayor Alemanno and nurtured a reciprocal trust. As Stasolla asserted (2012), Adzovic was the first Romani to embrace Alemanno's new strategy in public. Two years after being appointed, he was still expressing satisfaction about the results he had been able to achieve: '€600,000 was provided to the Romani cooperatives. This was a great success, because with the new administration Romanies became more and more the architects of their own future', he commented (ibid.: 56).

This upbeat attitude, directed at both the *Piano Nomadi* and the projects he appears to have been licenced to talk up, was again in evidence at the time of our interview. According to Adzovic, the municipality had invested substantially in setting up a number of Romani cooperatives within the camps. Basically, they were contracted to look after their own environment:

> If you go into any of these camps, you will see that there are Romani organisations in charge of cleaning up the camp areas and of the socio-educational services. [...] With this administration we have tried to make the Romani people feel responsible for their own lives and give them guidelines on how to move out of the camps. In the last 20 to 30 years this had never been accomplished. Today, Romani people have the chance to take part in meetings with City Hall, with the Mayor, the Deputy Mayor and the director of this department. Here they can discuss with them and plan the best strategies for getting out of the camps. This never happened before with the do-gooders of the Left under Rutelli or Veltroni. (Personal communication, April 16, 2012)

Personal attacks on Adzovic, as well as criticism of the activities he had already been engaged in, were already prominent at the beginning of his commission. But a year after his appointment, the failure of his efforts was even more conspicuous. Ulderico Daniele (as cited in Stasolla 2012)—a scholar of Romani issues whose specialty was Rome's metropolitan area—criticised the *Coordinamento Rom a Roma*, dismissing it as unrepresentative of the Romani population residing in the city: 'None of its members were democratically elected and some of the largest communities, such as the Romanian one, did not participate in its meetings' (ibid.: 55). In the autumn of 2010 Guarnieri, at that time still president of *Federazione Romani*, deemed Adzovic's statements and attitudes so damaging for Romanies that he forced him to resign from the federation (Stasolla 2012). The *Cooperativa Rom a Roma* met with criticism as well.

Like the 'Coordinamento', this cooperative was accused by Opera Nomadi of not being truly representative of the Romani communities in Rome and of acting only in the interests of a few families (Falcioni 2010, para. 18). It was the president of *Cooperativa Rom a Roma*, Halilovic himself, who had reported on the cooperative's shortcomings: 'Romanies seldom come to visit us, because we can only act as go-betweens, forwarding the requests we get to the department in charge' (Stasolla 2012: 56).

Significantly, Adzovic did not deny these critiques during our interview. At the beginning of the interview, his statements still reflected appreciation for the work conducted by the Alemanno administration during the *Piano Nomadi* and his time in office. As we conversed, though, the internal contradictions of Rome's Romani communities began to emerge. The biggest problem inside the Romani communities appeared to be a lack of sense of unity.

> I have promoted the creation of this *Coordinamento*, giving opportunity to all the Romani people in Rome, but we have been unable to find a common strategy to overcome the 'camps'. Every time I tried to bring them together they would only talk about their own problems: all they were interested in was their own business. There is not a single Romani who can say they were not allowed to talk with the administration. But lately our meetings have been suspended because I received several threats from certain members of the Romani communities. […] If I chose to give jobs to five or six people in a camp, all the others would just say, 'Why has Najo offered them a job? Why not us?' The prevailing mindset within the Romani communities is mutual hatred.

Another issue seemed to be the existence of widespread corruption.

> We, as management, provided many opportunities to several Romani co-ops and associations. These people took money from the city council, and guess what they did? They shoehorned members of their families into these cooperatives and basically created 'their own little empires'. Can these people be considered real leaders of their own communities? No. […] The projects we carried out [i.e., cleaning up the camp and conferring paid traineeships] were a kind of education. But if we launch these experiments in the camps, and you are irresponsible and unable to take care of your own living environ-

Between Self-Determination and 'Collective-Identity Closure'   **173**

ment, how can we be sure that tomorrow you will be responsible outside the camp? These co-ops today do not have the capacity to operate autonomously in the market.

Finally, Adzovic also pointed out an important element to consider, which will help to overcome the conceptualisation of the camp as an *istituzione totale* (total institution; see Nicola 2011), a space where Romanies are reduced to a 'bare life' (see Clough Marinaro 2009) upon which the state can inscribe its sovereign power without restriction. According to him,

> the problem is that there are people living in these camps who own cars worth €50,000 or €60,000, but they leave their kids get around dirty in the middle of the street. Why don't these people rent a house and get out of the camps? There are hundreds of people like this. Most of the Romani people you will find living in camps have a house. (Personal communication, April 16, 2012)

This point emerged from interviews conducted within the camps. A number of the 'camp-dwellers' interviewed revealed that they owned a house in their countries of origin. And yet, as Ca. (a Romanian Romani) argues, 'living in the camp is better than going back home. Life in Romania is much harder and Romanians are very racist towards us' (personal communication, April 11, 2012). In addition, during my previous experience as a social worker for a CSO working inside these camps, I was often shown pictures of the properties owned by 'camp-dwellers'. On a number of occasions, these individuals would leave and then return to their houses abroad for brief periods in order to attend to some family matter. Most of my Romani sources also admitted to investing some of the money they earn in Italy, back in their home countries.

In conclusion, the interview with Adzovic revealed the weakness of his strategy to empower the Romanies he claimed to represent. It was not easy to see how the initiatives activated under his supervision improved their situation. No evidence of their success was proffered. It looked as though there was a large gap between the declared goals of increasing participation and accountability and the actual results. At the same time

174 R. Armillei

Adzovic's statements showed how idle the administration had been when it came to tackling off-limits behaviour within the Romani camp-dwelling communities. Instead of promoting the introduction of a democratic model, from which all Romanies would have benefited, however indirectly, Najo Adzovic kept the old family-ruled system in place with the municipality's backing.

Romani People as 'Fighters' and 'Collective-Identity Closure'

An impressive body of literature on Romani life concentrates on the failures of successive Italian Governments vis-à-vis the 'camps policy'. The real failure lies in its euphemistic character: 'camps policy' here meaning a form of social control, containment and segregation that leaves no room for Romanies to exercise their political talent or for appraisal of their counter-strategies. However, the 'camp' is not just an exogenous institutional means of control and segregation. Even so, Romanies found a way to use it as a tool of 'resistance' to the Government's exclusionary efforts. In other words, while perceiving mainstream society as a threatening environment, the 'camp' became a powerful weapon to protect the in-group (us) against the out-group (them), producing what I call 'collective-identity closure'. The camp, in fact, could be better described as a 'battlefield', a conflict zone—and not in a sense that would allow valid solutions to emerge, but rather as a place where 'oppressor' and 'oppressed' form and crystallise their own identities as homogeneous entities and a mirror of the other. At the same time, the strategy adopted by the Romani 'camp-dwellers' is also part of a 'co-constitution' of identity that has been developing for centuries. For the dominant or mainstream culture, the 'Other', *par excellence,* is the *Zingaro,* the 'Gypsy', the 'Traveller', the Romani. For these people, the 'Other' corresponds to the *Gadje,* a derogatory term which in Romanies stands for 'the whole non-Romani population'. Hence, it is important not to overlook the persistence on both sides of a strong sense of belonging that is constantly being reproduced and reified. Especially since the 1970s, the 'battle' between *Zingari* and *Gadje* has become fixated on the 'camp' as a physical and socio-political space.

Romani Separateness/Distinctiveness

For centuries Romani history has been characterised by oppression and persecution. Romanies have long been subjected to repressive Government policies. These aimed either to keep them away from the rest of society or to eliminate them, be it culturally or physically. Through the former tactic, defining them as social outcasts led to their isolation and ghettoisation or, as recorded in Romania since the fifteenth century, to their exploitation as an 'economically valuable slave class' (Woodcock 2009: 2). The latter tactic set about eliminating them in the name of a 'civilising mission'. This was enforced with the secondary aim of assimilating them to the dominant culture. In many cases, elimination implied force: from forced expulsions to 'ethnic cleansing' and even systematic extermination, as occurred under the Nazi-Fascist regimes. Yet Romanies 'have resisted assimilation and managed to maintain a strong identity' (Silverman 1995: 43), by developing down the centuries, an ideology that mirrors the one mobilised by non-Romanies.

The existence of this separateness between Romani communities and mainstream societies led Gheorghe and Acton (2001: 55) to write about a 'Gypsy "archipelago"'. This expression evokes the diversity of various sub-groups and meta-groups, with their cultural, religious, linguistic and geographical affiliations. This diversity could explain why the leaders of Romani communities today are still striving to construct a coherent supranational Roma identity. As noted, conflicting interests, together with adverse policies in most national contexts, have so far prevented the creation of a unified movement, either at a national or at an international level (Boscoboinik 2009). Despite this great internal diversity, which bedevils Romani communities around the world, a unifying factor may be found in a binary opposition to the '*Gadje* world'. In Italy, for instance, the underlying rivalry between Roma and Sinti, the two major groups among the Romani population, was dispelled by a common attitude towards *Gadje*. They are the 'Other', the enemy. In other words, the *Gadjikane* dimension (being non-Romani) can be seen as the symbolic expression of a radical exclusion from *Romanipen* (Roma-being), a category that unites all Romani people (Fischer 2011). As Pissacroia (1998: 398) argued, the '*Gadje* people' hold up a mirror to the Romanies' own identity, while constituting the main source of their sustenance (Benedetto 2011).

The DNA of Romani distinctiveness takes on the form of a double helix, in which continuous internal negotiation among Romanies forms one strand, while interactions between Romanies and non-Romanies forms the other (Piasere 2004). According to Benedetto (2011), *Gadjikane* and *Romanipen* display two contrasting poles, which are reproduced through the sedimentation of prejudices cultivated by each group against the other. The picture that emerges from authors Asséo (1989), Piasere (2005) and Calabrò (2008), and more recently from the works of Armillei (2016, 2017a, b), Clough Marinaro (2014, 2015), Sigona (2015) and Maestri (2016, 2017), to name a few, is a stark reminder that Romani people should not be regarded as voiceless and passive victims of hostile societies. On the contrary, Romanies always resist the dominant culture. Gheorghe referred to the Romanies of the camps in Rome as 'fighters' (personal communication, July 21, 2012), in the sense that Romanies know how to take advantage of their marginal condition. According to him, they have learned to exploit old 'Gypsy stereotypes' to advance their personal interests, mainly as a way of obtaining welfare aid, while simultaneously blaming others for their predicament: Governments, CSOs and mainstream society. In many cases they were harming others, first and foremost members of their own communities.

Of course, as Stasolla pointed out, 'the condition of living in camps produces a perverse sub-culture. Anyone forced to experience the same type of social exclusion would respond in the same way' (personal communication, April 4, 2012). Romanies' resilience in the face of efforts to assimilate them has been an abiding theme with many variations. Carrasco (2011), for instance, used the concept of 'warriors' to underline the fact that for centuries the Romanies were able to resist the 'colonisation of their way of life by any means necessary' (para. 6). In 1989 Asséo coined the definition *peuples-Résistances* (resistant peoples), which described how the Romani people resisted assimilation and mounted what she called an 'internal counter-hegemony' (ibid.: 124). Rivera (2003) and Uzunova (2010) posited that a determination to resist was a sign of an isolationist and ethnocentric culture. Not surprisingly, Weber (1922, as cited in Pogány 2012) had described the Romanies as 'pariahs', acknowledging that the enactment of 'ritual segregation' from mainstream society was 'not necessarily, or exclusively, a function

Between Self-Determination and 'Collective-Identity Closure'   **177**

of discrimination by host communities […] [but could] also result from, or be reinforced by, religious or cultural norms instituted or maintained by the minorities themselves' (ibid.: 377). Almost a century on, the concept of 'pariah peoples' as elaborated by Weber still 'remains remarkably "modern"' (Pogány 2012: 389), aiding our understanding of the reasons behind the persistent marginality of Romanies within an enlarged EU.

'Romaniya', 'Anti-*Gadje*', Double Personality

Weyrauch (1999) has observed that modern society is not regulated exclusively by the law. According to him, 'a large body of unwritten law, based on oral legal traditions, coexists autonomously within any setting'. It is, he notes, 'supported by informal but effective sanctions' (ibid.: 1211). The existence of such 'unwritten laws' has always played a role in governing individuals' and groups' behaviours. With particular regard to Romanies, probably the best expression of their creative ability to resist external interference can be found in the 'hidden world of *Romaniya,* or Gypsy law' (Barnes 2003: 823). Weyrauch (2001, as cited in Uzunova 2010: 294) argues that all Romani communities share a similar normative code, 'an autonomous legal system, […] which operates outside the parameters of state law'. Over time, the existence of this 'invisible' legal system among Romanies has reinforced and legitimised their perception of the *Gadjikane* as an alien world. Calabrò (2008: 79) even maintains that, for many Romanies, knowing 'the rules of the dominant society [is important] all the better to elude them and to capitalise on the opportunities that they can offer'. The *Gadje* is basically stereotyped as 'a person who cannot be trusted and of whom it is only possible to ask and take as much as they can', she concludes (ibid.: 79).

Like normative 'anti-Gypsism', which developed within mainstream societies, an 'anti-*Gadje*' attitude has been collectively nurtured by Romanies. These two opposing approaches are so deeply ingrained in both majority and minority groups that, as Uzunova (2010) argued, they could somehow be interpreted as commonly accepted social norms. And 'because social norms are arguably much more powerful factors in shaping the dynamics of a society than its written legal rules, this process is extremely important, especially in the area of human rights' (ibid.: 307). In fact, she asserts, the introduction of any 'minority rights legal framework will be ineffective unless the nature of the social tension between Roma and non-Roma is first acknowledged and addressed' (ibid.: 286). The existence of a dualistic approach characterising the way Romanies relate with non-Romani societies was clearly visible within the Romani communities I conducted fieldwork with, especially among the individuals living in the camps. This aspect emerged also from Daniele's (2010) article, entitled 'Zingari di Carta' (Paper Gypsies), which describes the Romani world and its rules as a parallel system whose functioning is secretly and scrupulously hidden from host societies.

In his paper Daniele focuses particularly on recent works published by two of the leading Romani intellectuals and artists in Italy, the aforementioned Santino Spinelli (2005) and Bruno Morelli (2006). Daniele's aim was to analyse the type of narrative Spinelli and Morelli have used as part of their empowerment. Spinelli notes:

> Every member of the Romani population has basically developed a double personality: an 'external' one to be displayed in relation to *Gadje* peoples which is generally pitiful, submissive and reeking with victimhood; and an 'internal' one, based on pride, stainlessness and honour, which is deployed within one's own community. These two personalities are diametrically opposed and incompatible, and are kept neatly separated in these distinct contexts. (As cited in Daniele 2010: 69)

Similarly, the strategy adopted by the Romani people was described by Morelli (2006, as cited in Daniele 2010) as a *dualità di salvataggio* (survival ambivalence). Ambivalence allows the Romanies to use a social (thought of as an artificial) mask to conceal and protect their real identity. When permanent settlement was not possible, the choice of a nomadic lifestyle was adopted as a way to escape repressive dominant societies. According to Morelli, nomadism was used as a form of cultural and economic resistance (ibid.: 68).

Interestingly, both Spinelli and Morelli insist that the heterogeneity of the 'Romani world' should be seen as flowing from the capacity to adopt mimetic strategies to fit into, and survive inside, host societies. In turn, the combination of this mimetic approach and sustained separateness reinforces and perpetuates the idea of the Romani and the *Gadje* peoples as mutually antagonistic. Another factor should be considered, when seeking to comprehend the functional disconnection of Romanies from non-Romanies: ethnocentrism, the belief in one's own society and rules as something pure. This has been conveyed in the concepts of *vujo* (pure) and *marime* (impure), which constituted the basis not only of the *Romaniya* but also of Romani identity in general. According to Leeson (2010), for instance, any person who does not follow the *Romaniya* rules for ensuring ritual purity would be treated as *marime*. As a consequence, non-'Gypsies', 'who by definition do not follow these rules', are in a constant and full-blown state of defilement. Gypsies look on them with contempt' (ibid.: 10). From a very early age, Romanies adopt various ritual devices, such as avoiding unnecessary contact with *Gadje* and careful attention to bodily cleanliness so as not to be polluted and become *vujo* (Daniele 2010). And yet, during the last half century, a decline of belief in the *marime* concept has been also discernible in several Romani societies (Leeson 2010).

Absence of a Shared Understanding of 'Romaniness'

With respect to the differential degree of acceptance of Romani social structure, rules and traditions, Galati (2007) argues that it is possible to distinguish three main tendencies within Romani communities. There are Romanies who prefer to conform totally to the values their culture endorses. These Romanies will shun any form of relations with the 'Gadje' world (i.e. in education, employment, health) and its institutions, which implies that these individuals are often inevitably involved in criminal activity. Another group is composed of those who reject their own culture and identity, because basically they feel it is something to be ashamed of. Therefore, they choose to accept the host culture's values and try to assimilate to them. Finally, there is a third group that, deploying what might be termed a 'hybrid' behaviour, critically assesses the values championed by both the Romanies and the host society. This categorisation can be helpful because it introduces a new perspective to the understanding of intra-group co-operation, cultural identity and belonging. The remarkable heterogeneity of the Romani population throughout Europe should be regarded not only as an outcome of the pressure to conform emanating from the dominant culture, but also of the existence and proliferation of internal rivalries, as well as of a natural process of evolution and differentiation which over the centuries took place within Romani societies.

The striving for unity and the idea of ethnic uniqueness promoted by Romani elites have been under a constant challenge from the contemporaneous presence of widespread disunity within Romani populations and the elusiveness of a shared understanding of 'Romaniness' (Fischer 2011). According to Barany (1998: 313), for instance, 'Romani communities are such that it is not clear what the Romani identity is, since many Roma do not consider themselves members of a cohesive ethnic group but identify instead with the subgroup to which they belong'. Internal heterogeneity constitutes a clear obstacle to the realisation of the utopian dream of creating a 'Romani nation', which has been advocated since the 1970s. The feasibility of this project has been endangered, at different stages, by the difficult question of representativeness-cum-leadership. This emerged from the constant dialectic, or competition, between traditional communities, who commonly define themselves as the 'real' Romanies, and the modern, or more assimilated ones. The traditionalists would generally not co-operate with the non-traditionalists, whom they 'mostly considered inferior' (Council of Europe Romani Projekt [*ca* 2005]: 7). This problem was clearly highlighted by Romani scholar Ian Hancock (2000). At a number of World Romani congresses, Hancock had noted that on several occasions different Romani groups declared themselves 'traditional', each claiming for itself the mantle of legitimate representatives of what they defined as 'our true people'.

The statements by these groups aimed to highlight their opposition to those educated Romanies (the intellectual elite) who, according to Hancock, believed themselves to be 'in a better position to bridge the links with the non-Romani world' (para. 26). In this regard, Gheorghe's position was different. He argued (as cited in van Baar 2005: 15) that 'the relationship between the Romani elite(s) and the Romani grassroots […]

is to some extent debatable'. Although the emergence of Romani elites had raised consciousness of the Romani question in global political circles, their becoming increasingly articulate had widened 'the gap between them and their constituencies' until 'in many cases [it] proved to be unbridgeable' (Vermeersch 2001, p. 4). It is worth mentioning that in many circumstances these elites have played a key role in classifying Romanies as a distinctive ethnic group, probably underestimating (more or less consciously) the presence of significant internal differences. To this day, escalating internal conflict and greater cultural diversity among the Romani population has not delivered a system capable of promoting unity and dialogue. While Romani leaders laud the cause of strength through unity, many of them have to deal constantly with the contrary prospect. There are those who strive to inculcate internationalism in the Romani movement, and those leaning towards familism.

The key role of familism in Romani culture is elucidated by this observation from Matras ([*ca* 2007]: 1): 'Roma society is based around the group of close kin, which in most traditional Roma communities forms a single household'. This relation is generally reinforced by the common practice of marrying within one's own ethnic sub-group and the existence of extended families. Each sub-group aims to retain distinct cultural and linguistic practices, thus contributing to the growing heterogeneity within the Romani archipelago (Fischer 2011). At the same time, 'each Gypsy grouping tends to look upon itself as being the authentic [one]' (Fraser, as cited in Pogány 2004: 14). Despite the absence of a unifying national sentiment, umbrella organisations such as the International Romani Union (IRU) keep 'creating the framework of a Romani nation through top-down strategies of common-identity building' (Fischer 2011: 88). This happens although they are often self-appointed and most Romanies are unaware of the international political movement. It is therefore 'extremely difficult for Romani politicians and activists to establish a common platform within particular states' (Pogány 2004: 14). While Romani-related policies supporting integration have by now been introduced at a variety of institutional levels in many countries, their 'practical implementation has been evaluated as ineffective or counterproductive' (van Baar 2005: 2).

Essentially, only a small elite has benefited from the campaign to emancipate the Romani people. As Boscoboinik (2009: 187) has observed,

> the development of the Roma elite increasingly deepens the gap between educated and engaged Roma on the one hand and the poor, average Roma on the other. The Roma leaders have been much criticised by the non-elite Roma and are sometimes characterised by ethno-careerism, following their own interests.

Basing his analysis on the work of the anthropologist Jonathan Friedman, Fosztó (2003) also identified the existence of dualism within the Romani movement. Pan-European or transnational projects supported by more global elites run counter to the priorities of emergent diaspora identities that place the accent on nationalism and national minorities, as advocated by more traditional elites. This opposition between 'global elites' and 'diaspora elites' is reflected at the constituency level also (Fosztó 2003: 119). According to Fosztó, while an exemplar of the cosmopolitan elite 'communicates easier among his/her fellows, and identifies more with elite members in similar positions' (ibid.: 119), as previously suggested by Hancock (2000), lower-class Romanies tend to essentialise their positions (cut off from the dynamic of reflection about broader understandings of Romaniness), leading to political fragmentation, economic competition and the 'ethnicisation of poverty' (Fosztó 2003: 119).

The Camp as a 'Resistance Site'

Chapter 2 sketched the history of how Romani people were physically marginalised in Italy's *campi nomadi*. How the Government attempted to realise its strategic aspirations was outlined in its successive stages, from the notion of using the camp as means of 'protection' for Romani culture, through to its evolution into a 'system' of social control and segregation. In this section, attention will be paid to the realities of these establishments mainly using the perspective of the Romanies themselves, examining how they managed to exercise what remained to them of their free agency. In this context, the camp is not to be seen merely as a physical space separating its inmates from the outside world, living without prospect of escaping into that world. Here, rather, that paradigm is inverted, allowing the camp to be seen as the concrete consequence of a decision autonomously arrived at, if not the outcome of an explicit strategy. The power to influence the preservation and perpetuation of this system is unequal, it must be admitted, but also it cannot be denied that Romani 'camp-dwellers' have become dependent on the system's continuation for their survival. In this context, I argue that the daily struggle to make the best of a bad situation might be interpreted as a form of 'resistance'. This attitude could result, as Nicolae Gheorghe noted after his visit to Tor de' Cenci camp in June 2012, from a *sclerosi del pensiero collettivo* (a sclerosis of collective thinking).

He was struck by the fact that some of the Romani inmates owned houses back in their countries of origin yet they claimed, 'We are nomads and we want to live in this camp, in our caravan. This is our habitat and we are integrated now in the neighbourhood' (personal communication, July 21, 2012). Gheorghe was convinced that, having lived in 'ghetto-camps' for 30–40 years, many of these Romanies had developed an 'immunity' to social change:

> In one sense it is impossible not to empathise with them. But, on further consideration, I found their statements were used as a way of defending the *status quo*, for not wanting to move out. It is basically in place a situation of immobility. [...] There is a widespread culture of welfare dependency, even of victimhood. (Personal communication, July 21, 2012)

Gheorghe's description resonated with that of Stasolla, who explained that the Romanies of the camps and prison inmates were in the same psychological condition. He used the expression *sindrome del carcerato* (prisoner's syndrome), arguing that when people have been imprisoned for a lengthy period of time, they become accustomed to living in a prison and afraid to go out (personal communication, February 16, 2012). The Romani camp, he said, could justly be described as an 'open-air prison'. After all, prisons are built to prevent and punish crime, and the State has declared Romani people, in effect, a security threat from which the general population must be quarantined by confining the source of this threat to zones of control.

184   R. Armillei

However, not all the fallout of the State's 'camps policy' was detrimental. There is more to the tale than declining mental and physical health, psychological passivity and physical immobility, as emerged in another study conducted by Associazione 21 Luglio (2012a). On the contrary, Romanies have responded and found certain social and economic benefits can flow from 'campisation'. Many have grown more skilled in what Adzovic has defined as *arte della sopravvivenza* (the art of survival), a contest in which the conventional wisdom is that only the strongest will prevail. To quote Adzovic:

> Because of the camp, the Romani communities developed a system in which people are not merely prey but become predators too. Government politics can take credit for that. Romanies are just placed in a 'shipping' container and left to their destiny. Without consultation, necessity dictates every act. Under these circumstances Romanies have to battle on all fronts to succeed. (Personal communication, May 14, 2012)

On a similar note, Gheorghe posed the question, 'How can they live like this?' And he has worked out the answer: 'Like any human being, they simply try to maximise their personal interests' (personal communication, July 21, 2012). This attitude was prompted partly by the 'camps policy' and the tendency to categorise all Romani people as 'nomads'. But it was also produced by the Romanies themselves who have internalised the external logic and learned to go with it.

As he further explains, the 'Romanies of the camps have employed old clichés (e.g. living among rubbish and rats, exploiting their children) to paint an abstract portrait of their culture, thus going through what he defined "re-Tziganisation", a symbolic exploitation of the "Zingaro" stereotype' (personal communication, July 21, 2012). During a follow-up meeting to discuss his visit to Tor de' Cenci camp, Gheorghe said:

> It is commonly believed that Romani people are the victims of racism and persecution. Yes, they are victims, but they are also fighters. [...] I saw people in Romania, during Communism, hundreds of thousands of people of Romani origin, who worked in construction and other industries, received apartments, paid taxes, got 20-year loans from banks. [...] But

after the fall of Communism some people from those communities sold their apartments and re-entered a Romani ghetto in Romania or went to Italy to live in camps, becoming *Zingari* again inside those camps. [...] I am worried about these individual cases. There are not many but they are highly conspicuous. And, because of them, the stereotype continues, larger than life, while society, the political parties and the racists get the blame. But these people are also responsible for this situation. (Personal communication, July 21, 2012)

Another result of the 'camps policy' was highlighted by Stasolla and Brazzoduro. With some slight differences, they both branded the culture of 'camp-dwellers' a *cultura del sottoproletariato* (culture of the lumpenproletariat). According to Stasolla,

the people who live in camps are no longer Romanies. They have become part of the urban underclasses. They lost their culture in the cultural genocide unleashed by the camp, where they did not have the chance to live it. All the problems that developed within these communities, such as drug addiction and alcoholism, are the bitter fruit of an identity crisis. It is wrong to say that the Romani culture is the culture of those living in camps, because this would lead people to think that all Romanies are criminals, who steal cars and exploit their children. Any person, from any culture, living in a camp under those conditions would develop the same problems. (Personal communication, April 4, 2012)

Brazzoduro found analogies between the Romanies living in camps today and the Italian underclasses of half a century ago. The main problem, Brazzoduro argued, was that

their ghettoisation inside these camps paralyses any process of social inclusion. The existence of the camp has only one meaning: repudiation, rejection. It is beyond dispute: the government shuts Romanies away in a camp. These people need to formulate an immediate response, so they give vent to their anger. 'You dare to put me in a camp? You force me to live on the margins of society? Then I refuse to respect your laws!' (Personal communication, July 21, 2012)

The Case of M. (as Narrated by Romani Speakers)

M. is a Bosnian Romani who lives in Castel Romano 'equipped village' and has worked there for many years as cultural liaison for a CSO. He is also president of a Romani cooperative championing the rights of the Romani people. The city council contracted this organisation to run the 'cleaning projects' inside the camp area. 'Doing that for eight or nine years, M. earned €15,000 a month', a Romani informant of mine remarked (personal communication, June 26, 2012). In 2012, when fieldwork was completed, the city council was carrying out means-testing aimed at determining eligibility for State support and at removing from the camps those who could afford to live outside. M. was one of the Romanies who was going to be affected by this Government measure. As stated by a well-known Romani intellectual, a member of one of the federations of Romani organisations in Italy, 'M. was invited many times to participate in the activities and events launched by the federation, but he always refused to be involved. Only now that he is in trouble has M. decided to contact us, asking for help' (N. G., personal communication, April 21, 2012).

According to N. A., another Romani activist, 'in this camp, as in others, there are a number of empty, uninhabited 'shipping' containers. This is because some people are forced to leave the camp due to blood feuds between different factions' (personal communication, May 14, 2012). At that point, as reported by one of the inhabitants of the Castel Romano camp (as cited in Nozzoli 2013, para. 6),

> as soon as a 'camp-dweller' vacate a container in the camp, disputes amongst Romanies begin. The container gets occupied and sold to other people in the camp. But the occupation can also lead to wars between rival groups which are often fought by setting containers on fire. In some cases, burning containers might be a precise strategy that Romanies enact in order to leave the camp and go back to the places from which they had been previously evicted. (para. 5)

An operation conducted by the local police in the Salone camp in July 2014 brought to light an illegal system of trade and rental of these containers. However, this is an activity which cannot be ascribed to the Romani 'camp-dwellers' only. In fact, two policemen were also accused of

Between Self-Determination and 'Collective-Identity Closure'

being involved in the criminal allocation of camp dwellings. As Pierucci (2014) reported, these officials, in collaboration with a number of camp inhabitants, would bribe Romanies to pay up to €2000 for a container. The trade and rental of containers has become big business for a number of Romani families and persists to this day (Bisbiglia 2017). It is worth noting that this activity is not only Rome-based, as similar cases were also reported in Romani encampments in other Italian cities (for Milan see Lodigiani 2010: 179).

M. was one of those who had 'squatted' in a few of those containers. When the city council intervened to solve the issue, giving the containers back to the rightful claimants, a *guerra tra poveri* (war among the poor) ensued, and only then did M. decide to request help from the federation and some friends, CSOs and non-Romani intellectuals as well (N.G., personal communication, April June 21, 2012). He tried to create a committee whose members were Romanies living in a number of camps scattered throughout the capital territory, but his strategy to unite all the Romani leaders and defy the Government's decision was unsuccessful in the end. In a number of meetings I participated in between May and July 2012, which brought together both Romani and non-Romani activists, M. was accused of promoting this committee only because his own interests were in danger.

Because corruption became a widespread issue within the camps, N. A. argued that

> it is high time we fight some of the Romani organisations as well. If you take even 1 Euro from the government, you have to explain how you are going to use it. For many years we criticised the non-Romani organisations because they were using public funds improperly. Why should we not now condemn the Romani organisations or individuals if they are doing the exact same thing? (Personal communication, June 26, 2012)

The Case of E.

E. also lives in Castel Romano camp. Like M., she has worked for many years as a cultural liaison with a CSO in this camp. E.'s story was presented by the CSO she was working for as one of the best examples to have come to their notice since they had begun working with Romanies. This was during a private meeting in the presence of a number of public-utility and Third Sector representatives. The informant's intention was to celebrate the courage of a woman who, despite the many difficulties of living in a camp, raised and educated her children and, in the end, bought her own house. According to him,

> E. is a woman, a friend and our employee. Her husband is a layabout while she has managed to raise her children and helped get them Italian citizenship. Fifteen years ago she bought a house in the city of T. She sold a house she still owned in Bosnia and made a downpayment on it with this money. Eventually she managed to repay the balance. She asked us for help and we were delighted to support her loan request. She was the first Romani woman to get micro-credit from the Regione Lazio [the regional government]. She received €10,000 and now she is trying to repay it. We also helped her in other ways, because the city council financed several of our projects. She has been working on these, so we could give her more money. Six months ago, I experienced one of the greatest satisfactions I have had since beginning work with the Romanies. This lady invited us to see her house and it was beautiful: 175 sq. m., two floors and a garden all the way around. This goes to show that a woman with character, given a helping hand by certain institutions and associations, can realise her dream. (Personal communication, July 21, 2012)

The interviewee, formerly president of this organisation, summed up this account of her experiences as a *percorso di emancipazione bellissimo* (a beautiful emancipation story). Yet, despite the decision to give prominence to E.'s story, several aspects remain unclear. For instance, the not-so-wonderful side of the story, as the speaker admitted at some point, was that E. and her family were still living in the camp. So, the insight provided by the informant was quite confusing and a number of questions arose: How to present this story as a positive example of social inclusion from the CSO perspective? How could anyone talk about emancipation if this woman owned a house and was still living in a 'shipping' container inside a *campo nomade*? Why in 15 years had this organisation not been able to let this person and her family leave the camp, and stand on their own feet? This person had owned a house in Bosnia but she came to Italy

The Case of B.

B. is a Romani from Romania. He has been living in *campi nomadi* for 20 years. At the moment he lives at Candoni 'equipped village' and for the past eight years he has been working as cultural liaison with one of the CSOs in the camp. According to him, 'most of the Romanies in Candoni (about 70 percent of them) have a job. Yet, they all make their homes in containers in the camp' (personal communication, April 4, 2012). This is because, as B. argues, their salaries are not high, and so they would not be enough to cover rent and other basic costs. He discloses that the decision not to move out is basically down to convenience:

> Although there are a number of Romani families who would like to move out and live in a house, there are also many others that prefer to stay in the camp. They say: 'Why should I leave if here I do not have to pay anything (rent, electricity, etc.)?' (Personal communication, April 4, 2012)

B., for instance, owns a house in Romania, where he and his relatives go from time to time. He admits that the reason for not moving back to Romania is because the situation over there is worse than in Italy. Salaries are even lower there—about €200 a month—and this would not be enough to support his family. B. said nobody was forcing him to live in Candoni. For him, living there was the best way to take care of his family.

B. blamed the political classes and the CSO network for the abysmal conditions in the camp. He was quick to point out that the Government was squandering an EU grant on the 'National Strategy'. Then he also warned that disunity among the CSOs was directly affecting them: 'If the

CSOs that deal with Romani issues would co-operate with one another they would probably have solved these problems by now' (personal communication, April 4, 2012). According to him, not only should the Government be spending tax revenue to build council houses rather than camps, but public institutions and the CSOs should involve the Romanies in developing long-term strategies too. Up until this point, he said, 'Nobody has come to us and asked how we want to live or what we want!' (personal communication, April 4, 2012).

As well as individual choice, the interview revealed a lack of political consciousness on the part of Romanies. B. admitted that the leaders of this and other camps in Rome met regularly (every two weeks). But he also explained, with surprising candour, why they could not secure political representation: 'We are neither politically organised nor united. We are envious of each other' (personal communication, April 4, 2012).

The Case of Co.

Co. is a Romani woman from Serbia who lives in the Via dei Gordiani authorised camp. Her partner, also from Serbia, is completely disabled. They met back in Serbia but then she decided to follow him to Italy, where he was already living. She was 25 years old (she is now 40) and she did not know that he was living in a 'nomad camp'. She still cannot believe that she left a real house for life in a container. She still has not accepted it. According to her, 'being in a camp is like living in hell' (personal communication, June 29, 2012). When she migrated, he had been on dialysis for several years already, but she did not know that either. She argues that, although he would be entitled to compensation for that, the only benefit he gets from the Government is free treatment in hospital where he has to go three times every week. A lawyer for the CSO managing the camp where they live is following their case, but so far their efforts have not been successful.

In May 2012, she started a *borsa lavoro* at a local tailor's shop. This is a workers cooperative which runs a number of projects that promote women's employability, particularly those in vulnerable positions. As part of the contract agreement, Co. will be doing this paid traineeship for a few months. The cooperative was only founded in early 2012 and they are still a start-up. Cr., the manager of the cooperative, reveals that at the moment they are having some financial difficulties. This explains why Co. has not received any salary as yet. As Cr. further explains, the CSO who is officially in charge of the *borsa lavoro* on behalf of the local administration knew from the beginning that there were not going to be any employment opportunities. Despite that, she thought that this was a good opportunity, where she could learn something new. Co. mentioned having participated in the *borse lavoro* scheme in the past, but this never led to fixed-term position.

Together with this form of employment, she had several other work-related experiences as well, but as soon as employers discovered she was Romani and living in a camp, she immediately lost her job. Nevertheless, she has been continually looking for a job. According to her, this is in contrast with the predominant attitude among a number of other Romanies living in the camps. Using her words:

> Not many Romanies are motivated and want to change. Only a few of them try hard to find a job, take their children to school and respect the laws. They are too used to getting 'easy' money. They would never go to work. But if you really want a job, you can find something. The other women laugh at me when I say that I go to work. They just wait for their husbands to come back with the money they have earned illegally. Many of them, for instance, get a lot of money begging on the street. And in some cases, they invest their money buying properties in their country of origin. But I prefer not to argue with these people, because as soon as you raise your voice dozens of them surround you. I just pretend to agree when they talk like that and try to look at my own things. In a way, I feel they are luckier than me. First, because they do not make a fuss over this situation (living in a camp in such conditions), like I do. And secondly, because in the end they have all the things I don't have. I should probably follow their example, but I am not able to steal, I have never done it. Sometimes the other Romanies make jokes and say 'Are you really a Romani'? (Personal communication, June 29, 2012)

The encamped experience for Co. is quite emblematic. It reveals the existence of a 'dual mechanism of exclusion'. On the one hand, she experiences exclusion in relation to Italian institutions and, moreover, mainstream society. On the other hand, she is also marginalised within the 'camps system' as a result of practices of exclusion carried out by Romanies themselves. She cannot get out from the camp, mainly because of the obvious difficulty of having to take care of herself and her husband. At the same time, she also feels a sense of not belonging to the camp community. Therefore, she feels trapped in this 'in-between space'.

The Case of Ti.

Ti. is a Romanian Romani man living in the authorised camp in Via Candoni. Before migrating to Italy in the early 1990s, he had tried, unsuccessfully, to settle in Poland and Germany. His migration coincided with the fall of Nicolae Ceaușescu's dictatorship in 1989. He still has positive memories of Ceaușescu's regime. At that time, he argues, 'Romanies were integrated, lived in houses, went to school and the Government would provide jobs as well' (personal communication, June 6, 2012). In Italy, instead, he has constantly struggled to find a job and to feed his large family (nine children). Despite everything, though, life in Italy is much better than in Romania. Back home, he argued, there is more racism against the Romanies.

Since his first arrival in Italy he has been living in different encampments, Salone and Cervara among others, before taking up residence in the Candoni camp. His reason for coming to Rome is because his sister was already living in the Salone camp. Along with his wife, his main activity is to go around the city and collect all sorts of recyclable material and objects from the bins. He and his wife do not own a van like many other Romanies, so they use strollers instead. He is a very religious person (Catholic) and is proud to tell me that he does not carry out any illegal activities, unlike other Romanies living in camps. That explains the nickname they gave him 'il Prete' (the Priest). He is also an activist and showed me newspaper articles in which he is depicted promoting Romani rights.

Quite alarming is the way he describes life in the camp:

> The camp is like a little jungle. When you enter here you are not in Italy anymore. It is a place where people become *cannibali emancipati* (emancipated cannibals). Everyone lives to the neighbour's disadvantage. In the Salone camp there were a lot of Mafia-type criminal activities. In the

Candoni camp, where I have been living for the last two years, there are lots of problems as well, particularly between the two major rival groups (Slavic and Romanian peoples). I moved here because I heard that there was an empty container. This had been assigned to another person, but then he ended up in jail, and my wife and I decided to occupy it. Yet, by doing so we broke an internal code among Romanies. And we had to pay for it if we wanted to stay. (Personal communication, June 6, 2012)

He also talked about his constant quest for a proper job, which over the last ten years has been elusive. He admitted that he has been trying hard, but none of the so-called Pro-Romani organisations managing the camps have helped him to get a job (although this is part of their institutional mandate). I have met with Ti. several times. On a few occasions we decided to go together to both private and public job agencies. However, a number of problems emerged when discussing job opportunities: he is illiterate, he does not hold any qualifications, and he does not have a driving licence. Consequently, we could not find anything that might have suited the agencies' requirements. These seemed to be the major issues that need to be addressed, before he embarks on another job hunt. He confessed that the only organisations that are trying to help him at the moment are the Catholic charity ones. Despite their support, though, they too have not been successful in finding an alternative housing solution for him, or gainful employment.

The case of Ti. is revealing of the lack of any coordinated intervention which during that time could have addressed his basic needs (mainly education and job qualifications). In addition, just as in Co.'s case, Ti. is facing the same type of difficulties, occupying a sort of in-between position of 'Other' in relation to mainstream Italian society but also to his own community. The camp becomes a threatening environment where only the fittest survive.

The Case of the E., W., B. and G.: The Italian Sinti

E. is an Italian Sinto living at La Barbuta camp. He is originally from the Umbria region, but moved to the Lazio region, where he met the woman he later married, while travelling. She used to live in a council house in

Rieti. For a time he tried to live there, but he soon realised that living in a house was too constraining for him. In his words:

> I could not live in an apartment building. I needed open spaces, fresh air and sharing life with my community. In that place you could not even play music that would immediately annoy the other residents. Of course, even in a camp there can be issues. In the Casilino 900 camp, for instance, the Korakhane group [Muslim Romanies] would always leave their rubbish out of their house instead of using the common bin. I come from a family whose main activity was the 'travelling show'. I was born in a camper. Sadly, my job now is to go around the city with my truck to collect metal or to clean and empty basements of all sorts of material. (Personal communication, May 25, 2012)

According to him the situation for the Romanies in Italy has worsened since the 1990s, after a massive influx of what he calls 'foreigner Romanies'. This created friction among the Italian Romani population. Divisions between Italian 'Rom' and 'Sinti' already existed, but the centuries' old coexistence mitigated their relationship. The arrival of many Romanies with different traditions and languages increased tensions between Romani groups, he argues. One of the main issues for them is that only recently has there been more talk about the Sinti as a specific Romani group. For a long time Romanies in Italy were all called indiscriminately 'Rom'. The worsening of their living conditions, though, galvanised the Sinti to come out and be more vocal. Yet, up until now, not much has been achieved, chiefly because all the attention goes to the 'foreign Romanies', instead of the 'Italian' ones.

> Before the 1990s different groups of Sinti were scattered across Italy. They could travel while practising their traditional activities mainly unnoticed. But the new Romanies brought a number of problems, such as drug and arms trafficking, prostitution and the trading of containers. (Personal communication, May 25, 2012)

G. has been living at La Barbuta camp for the past 17 years. His main activity also entails the collection of metal from around the city. The main problems raised by G. were all related to camp life and his own professional activity. According to him, La Barbuta camp is one of the

Between Self-Determination and 'Collective-Identity Closure'   195

most polluted camps in Rome, not only because of its proximity to the Ciampino airport, but also because of the Korakhane group, who have a habit of burning dangerous waste inside the camp, ladling the atmosphere with harmful smoke. This situation is aggravated by the fact that despite their differences, Sinti and Rom have been basically forced to live together since the time of the Rutelli administration. As for the profession he and many other Romanies carry on 'illegally', his comments point out the potential revenue that the collective may have from them[2]:

> We want to work, we clean Rome and recycle unwanted things, but we need the possibility to do this job legally. We need authorisations but the city council refuses to legalise our activity. (Personal communication, April 5, 2012)

W. and B., unlike E. and G., are still in the 'travelling show' business. They live in different cities; W. in Rome and G. in Ravenna, but they both experience the same types of problems that seem to plague the whole Sinti population. W., B., G. and E. all complain about the fact that over the years the introduction of a number of new legislative measures has considerably affected their profession. After having spent many years in a camp, W. now lives in a council house on the periphery of Rome. He is the owner of a small *giostra* (carousel). According to him,

> many of the Sinti found themselves drowning in an ocean of new laws (often involving costly procedures). They didn't know how to navigate their way around them. At the same time the opening of huge amusement parks has also endangered our small, mainly family-run, businesses. As a consequence, 70 percent of our people do not own a *giostra* anymore. We have been forced to quit our profession. [...] We don't want to end up being recruited by the Mafia like many 'Rom' people. (Personal communication, April 14, 2012)

---

[2] According to Aleramo Virgili, of the Rete Onu (the National Network of Second-hand Goods Handlers), as recently as 2012 tens of thousands of informal-sector garbage pickers were identified by the Municipal Police (Rete di Sostegno Mercatini Rom 2012). This activity represents the main source of food for many Romanies living in camps. Despite this, the Government's practice has always been to adopt measures to suppress it, rather than to consider the alternative of legalising it (Santilli 2017).

B.'s story is not dissimilar from W.'s. B. proudly defines himself as a *giostraio* (carousel holder). Despite the difficulties, he refuses to give up. In the city of Ravenna, where he resides, he has been fighting with the council, because they are refusing to comply with Law no. 337/1968 which establishes that certain areas should be devoted to the temporary running of their activities/shows (personal communication, April 5, 2012). The lack of explicitly designated spaces for this purpose, along with excessive taxation, forced many Sinti to simply quit their profession (Pecini 2016).

One of the issues that seems to emerge from these interviews is a clear opposition between Rom and Sinti groups. W. often referred to them using the term *gli altri* (the Others). This explains why the Mayor's decision to nominate Najo Adzovic as his personal liaison with Rome's Romani communities was highly criticised by the Sinti. As W. states, 'we did not feel represented by a foreign Romani'. At the same time, the Rom groups also discriminate against the Sinti, by identifying them with the 'Gadje' people, 'because we show a great fluency in Italian, while a consistent part of the "foreign Romanies" cannot speak Italian' (W. personal communication, April 14, 2012). The division between these two major Romani groups in Italy is not only defined by different customs and traditions, but also by a language factor. As for their traditions, most of the Sinti would like to preserve their itinerant business, and as W. maintains, unlike many Rom groups, they still consider themselves as nomadic. E., G., B. and W. all consider themselves Italian. Yet, they claim, 'despite being Italian citizens, we still live at the margins of the Italian society' (personal communication, April 14, 2012).

The Case of the Former Inhabitants of Casilino 900

In January 2010, after having personally reached an agreement with the camp's inhabitants, Alemanno ordered the closure of Casilino 900. The previous year, the camp's spokespersons had signed a written paper in which they agreed to support the city council's wishes during the relocation. More than 600 Romanies were transferred in partnership with the CRI to several 'equipped villages' around the city: 200 in Salone, 96 in Candoni, 173 in Camping River, 40 in Gordiani and 64 at a homeless shelter in Via Amarilli. A month later, the mayor had officially guaranteed that the city council would provide this group with work and houses (Stasolla 2012). In May 2012, however, a group of residents of the former Casilino 900 started planning to reoccupy the area.

The Romanies' representatives organised an informal meeting to examine whether the conditions were suitable to do so. I was also invited to attend the meeting. During the consultation, Najo Adzovic as leader of this group maintained that this action had received approval from the Romani 'Council of Elders'. According to him, 700 Romanies, mostly from the ex-Casilino 900, and certain Catholic organisations were supporting the occupation. A number of non-Romani intellectuals and activists, mainly belonging to the leftist political bloc, took part as well. Most of them had been defending the cause of the inhabitants of Casilino 900, at least until they did a u-turn and supported Alemanno's relocation plan instead.

For many years there was a close collaboration between Casilino 900 'camp-dwellers' and a number of local organisations: Stalker/On, in particular, had been supporting self-organisation processes in areas of extreme marginalisation. Bringing together people of different backgrounds and disciplines, their main idea was to propose valid alternatives to 'nomad camps' through the employment of self-construction methods. This would have enabled mutual learning between Romanies and 'Gadje' while triggering a 'responsibilisation' process among the Romani people (Fioretti 2011: 552). *Savorengo Ker*, which in the Romani language means 'the house for everyone', was one of their projects. Designed and built together by Romanies and non-Romanies, the project aimed to use 'Romani people's own distinctive practices of dwelling and building and embedding them in a proposal comprehensible and acceptable to non-Roma' (Laboratorio Arti Civiche n.d.: para. 5).

Despite showing a housing solution which was safer, more ecological and less expensive than a container, the initiative met strong opposition: not only from the surrounding Italian populace, who were against the existence of the camp itself, but also from the public administration which accelerated the process of clearing the area (Fioretti 2011: 552). What has been termed 'a manifesto house' produced by the Romanies, the wooden structure was completed in July 2008 but never officially opened, would meet its end at the hands of an unknown aronsist. Some of the Romani 'camp-dwellers' suggested that the fire might have been started by Romanies themselves. In fact, there was at the time an ongoing feud among Casilno 900 inhabitants: some supported Alemanno's project of moving camp inhabitants elsewhere; while others did not want to leave the camp area ('Casilino 900, brucia' 2008). Adzovic and the other Romanies had all been publicly involved in this project.

During the meeting, the non-Romani participants were naturally suspicious of Adzovic's real intentions: Najo had supported Alemanno's strategy and now he was suddenly hurling accusations at the mayor. They liked the idea of a symbolic occupation of Casilino 900, but their main concern was that this action had to be part of a larger political strategy. They would have supported it in the context of the mayoral election campaign due in June 2013. But this time they also wanted to be sure that the Romanies were not going to change their political allegiance again. For this reason they asked Najo to take a public position against the current mayor and his politics, as a way to redeem himself after his 'betrayal'. On this occasion, Najo presented the rationale for plotting against Alemanno. He complained that the administration had not solved the Romani question. But he also criticised the Romanies. Through Najo's own mediation, many of them had received financial aid from the local administration, but, unfortunately, they had used this assistance to pursue their own interests.

His major plan was to return to Casilino 900 and mount a 'permanent occupation', restoring the traditional Romani presence in that vicinity. The plan implied the transfer of hundreds of Romanies (most of them former inhabitants of Casilino 900) from 'equipped villages' (where at least they now had containers and some basic infrastructure) to an urban desert. Some of the participants agreed, at least hypothetically, with Najo's idea, while others were more sceptical. They felt this plan was either too starry-eyed or deficient in political vision. Some suggested it would be more useful to 'squat' in a vacant building or houses instead of going back to nothing. Overall, the Romani representatives looked disorganised with no cohesive plan to speak of. Occupying Casilino 900 seemed to be their only objective.

At some point one of the Romani participants made a statement that unveiled the real rationale behind the plan. According to him, the closure of Casilino 900 and the transfer of hundreds of Romanies had upset the balance of power between different Romani groups in all the 'equipped villages' affected by the relocation. He confessed that on several occasions older residents of the other camps had harsh words for the newer arrivals. 'They said, "We do not want you here. You cannot come here and dictate your own rules". This was happening all over the place: that is why now we are examining the feasibility of returning to our old homes' (personal communication, May 14, 2012). A few significant points logically emerged from the meeting.

First of all, the Romanies who gathered here demonstrated clear political capacity. They had supported the Alemanno administration while they believed this could secure them some advantages. As soon as it became clear this was a chimaera, they decided to occupy Casilino 900 again (which was offered to their non-Romani supporters as a political tool against Alemanno). Romanies have also shown the ability to explore potential agreements with activists and CSOs of the Left and Right alike. Secondly, their strategy implied faith in the 'logic of power by possession'. In this variation of the 'squatter's charter', they reasoned that if they could settle in one place long enough and resist attempts to move them out, they would somehow have earned the right to 'own' it. This is a logic that is shared by many Romani communities in different parts of the city. An interview with a representative of the Cesare Lombroso camp confirmed this point. H. criticised Najo Adzovic for having 'sold out' his community: 'He did not have to do it. That area [already] belonged to the Romani people, who had occupied it for many years', he had noted (personal communication, April 2, 2012).

Final Observations

This chapter can not and will not present an encouraging picture of the Romani movement in Italy. Certainly, the policy adopted by the Government did not help them find their own voice. A number of issues still await action at the national level: among them legal status, cultural recognition and the camps. The 'National Strategy', for instance, which should have finally ushered in real change, failed to adequately address the issue of securing authentic political representation for Romanies. The situation of the Romani movement in Rome is particularly drastic. The boom in cooperatives and associations in the capital over the past decade now resembles a short-lived bubble. These organisations are still lacking real political awareness, not to mention an agreed strategy, and were principally motivated by the need to access State funds. Competitiveness lay at the heart of these experiences, where different groups were generally more oriented to protecting their own family interests, rather than the Romani cause.

Life within the camps was also characterised by widespread corruption. This was also instigated by the Italian political class and institutions who found preserving this situation advantageous (see Chap. 4). A sense of victimhood and an incapacity for consensus reinforced the need to depend on this or that politician or CSO. Paradoxically, the camp became the only place where Romanies felt secure and protected. Mainstream society was still perceived as a threatening environment where it would have been more difficult to survive without community support. Nevertheless, in contrast to a prevailing belief that Romani people were merely passive players, institutionalised by the Government and forced to live inside the *campi nomadi*, this chapter showed a different reality. Many of them, in fact, had a house and a job but chose to live in the camp as a deliberate survival strategy. The *campi nomadi* should be seen as a protective shield and a tool of 'resistance', where Romanies constructed and reified a strong sense of belonging in opposition to non-Romanies.

Government and CSOs have made a lucrative business out of the Romani issue, but the Romanies have also learned to use the 'camps system' to achieve their own goals. In fact, as an anthropologist who worked with Romanies in Rome for many years has contended:

> We should not underestimate the capacity of the Romani people for self-consultation. The capital city went through a traumatic period because of Najo Adzovic. But Romanies never stopped meeting and consulting each other even during this time. They tried to create a sort of 'lobby', even if this was unsuccessful in the end. That is why when I hear of Romani people asking *Gadje* individuals and organisations for help I am immediately

suspicious: their access to funds – for either the 'schooling projects' or 'cleaning up the camp' – has probably been stopped, so they need to find new ways to support themselves. (Personal communication, June 26, 2012)

It is surely important to recognise that the existence of a top-down approach adopted by the Government and CSOs was always going to leave slender scope for the Romani voice. Nonetheless, it has to be acknowledged that bottom-up opposition, as voiced by the Romani communities living in camps, does exist. 'Resistance' has played a key role in pushing the Government and the CSOs to adopt a self-justifying paternalism. The Government embarked on a strategy that reproduced marginality. The Romanies were 'racialised' as a pretext for introducing specific ethnic policies, in which contracted CSOs would deliver an array of social inclusion programmes, creating a 'social mechanism of complicity' (Gheorghe, personal communication, July 21, 2012). This in turn assisted 'camp-dwellers' in keeping the 'ghetto economy alive', as Gheorghe dubbed it (personal communication, July 21, 2012). Within this context, the Romanies reverted to old stereotypes in order to evoke pity and promote assistentialism.

The saga of the camps not only shows the human genius for creating a complex system in which everyone gets some advantage, but also reinforces and crystallises the centuries-old contrast between Romanies and non-Romanies. Yet, while the 'Romani of the camps' have been fighting an 'invisible battle' with the mainstream society—becoming visible only in negative terms, when bad news floats our way, the greater proportion of the Romani population remains invisible. They prefer to hide their cultural background, avoid the risk of being discriminated against and shun comparisons with the 'visible' Romanies. What is needed, as suggested by Gheorghe, is an 'epistemological fracture', a new language: 'Romanies should no longer be the objects of assistance. The main aspiration now must be to see them become the main actors in their own lives. After a long period of involution the Romanies need to re-mobilise (personal communication, July 21, 2012). No one expects the road ahead to be easy. Effecting real social change in a time of economic crisis, widespread populism and resurgent racism will be a formidable challenge into the future.

Bibliography

Armillei, R. (2016). Reflections on Italy's contemporary approaches to cultural diversity: The exclusion of the 'Other' from a supposed notion of 'Italianness'. *Australia New Zealand Journal of European Studies, 8*(2), 34–48.

Armillei, R. (2017a). The 'Piano Nomadi' and its pyramidal governance: The hidden mechanism underlying the 'camps system' in Rome. *Romani Studies, 27*(1), 47–71.

Armillei, R. (2017b). The Romani 'camp-dwellers' in Rome: Between state control and 'collective-identity closure'. In C. Agius & D. Keep (Eds.), *Identity making, displacement and rupture: Performing discourses of belonging, being and place* (pp. 107–122). Manchester: Manchester University Press.

Asséo, H. (1989). Pour une histoire des peuples-Résistances [For a history of resistance-peoples]. In P. Williams (Ed.), *Tsiganes: identité, évolution* (pp. 121–127). Paris: Syros.

Associazione 21 Luglio. (2012a). Anime Smarrite. Il piano degli sgomberi a Roma: Storie quotidiane di segregazione abitativa e di malessere [Lost souls. The evictions plan in Rome: Ordinary stories of housing segregation and sickness]. Retrieved from http://www.21luglio.org/images/anime_smarrite_def.pdf

Associazione 21 Luglio. (2012b). Lavoro Sporco: Il Comune di Roma, i rom e le 'borse-lavoro' [Dirty job: The Municipality of Rome, the Romani people and the 'paid traineeships']. Retrieved from http://www.21luglio.org/images/Report/lavorosporco.pdf

Associazione Thèm Romanó. (2010). Un evento da non sottovalutare [An event which is not to be underestimated]. Retrieved from http://www.associazione-themromano.it/albumquattrosettembre.htm

Barany, Z. (1998). Ethnic mobilization and the state: The Roma in Eastern Europe. *Ethnic and Racial Studies, 21*(2), 308–327.

Barnes, A. (2003). Gypsy law: Romani legal traditions and culture. *Marquette Law Review, 86*(4), 823–844.

Benedetto, I. (2011). Le minoranze Rom e Sinte: Alla ricerca di uno status giuridico [Roma and Sinti minorities: The pursuit of legal status]. Doctoral dissertation. Retrieved from http://www.stranieriinitalia.it/briguglio/immigrazione-e-asilo/2011/dicembre/tesi-irene-benedetto.pdf

Bisbiglia, V. (2017, May 31). Roma, tra tensioni, roghi ed esempi virtuosi [Rome, between tensions, blazes and best practices]. *Il Fatto Quotidiano*. Retrieved from http://www.ilfattoquotidiano.it/2017/05/31/roma-tra-tensioni-roghi-ed-esempi-virtuosi-ecco-la-mappa-dei-19-campi-che-accolgono-i-rom/3580993/

Boscoboinik, A. (2009). Challenging borders and constructing boundaries: An analysis of Roma political processes. In V. Ciubrinskas & R. Sliuzinskas (Eds.), *Identity politics: Histories, regions and borderlands* (pp. 181–193). Klaipeda: Klaipeda University.

Calabrò, A. R. (2008). *Zingari: Storia di un'emergenza annunciata* [Gypsies: The history of an announced emergency]. Naples: Liguori.

Carrasco, O. (2011, August 23). Racist removal: The ongoing hate of Roma peoples in Europe. *POOR Magazine*. Retrieved from http://poormagazine.org/node/4049

Casilino 900, brucia. (2008, December 12). Casilino 900, brucia la 'casa dei sogni' [Casilino 900, the 'dream house' burned down]. *La Repubblica*. Retrieved from http://roma.repubblica.it/dettaglio/casilino-900-brucia-la-casa-dei-sogni/1560445

Clough Marinaro, I. (2009). Between surveillance and exile: Biopolitics and the Roma in Italy. *Bulletin of Italian Politics, 1*(2), 265–287.

Clough Marinaro, I. (2014). Rome's 'legal' camps for Roma: The construction of new spaces of informality. *Journal of Modern Italian Studies, 19*(5), 541–555.

Clough Marinaro, I. (2015). The rise of Italy's neo-ghettos. *Journal of Urban History, 41*(3), 368–387.

Council of Europe. (2008). Go beyond prejudice, discover the Roma! Retrieved from http://www.coe.int/t/dg3/romatravellers/jp3/arc/EnglishDOSTA.pdf

Council of Europe Romani Projekt. (ca. 2005). Institutionalisation and emancipation [Fact Sheet]. Retrieved from http://romafacts.uni-graz.at/index.php/history/prolonged-discrimination-struggle-for-human-rights/institutionalisation-and-emancipation

Cugusi, M. C. (2011, May 18). 'Generazioni rom rovinate dall'assistenzialismo': Intervista a Dijana Pavlovic [Romani generations damaged by welfare dependency: Interview of Dijana Pavlovic]. Diritto di critica. Retrieved from http://www.dirittodicritica.com/2011/05/18/rom-pavlovic-assistenzialismo-57035/

Daniele, U. (2010). Zingari di carta: Un percorso nella presa di parola rom ai tempi dell'emergenza [Paper Gypsies: A route towards the empowerment of Romanies during the emergency]. *Zapruder, 22*, 56–72.

Falcioni, D. (2010, July 29). Piano Nomadi di Roma: Il punto dopo un anno [Nomad Plan in Rome: The situation after a year]. InviatoSpeciale. Retrieved from http://www.inviatospeciale.com/2010/07/piano-nomadi-di-roma-il-punto-dopo-un-anno/

Fiano, F., & Sacchettoni, I. (2016, June 16). Tangenti sui campi rom [Bribes regarding the Romani camps]. *Corriere della Sera.* Retrieved from http://roma.corriere.it/notizie/cronaca/16_giugno_29/tangenti-campi-rom-indagati-15-dirigenti-campidoglio-819c44c6-3d66-11e6-922f-98d199acd386.shtml#

Fioretti, C. (2011). Do-it-yourself housing for immigrants in Rome: Simple reaction or possible way out. In F. Eckardt & J. Eade (Eds.), *The ethnically diverse city* (pp. 535–558). Berlin: Berliner Wissenschaftsverlag.

Fischer, A. M. (2011). Between nation and state: Examining the International Romani Unions. Senior Projects Spring, Paper 12. Retrieved from http://digitalcommons.bard.edu/senproj_s2011/12

Fosztó, L. (2003). Diaspora and nationalism: An anthropological approach to the international Romani movement. REGIO Minorities, Politics, Society, 1: 102–118.

Galati, M. (2007). *Rom cittadinanza di carta: Metodologie di ricerca e di intervento sociale per apprendere parola e rappresentanza.* [Romani citizenship made of paper: Methodologies of research and social practice to learn self-representation]. Soveria Mannelli: Edizioni Rubbettino.

Gheorghe, N., & Acton, T. (2001). Citizens of the world and nowhere: Minority, ethnic and human rights for Roma. In W. Guy (Ed.), *Between past and future: The Roma of Central and Eastern Europe* (pp. 54–70). Hatfield: University of Hertfordshire Press.

Hancock, I. (2000). Speech presented at the panel discussion 'The Romani movement: What shape, what direction?', Budapest. Retrieved from http://www.errc.org/cikk.php?cikk=1292

Howe, B., & Cleary, R. (2001, January). *Community building: Policy issues and strategies for the Victorian Government.* Melbourne: Victorian Department of Premier and Cabinet.

Laboratorio Arti Civiche. (n.d.). Savorengo ker. Retrieved from http://www.articiviche.net/LAC/works___savorengo_ker.html

Leeson, P. T. (2010). Gypsy law. Retrieved from http://www.peterleeson.com/Gypsies.pdf

Lodigiani, R. (Ed.). (2010). *Rapporto Sulla Città Milano 2010: Welfare ambrosiano, futuro cercasi* [Report on the city of Milan 2010: Ambrosiano Welfare, looking for future]. Milano: Franco Angeli.

Maestri, G. (2016). Persistently temporary. Ambiguity and political mobilisations in Italy's Roma camps: A comparative perspective. Durham theses, Durham University. Retrieved from Durham E-Theses Online: http://etheses.dur.ac.uk/11881/

Maestri, G. (2017). Struggles and ambiguities over political subjectivities in the camp: Roma camp dwellers between neoliberal and urban citizenship in Italy. *Citizenship Studies, 21*(6), 640–656.

Matras, Y. (ca. 2007). Roma culture: An introduction. Retrieved from http://romafacts.uni-graz.at/index.php/culture/introduction/roma-culture-an-introduction

Morelli, B. (2006). *L'identità zingara* [The Gypsy identity]. Rome: Anicia.

Musgrave, S., & Bradshaw, J. (2014). Language and social inclusion: Unexplored aspects of intercultural communication. *Australian Review of Applied Linguistics, 37*(3), 198–212.

Nicola, V. (2011). *I ghetti per i rom. Roma, via Di Salone 323. Socianalisi narrativa di un campo rom* [The ghettos for Romani people. Rome, Di Salone road, 323. Socio-analysis account of a Romani camp]. Cuneo: Sensibili alle Foglie.

Nozzoli, G. (2013, July 5). Campo Castel Romano e gli incendi dei rom: 'Non solo guerra etnica' [Castel Romano camp and Romanies' fires: 'Not simply an ethnic war']. *Roma Today*. Retrieved from http://eur.romatoday.it/campo-castel-romano-incendi-perche.html

Nye, M. (2007). The challenges of multiculturalism. *Culture and Religion, 8*(2), 109–123.

Officina Genitori. (2008). La questione rom a Milano [The Romani issue in Milan]. Retrieved from https://www.officinagenitori.org/index.php?option=com_content&view=article&id=1968:la-questione-rom-a-milano&catid=90&lang=it&Itemid=248

Osservatorio Sociale Regionale. (2007). Il presidente dell'Opera Nomadi Abruzzo ai dirigenti nazionali: 'Dimettetevi e consegnate l'associazione a Rom e Sinti' [The president of Opera Nomadi Abruzzo to the national leadership: 'Resign and hand over the organisation to Romani people']. Retrieved from http://www.osr.regione.abruzzo.it/do/index?docid=3857

Pecini, C. (2016, January 18). Esercenti dello spettacolo viaggiante: i tratti di un'identità incerta [Travel business owners: the traits of an uncertain identity]. Parksmania. Retrieved from https://www.parksmania.it/articoli-tecnici/esercenti-dello-spettacolo-viaggiante-i-tratti-di-unidentita-incerta/

Piasere, L. (2004). *I Rom d'Europa: Una storia moderna* [The Roma of Europe: A modern history] Rome: Laterza.

Piasere, L. (2005). *Popoli delle discariche: Saggi di antropologia zingara* [Peoples of the dumps: Essays in Gypsy anthropology] (2nd ed.). Rome: CISU.

Pierucci, A. (2014, July 10). 'Mille euro per una baracca ai rom': Accusati di corruzione due vigili urbani [A thousand Euros for a shanty house: Two municipal officers investigated for corruption]. *Il Messaggero*. Retrieved from http://www.ilmessaggero.it/ROMA/CRONACA/mille_euro_baracca_rom_accusati_corruzione_vigili_urbani/notizie/789408.shtml

Pissacroia, M. (1998). *Trattato di psicopatologia della adolescenza* [Essay on psychopathology of adolescence]. Padua: Piccin-Nuova Libraria.

Pogány, I. (2004). Legal, social and economic challenges facing the Roma of Central and Eastern Europe. Queen's Papers on Europeanisation, 2, Queen's University Belfast, Belfast.

Pogány, I. (2012). Pariah peoples: Roma and the multiple failures of law in Central and Eastern Europe. *Social & Legal Studies, 21*(3), 375–393. https://doi.org/10.1177/0964663911429152.

Rete di Sostegno Mercatini Rom. (2012). Comunicato stampa rovistatori [Press release garbage bin pickers]. Retrieved from http://retedisostegnomercatini-rom.over-blog.it/

Rivera, A. (2003). *Estranei e nemici* [Aliens and enemies]. Rome: DeriveApprodi.

Romano Lil. (2007, September 8). Spinelli e Guarnieri: Il pre-giudizio degli 'zingari' [Spinelli and Guarnieri: The prejudice of the 'Gypsies']. *Romano Lil*. Retrieved from http://romanolil.blog.tiscali.it/2007/09/08/spinelli_e_guarnieri__il_pre_giudizio_degli__zingari__1797483-shtml/

Santilli, C. (2017). I rom che raccolgono il ferro a Roma [Romanies collect metal in Rome]. *ANUAC, 6*(1), 141–163.

Sigona, N. (2009). The 'Problema Nomadi' vis-à-vis the political participation of Roma and Sinti at the local level in Italy. In N. Sigona & N. Trehan (Eds.), *Romani politics in contemporary Europe: Poverty, ethnic mobilization, and the neoliberal order* (pp. viii–xiii). New York: Palgrave Macmillan.

Sigona, N. (2015). Campzenship: Reimagining the camp as a social and political space. *Citizenship Studies, 19*(1), 1–15.

Silverman, C. (1995). Persecution and politicization: Roma (Gypsies) of Eastern Europe. *Cultural Survival Quarterly, 19*(2), 43–49. Retrieved from http://www.culturalsurvival.org/publications/cultural-survival-quarterly/albania/persecution-and-politicization-roma-gypsies-eastern

Spinelli, S. (2005). *Baro romano drom*. Rome: Meltemi Editore.

Stasolla, C. (2012). *Sulla pelle dei Rom: Il Piano Nomadi della giunta Alemanno* [On the skin of the Romani People: The Nomad Plan of the Alemanno administration]. Rome: Edizioni Alegre.

Tonkens, E., & Hurenkamp, M. (2011, July 7–9). The nation is occupied, the city can be claimed. Paper presented at the Annual Conference of the Sociology of Urban and Regional Development of the International Sociological Association, University of Amsterdam, The Netherlands.

U Velto. (2012a, May 15). Rom e Sinti, Fornero: Uscire da gestione emergenziale [Roma, Sinti, and Fornero: Let's drop the emergency approach]. *U Velto*. Retrieved from http://sucardrom.blogspot.com.au/2012/05/rom-e-sinti-fornero-uscire-da-gestione.html

U Velto. (2012b, May 28). Rom e Sinti, l'associazionismo: Parliamo di interazione [Romani associationism: Let's talk about social interaction]. *U Velto*. Retrieved from http://sucardrom.blogspot.com.au/2012/05/rom-e-sinti-lassociazionismo-parliamo.html

Un rom delegato di Alemanno. (2010, July 27). Un rom delegato di Alemanno [A Romani person as Alemanno's delegate]. La Repubblica. Retrieved from http://roma.repubblica.it/cronaca/2010/07/27/news/nomadi-5869812/

Uzunova, I. (2010). Roma integration in Europe: Why minority rights are failing. *Arizona Journal of International and Comparative Law, 27*(1), 283–323. Retrieved from http://academos.ro/sites/default/files/biblio-docs/845/roma_integration_in_europe.pdf

van Baar, H. (2005). Romany Countergovernmentality through transnational networking. Paper presented at the Oxford Symposium on (Trans-) Nationalism in South East Europe, University of Oxford, Oxford.

Vermeersch, P. (2001). Roma identity and ethnic mobilisation in Central European politics. Paper prepared for the workshop on identity politics at the ECPR, Grenoble.

Weyrauch, W. O. (1999). Unwritten constitutions, unwritten law. *Washington and Lee Law Review, 56*(4), 1211–1244.

Woodcock, S. (2009). What's in a name? How Romanian Romani were persecuted by Romanians as Tigani in the Holocaust, and how they resisted. Interstitio. Retrieved from http://www.academia.edu/207265/Whats_in_a_name_How_Romanian_Romani_were_persecuted_by_Romanians_as_Tigani_in_the_Holocaust_and_how_they_resisted

6

Conclusions

Italy today is awash with an 'excess' of information about the Romanies. Most of it is framed in a very pejorative and negative way, thanks to a sensationalist media and a populist political class. The politicians make free use of xenophobic rhetoric in addressing the 'Romani problem', often portrayed as a mere security issue. This keeps reviving old stereotypes (e.g. 'nomads', 'dirty', 'lazy', 'criminals'), while also legitimising discriminatory, and even violent, actions against them. In 2015, Associazione 21 Luglio (as cited in Zandonini 2016) recorded 265 'hate speech' cases across Italy, of which 89 per cent were caused by politicians. As for the media, they have a tendency to endorse 'sensationalism' rather than a deep analysis of a complex phenomenon (Di Grazia 2017). Not surprisingly, 82 per cent of Italian people have a negative perception of the Romani people, which is a much higher percentage compared to other minority groups, who suffer discrimination, such as Muslims and Jews (Pew Research Center 2016). The Government's attentiveness to the Romanies' plight is of recent provenance. Only in February 2011, in fact, was the first research by the Italian Parliament on the conditions of Romani communities in Italy ever published. To this day, not many scholarly works have appeared on Romani culture and history. Romani studies, in fact, still form a very marginal area of interest (Rossi 2010).

© The Author(s) 2018
R. Armillei, *The 'Camps System' in Italy*, Mapping Global Racisms,
https://doi.org/10.1007/978-3-319-76318-7_6

Besides which, the history and memories of the Romani peoples are always narrated by Italian 'experts' and researchers rather than by the Romani themselves. Hence, this topic is under-studied and marked by widespread confusion.

A confusion which is certainly deepened by the contest between opposing political alignments, either left wing or right wing, which have always supported the highly criticised 'camps policy'. In this context, public administrations have been delegating Romani issues to Third Sector and/or Catholic organisations (according to which coalition is in power) rather than to Romani agencies, which often conceal the existence of special agreements and political patronage. The Italian Government recently adopted a 'National Strategy' regarding the social inclusion of these minority groups. Its commitment, though, was merely a response to the EU's request to improve the Romanies' situation by addressing the causes of their marginalisation. On top of that, the whole project still looks vague, as recognised by a number of both Romani and non-Romani commentators. This initiative has emerged in the context of legislative and policy factors which thwart any real change. For instance, the lack of a transparent and accountable apparatus that can monitor Government proposals; patronage-ridden politics; absence of any comprehensive national legislation regarding dealing with Romani issues; failure to empower the Romanies (or, more to the point, a strategy of disempowerment) and their lack of self-representation (ventriloquism). This contradictory approach by the Government is harming Romani communities, whose situation has got worse, not better. The Government's and Third Sector's incapacity to solve this issue may well reflect the difficulty Romani communities face in co-operating with each other due to their internal differences, as well as the practices of 'resistance' developed within the camps.

Therefore, the major contribution this book will make is to provide a clearer picture of what has been termed as the 'camps system' in Italy (made up of the public sector, CSOs and Romani organisations), while highlighting the main causes of this minority's social exclusion and marginalisation. This study was driven by the observation that the dominant views on Romani-related issues were mainly shaped by the proliferation of 'one-sided' types of analyses. International advocacy organisations have criticised Italy's public institutions, a view supported by influential Italian scholars, who often portray Romanies as victims and the *campo nomade* as an institution that objectifies its inhabitants. CSOs, mainly those working inside the camps, have also criticised the Government, but over the years they have become powerless to stop its policies being implemented. Finally, Romani peoples, backed by intellectuals/activists, generally blame the Government and Third Sector organisations for exploiting and disempowering them. As it was, the context in which I operated was one dominated by conflicting stances. The guiding principle of my research strategy therefore was not to undermine or deny the validity of anyone's opinion but to emphasise the fluidity, rather than the theoretical rigidity, which seemed to characterise the Romani issue. This required separate analysis of each agent, in order to have a better understanding of the camps' reality. My analysis will deliver a new theory about the predicament of Romanies living in Italy, while also suggesting possible courses of intervention that could make existing policy initiatives more effective. At the same time, presenting and analysing the Italian experience can shed light on processes which are observable in other member states of the EU (for France see Armillei and Maestri forthcoming; Doytcheva 2016).

Between Institutional Racism and Practices of Resistance

The Romani communities constitute a very small proportion of the Italian population. Of this portion, about 3 per cent actually maintain a 'nomadic' lifestyle (La Stampa 2017). Still, as illustrated throughout this book, the Italian Government, despite being strongly criticised by the International Human Rights organisations and EU institutions, has based an important part of its national policy on a definition of 'Romanies' that makes the word co-terminous with *nomadi*. Such a designation implies that they are unwilling or unable to settle within their host society 'resisting the norms of territoriality and cultural normalisation' (Balibar 2009, foreword). Because of this, they are looked (down) upon as a national 'problem' that must be addressed with extraordinary measures, as discussed in Chap. 3. Seventy years after the end of the Second World War, public discourse about what Italians have come to call their *Problema Nomadi* still revolves around the same three key concepts of 'nomadism', 'asociality' and 're-education', all of which have been touchstones of discrimination against these peoples throughout history (Bravi and Sigona 2006: 858). The existence of major 'gaps' in the Italian collective memory, a tendency to ignore or deny the reality of moments of national shame, historical revisionism, and a preparedness to play down the persecution of Romani peoples are all salient characteristics of contemporary Italian public discourse, just as they were during the Fascist era (Armillei 2014, 2016).

Probably the most dramatic result of the strategic interpretation that incorrectly views Romani culture as inherently 'nomadic' has been the ghettoisation of part of the Romani population within the *campi nomadi*, where still to this day, they live in conditions of practical segregation from the rest of society. In these confined spaces Italian-Romani citizens and Romani citizens of other EU member states, as well as stateless persons, are thrown together without distinction or consultation:

> The building of these camps has generally been accomplished without negotiation or involvement of the clients; people of different origins, ethnic or cultural backgrounds, have been literally piled up all together in the same space. The fact that these groups were incompatible with each other has often fuelled internal conflict and deviant behaviours. (UNAR 2011, p. 42)

Violent episodes within these establishments are indeed linked to a raft of socio-economic factors: people of diverse cultures crammed into confined spaces; the physical isolation of being on the urban outskirts, where under-serviced or un-serviced districts are bedevilled by chronic poverty and unemployment; and widespread racism and no history or pattern of social inclusion.

This situation has deteriorated since May 21, 2008, when, as discussed in Chap. 3, the Berlusconi Government decreed a 'State of Emergency' to counter the presence of 'nomad communities' in the Campania, Lazio and Lombardy regions (Ministero dell'Interno 2011). But this dispensation merely signalled a concerted strategy to tackle the *Problema Nomadi* with one important difference. In the 1980s and 1990s, as illustrated in Chap. 2, there was a declared intention to preserve a supposedly 'nomadic culture' by creating Romani settlements in authorised areas as a way station to integration. By the late 2000s, this policy had evolved into permanent 'institutional segregation' (ERRC 2000; Fiorucci 2010). Chapter 4 explored how Romanies were now institutionalised under a 'patrol and surveillance' mechanism whose symbol was the camp, not just a structure or space of repression but one link in a chain of such institutions organically connected for the operation and preservation of the entire mechanism. As described in Chaps. 3, 4 and 5, the inevitable result was a form of 'ethnic or racial segregation' (Associazione 21 Luglio 2011), a throwback to the type of forced seclusion associated with the first ghettos, founded by the Venetian Republic as a place of captivity for Jews in 1516 (Nicola 2011).

Branding the Romani individual as 'Other' and 'nomad' is reinforced in our time with a number of other official measures. Several city councils throughout Italy have special offices dedicated to 'immigrants and nomads', or just to 'nomads'. A few examples will suffice to make the point: the city of Turin has an *Informa Stranieri e Nomadi* (Information Desk for Immigrants and Nomads; Comune di Torino n.d.); the city of Reggio Emilia, an *Ufficio Nomadi, Prostituzione e Carcere* (Nomads, Prostitution and Prison Office; Comune di Reggio Emilia 2017); the city of Asti, a *Sportello Stranieri e Nomadi* (Immigrants and Nomads Office; Comune di Asti 2014); the city of Palermo, a *Nomadi e Immigrati* (Nomads and Immigrants) division (Comune di Palermo 2016); and the city of Padova, a *Servizio Sociale per i Nomadi* (Social Services for Nomads; Comune di Padova 2015). The city of Rome also had its *Ufficio Nomadi*, which only recently has been renamed *Ufficio Speciale Rom, Sinti e Caminanti* (Comune di Roma 2017). It is clear that Romani peoples, as Chap. 2 in particular recognised, are commonly perceived and categorised as foreigners, and deemed different from the rest of the population.

This Othering process is self-publicised by the constant stream of forced evictions. The constant displacement of hundreds of Romani families, often in violations of international law (Amnesty International 2017), has also become a lucrative business. Between November 1, 2016, and June 30, 2017, the city council carried out 28 forced evictions involving 478 individuals at a cost of around €600,000. Because these measures are not part of a broader inclusion project, they do not and cannot solve the marginalised condition of these people once and for all; they simply move the problem from one suburb or area to the next (Stasolla 2017). All this is assumed to have contributed towards their 'unsettledness', which not only ends up confirming the sense of superiority felt by society's power cliques towards the overt misery of the Romani peoples, but that sense is also recycled into further justification of the 'camps policy' and the enactment of emergency-type of measures. As Clough Marinaro (2009: 267) argued, amid a dread of police 'swoops' and mass deportations, 'the Roma are trapped in a dual predicament of "rightlessness"', between the biopolitical confines of the official camp and the life of a constant fugitive from violence, potentially leading to death. Carlo Stasolla has found an apt metaphor for the current situation: 'It is like a snakes-and-ladders game: if Romanies make it all the way [off the board], then so does the money' (as cited in Castri and Aversano 2011, p. 31). In other words, public funds are used to promote a 'fake' inclusion of the Romani people (Armillei 2015).

Over the past decade, the Italian Government has signed a number of national and international agreements. As one of its flagship national objectives, it has committed itself to the empowerment of Romani groups. In the face of this commitment, this book has assembled evidence of a policy drive in the opposite direction—one that has curbed Romani involvement in influencing the politics that will directly affect them. Implementation of the 'camps policy' amounted to the most obvious example of political single-mindedness to push the Romani population beyond the margins of mainstream society, and exclude it as much as possible from public life. As discussed in Chap. 4, the Romani issue was largely used, by public and Third Sector bodies alike, to build up a lucrative business. Basically, most of the money authorised for tackling the inclusion of the Romani people was spent on forced evictions, running the camps and keeping them under surveillance. The way each party behaved has been shown to establish a mechanism of 'inclusive exclusion', in which the 'Romani problem' became a precondition for its replication. Within this context, the financial dependence on the Government has placed some CSOs in what could be defined as 'operational limbo': they criticised the system but kept working for it. In turn, while developing an 'institutional organisational isomorphism' (Lori 2010), these organisations were able to survive, but at the expense of its constitutive principles. Loss of independence, a growing detachment from the needs of its target groups and a derailment from its social mission ensued.

During the 'Nomad Emergency', in particular, Third Sector organisations were not mere 'victims' of short-sighted public policies; they also suffered from their own incapacity to become self-sustaining. Fundraising is surely a big issue for non-profit organisations (Crescenzi 2008: 2). But if the social sector subscribes to an ethical code, how can they justify taking money from administrations that carry out forced evictions, perpetuate these camps and violate human rights, instead of working for social inclusion? The sector is undoubtedly confronting an image and identity crisis.[1] While lacking appropriate accountability mechanisms, they prioritise their self-interests rather than the well-being of the people they say to represent. Inside the camps, any CSO-led social inclusion projects become irrelevant. The camps are completely neglected by local authorities. During the fieldwork for this book, I saw litter lying scattered throughout the camp areas. There was a time when the city council assigned particular Romanies in each camp to muster hygiene patrols, not only for the sake of good sanitation but to give those residents some responsibility, even if it was just running 'pseudo-cleaning projects'. In reality, said one social worker, this was 'just a way for the Government to buy agreement from the families who dominate the camp. Nobody can really guarantee the outcomes of these agreements' (Ermes Cooperativa Sociale representative, personal communication, May 3, 2012). A number of the informants, who were interviewed, were all well aware of the existence of this bribing mechanism and other forms of corrupt practices. However, only thanks to the *Mafia Capitale* investigation did those rumours were proven to be reality, with several city council's and CSOs' representatives arrested.

However, the Romanies themselves have also learned to use the 'camps system' for their own ends, as discussed in Chap. 5, which attempted to survey the 'camps policy' from Romani perspectives. This element in the equation contradicts a well-established view of them as merely passive

---

[1] Worth noting that CSOs have become the focus of criticism in other contexts too (e.g. Lewis 2014; Piotrowski 2017).

216   R. Armillei

actors, institutionalised and made powerless by a Government that has forced them into a type of *campi nomadi*-based captivity. This book was premised on a new approach to the Romani communities living in State-sanctioned camps. The circumstances of these communities were portrayed as part not only of a broader mechanism of control and marginalisation but also of 'resistance' and 'collective-identity closure'. The work of Foucault (1990) on power and resistance proved helpful in the analysis of the Romanies' interaction with the majority. A CRI worker said that, ever since he could remember, there was a longer queue to enter the camp than to escape it: 'although the great majority of its Romani inhabitants (between 60 per cent and 70 per cent) might have the chance to get out and rent a house or apartment, they preferred to stay' (personal communication, April 21, 2012). A 'pro-camps' delegate confirmed this point: 'There are examples of Romani individuals with jobs who stay on in their camp instead of looking for a different housing solution' (personal communication, April 11, 2012). A social worker explained why: 'This is because inside the camp they have someone who can protect them. Everyone has a specific role in the camp, while outside they are just "Zingari" (Gypsies)' (Personal communication, May 14, 2012).

In other words, the existence of these official camps has become an incentive for many Romani families to live there. Another key informant of a CSO working inside the institutional camps denied they were 'mere victims': according to him 'they stay because they know that they can live there for free' (Personal communication, April 2, 2012). Nazzareno Guarnieri was also strong in recognising the responsibility Romani peoples had for themselves. Those living in camps have developed a welfare dependency and feelings of persecution.

> Because they are Romanies, they now automatically think they are persecuted, so they have to be helped. There is this guy in Rome who has been working for years as part of the schooling projects one of these CSOs carries out. His salary is around €900–1,000. His wife also works, as a cleaner, she brings in another €500–600. They both live in a nomad camp. One day I met him and asked: 'Is it not time you two found a little house of your own?' He replied: 'Are you crazy? How would I pay all the bills and the rest?' I live on a monthly salary of €1,500 and he cannot get by with

€1,600? Many Romanies have no desire to leave the camps, because it is easier for them! They do not have to think about rent and bills etc. (Personal communication, April 21, 2012)

Closing Observations

The *campo nomadi* represents today a weapon for the social control of an allegedly dangerous people. In the public mind, this allegation has gradually crystallised into 'a state of exception' where the rule of law is suspended by the state and power operates directly to bodies who have become 'bare life'—their lives are outside the law (Colebrook and Maxwell 2016). Manufacturing an *Emergenza Nomadi* was the juridical precondition for its proclamation. Dilapidated and abandoned infrastructure—by now a common sight in these encampments—is generally the consequence of officialdom's paralysis and indifference to the living conditions of human beings once defined as 'peoples of the rubbish dumps' (Piasere 2005). The true answer to the question of what produced this 'emergency' and the grounds for such extraordinary measures is therefore *vuoto istituzionale*, an official and political vacuum—an absence of rational and analytical thought among the political and administrative elites, as argued in Chaps. 2, 3 and 4. For years, the Government has basically allowed a corrupt system to survive and prosper. This tolerance has come about through the politics of absolute neglect and a policy of marginalising everyone. The State's decision to isolate the Romanies reinforced the popular perception of them as 'alien/exogenous' communities. Using Marotta's (2011) work, the camp became an 'ethnic place' as a result of the 'social sorting' indulged in by political and economic forces with implications that transcend, but certainly include, control of the Romanies.

In turn, the existence of an inhospitable environment dominated by racism and discrimination has provoked the target group to develop a sort of 'reactive ethnicity' (Marotta 2011: 202–203). It was not only institutional actors who depicted them as the 'stereotypical Gypsy', to simplify a very complex cultural universe, but also camp-dwelling members of the minority group who at times exploited this caricature for their own personal interests. The stereotype was perpetuated by the Government and Third Sector organisations via the 'camps system'. Change must now come from the comprehensive reform of institutional approaches and Third Sector practices, as well as from within Romani civil society. The last decade was characterised by intense cultural and political turmoil among the Romani communities in Italy. This triggered a 'boom' in the formation of Romani organisations all over the country. As discussed in Chap. 5, though, arguing that the Romani movement is strong, cohesive and monolithic would be a misrepresentation. Not only is there marked disunity between 'Italian' and 'foreign Romanies', but conflict is common in the camp-dwelling communities as well. My research has revealed that the condition of Romani associationism is particularly weak in the city of Rome. This fact may be related to another: that of the considerable number of so-called projects founded in recent years, the overwhelming majority of which were established with the single aim of accessing public funds rather than progressing real strategies for the social inclusion of their communities. A genuine political awareness and a jointly agreed strategy were nowhere to be seen.

In conclusion, this book has uncovered sufficient repetition of discursive patterns to establish that the 'incarceration' of Romanies in camps has been spectacularly good for business—involving a number of agencies, public and private, Romani and non-Romani. This study has produced a clearer picture of this complex system, helping to highlight the main causes of the social exclusion and marginalisation of this minority group:

- firstly, a democratic deficit in the way local authorities and agencies operated, particularly during the past decade;
- secondly, it emphasised the responsibilities of some CSOs, mainly those working inside the *campi nomadi*. Their funding dependence and a tendency to mediate with local authorities have prevented them from responding adequately to the Romanies' needs, reinforcing welfare dependency among the 'Romanies of the camps'; and
- finally, it uncovered within these communities 'resistance' practices, modes of defiance and acts of self-assertion, which are identifiable as side effects of self-ghettoisation produced by the existence of the 'camps system'.

It is in light of all these elements that a more or less open state of conflict between *Gadje* and *Zingari* has developed. Both communities have for years regularly 'constructed' and reified a strong sense of their own identity, each in opposition to the other. The 'camps system' represents today the highest expression of this opposition. Overcoming this system can be only achieved through the enactment of a holistic treatment, one that recognises the multidimensional character of its complex mechanism.

Possible Directions for Future Analysis

In Italy, Romani communities, and immigrants more generally, are still considered 'security' issues and treated solely through the application of extraordinary actions. Politicians refer to the idea of national 'insecurity' in order to convey a political willingness to pursue a more 'muscular' approach towards diversity and 'Othered' communities. The issue of borders and invasion from outside has often created a sense of 'ungovernability' and 'insecurity' (Armillei and Mansouri 2017). As a consequence, scapegoating attitudes emerged particularly towards the Romanies, often depicted as public enemies. The role of nationalism in this governing of marginal populations is not the main focus of this book—this is more about the variegated world circulating inside and around 'nomad camps'—but it is surely central to the way the Italian Government has been constant enacting emergency approaches in order to deal with Romani issues, and immigration more in general. The book provides a comprehensive but broad normative analysis of the 'camps system', but it could be further elaborated by placing it in the context of democratic theory. The present study also does not address enough the new kinds of stereotypes that make these interventions possible. For the Romanies, their culture is pathologised and is what makes them ungovernable or prone to violence, crime and social collapse. Thus, reflecting upon democratic and identity theories might be helpful in analysing the applicability of the 'model of ethnic democracy' theorised by Smooha (2009).

The Italian socio-political context, in fact, is characterised by a new form of racism that moves from 'biology' to making 'culture' the site of pathology and the reason for state intervention. The proliferation of discourses and practices of exclusion not limited to the Romanies—their case could be compared to the case of Muslim citizens—gained strength and are no longer limited to extreme right movements. Smooha's work can help to frame the presence of people forced to live within a society but with no recognised right of belonging. Instead of renouncing its traditional, structured dominance, there are clear signs of an Italian 'core ethnic' majority trying to make the new emerging democracy serve them in a form of 'ethnic democracy' (see Armillei 2016; Armillei and Mansouri 2017). Recent authoritarian approaches, particularly directed against 'non-core' ethnocultural groups, promote an ongoing sense of threat which represents one of the conditions for this type of democracy to survive. According to this theory some of the different ethnic groups are viewed as inassimilable into mainstream society, allowing the ethnic majority to install a form of democracy with a strong ethno-nationalist drive. Rather than serving all its citizens equally, an 'ethnic democracy' privileges a supposed ethnic majority and its interest. The fact that institutions in supposedly liberal democratic societies like Italy (for Australia see Armillei and Lobo 2017) engage today in 'inclusive exclusion' makes this book a necessary tool for a more analytical inquiry.

Bibliography

Amnesty International. (2017). Italy 2016/2017. Retrieved from https://www.amnesty.org/en/countries/europe-and-central-asia/italy/report-italy/

Armillei, R. (2014). 'Emergenza nomadi': Institutional continuities in Italian government policy towards the Romanies. *Australian and New Zealand Journal of European Studies, 6*(1), 28–42.

Armillei, R. (2015). A multicultural Italy? In F. Mansouri (Ed.), *Cultural, religious and political contestations: The multicultural challenge* (pp. 135–151). Cham: Springer International Publishing.

Armillei, R. (2016). Reflections on Italy's contemporary approaches to cultural diversity: The exclusion of the 'Other' from a supposed notion of 'Italianness'. *Australia New Zealand Journal of European Studies, 8*(2), 34–48.

Armillei, R., & Lobo, M. (2017). 'Parallel emergencies' in Italy and Australia: Marginalised and racialised Romani and Aboriginal 'camp dwellers'. *Journal of Intercultural Studies, 38*(5), 560–575.

Armillei, R., & Maestri, G. (forthcoming). Camps, civil society organisations and the reproduction of marginalisation: Italian and French 'solidarity/integration' villages for Romani people. In I. Katz, D. Martin, & C. Minca (Eds.), *Camp geographies today: Contemporary spatialities of a modern political technology*. London, UK: Rowman & Littlefield International.

Armillei, R., & Mansouri, F. (2017). 'Ethnic Democracy' and authoritarian legacies in Italy's and Australia's contemporary policies towards 'Boat people'. *Journal on Ethnopolitics and Minority Issues in Europe, 16*(2), 13–40.

Associazione 21 Luglio. (2011). Linea 40: Lo scuolabus per soli bambini rom [Line 40: The school bus for Romani children only]. Retrieved from http://www.21luglio.org/index.php/notizie/9-lassociazione-21-luglio-presenta-la-ricerca-qlinea-40q

Balibar, E. (2009). Foreword. In N. Sigona & N. Trehan (Eds.), *Romani politics in contemporary Europe: Poverty, ethnic mobilization, and the neoliberal order* (pp. viii–xiii). New York: Palgrave Macmillan.

Bravi, L., & Sigona, N. (2006). Educazione e rieducazione nei campi per 'nomadi': Una storia [Education and re-education inside camps for 'nomads': An overview]. *International Journal of Migration Studies, 43*(164), 857–874.

Castri, C., & Aversano, L. (2011). Piano Nomadi: Questione di integrazione o di ordine pubblico? [Nomad Plan: A matter of integration or rather public order?]. *Reti solidali, 1*, 21–35. Retrieved from http://it.calameo.com/read/0 00605228b53276e869f6

Clough Marinaro, I. (2009). Between surveillance and exile: Biopolitics and the Roma in Italy. *Bulletin of Italian Politics, 1*(2), 265–287.

Colebrook, C., & Maxwell, J. (2016). *Agamben*. Milton, Australia: John Wiley & Sons.

Comune di Asti. (2014). Sportello Stranieri e Nomadi [Immigrants and nomads office]. Retrieved from http://trasparenza.comune.asti.it/archivio16_procedimenti_-1_9330_22_1.html

Comune di Padova. (2015). Servizio sociale per i nomadi [Social services for nomads]. Retrieved from http://www.padovanet.it/informazione/servizio-sociale-i-nomadi

Comune di Palermo. (2016). U.O. Nomadi e Immigrati [Nomads and immigrants division]. Retrieved from https://www.comune.palermo.it/noticext. php?id=9953

Comune di Reggio Emilia. (2017). Ufficio nomadi prostituzione e carcere [Nomads, prostitution and prison office]. Retrieved from http://www.municipio.re.it/retecivica/urp/retecivi.nsf/PESUfficiTabellaWeb/8B6E6C5F9230 DCB6C1256698003A08CC?opendocument

Comune di Roma. (2017). Ordinanza Sindacale n. 102 del 4 luglio 2017 [Mayoral Law no. 102 of July 4, 2017]. Retrieved from https://www.comune.roma.it/pcr/it/dip_sss_ufficio_nomadi.page

Comune di Torino. (n.d.). Informa Stranieri e Nomadi [Information desk for immigrants and nomads]. Retrieved from http://www.comune.torino.it/stranieri-nomadi/nomadi.htm

Crescenzi, M. (2008). La qualità del non profit e dell'impresa sociale: Casi esemplari del Terzo Settore italiano [The quality of not-for-profit sector and of social enterprise: Case models of the Italian third sector]. Rome: ASVI Edizioni.

Di Grazia, D. (2017, September 9). Rom, quando è la stampa a diffondere gli stereotipi. *Ultima Voce*. Retrieved from https://www.ultimavoce.it/rom-quando-e-la-stampa-a-diffondere-gli-stereotipi/

Doytcheva, M. (2016). Between infra-right and public hospitality: Ambiguity in local policies towards Roma migrant families in France. *International Journal of Migration and Border Studies, 2*(4), 365–381.

European Roma Rights Centre. (2000). Campland: Racial segregation of Roma in Italy. Retrieved from http://www.errc.org/cms/upload/media/00/0F/m0000000F.pdf

Fiorucci, M. (2010). Un'altra città è possibile. Percorsi di integrazione delle famiglie Rom e Sinte a Roma: Problemi, limiti e prospettive delle politiche di inclusione sociale. [Another city is possible. Integration trajectories of Roma and Sinti families in Rome: Problems, limitations and perspectives of social inclusion policies]. Roma, Italia: Geordie onlus.

Foucault, M. (1990). *The history of sexuality: An introduction* (trans: Hurley, R.). New York: Vintage Books.

La Stampa. (2017, May 11). Rom e Sinti in Italia. *La Stampa*. Retrieved from http://www.lastampa.it/2017/05/11/multimedia/italia/cronache/rom-e-sinti-in-italia-DQyWN5m5PGilUEqGhvnzJK/pagina.html

Lewis, D. (2014). *Non-governmental organizations, management and development.* (3rd). Abingdon, Oxon: Routledge.

Lori, M. (2010, July). Autonomous or dependent: Isomorphic effects of public regulation on voluntary organisations. Paper presented at 9th International Conference of the International Society for Third Sector Research (ISTR), Istanbul. Retrieved from http://www.istr.org/?WP_Istanbul

Marotta, V. (2011). Home, mobility, and the encounter with otherness. In F. Mansouri & M. Lobo (Eds.), *Migration, citizenship, and intercultural relations: Looking through the lens of social inclusion* (pp. 193–209). Aldershot: Ashgate.

Ministero dell'Interno. (2011). Dichiarazione dello stato di emergenza in relazione agli insediamenti di comunita' nomadi nel territorio delle regioni Campania, Lazio e Lombardia [Declaration of the state of emergency in relation to the settlements of the nomads communities in the territory of the Campania, Lazio and Lombardia]. Retrieved from http://www.governo.it/Governo/Provvedimenti/testo_int.asp?d=39105

Nicola, V. (2011). *I ghetti per i rom. Roma, via Di Salone 323. Socianalisi narrativa di un campo rom* [The ghettos for Romani people. Rome, Di Salone road, 323. Socio-analysis account of a Romani camp]. Cuneo: Sensibili alle Foglie.

Pew Research Center. (2016). Europeans fear wave of refugees will mean more terrorism, fewer jobs. Retrieved from http://assets.pewresearch.org/wp-content/uploads/sites/2/2016/07/14095942/Pew-Research-Center-EU-Refugees-and-National-Identity-Report-FINAL-July-11-2016.pdf

Piasere, L. (2005). *Popoli delle discariche: Saggi di antropologia zingara* [Peoples of the dumps: Essays in Gypsy anthropology] (2nd ed.). Rome: CISU.

Piotrowski, T. (2017, February 26). The seeds of volunteering. *The Grassroots Journal*. Retrieved from http://www.thegrassrootsjournal.org/single-post/2017/02/25/The-Seeds-of-Volunteering

Rossi, M. (2010). The city and the slum: An action research on a Moroccan and a Roma Xoraxanè community in Rome. Doctoral dissertation. Retrieved from http://etheses.bham.ac.uk/1263/

Smooha, S. (2009). The model of ethnic democracy: Response to Danel. *The Journal of Israeli History, 28*(1), 55–62.

Stasolla, C. (2017, July 13). Campi rom e sgomberi, a Roma la musica è davvero cambiata. *Il Fatto Quotidiano*. Retrieved from http://www.ilfattoquotidiano.it/2017/07/13/campi-rom-e-sgomberi-a-roma-la-musica-e-davvero-cambiata-purtroppo/3726875/

Ufficio Nazionale Antidiscriminazioni Razziali. (2011). Vai oltre i pregiudizi, scopri i Rom: Go beyond prejudice, discover the Roma. Retrieved from http://www.cominrom.it/wordpress/wp-content/uploads/2011/11/Volume_Campagna-Dosta_UNAR.pdf

Zandonini, G. (2016, April 16). Rom e Sinti, arrivata a metà corsa, la Strategia Nazionale per l'inclusione ha già il fiato corto. *La Repubblica*. Retrieved from http://www.repubblica.it/solidarieta/diritti-umani/2016/04/10/news/rom_arrivata_a_meta_corsa_la_strategia_nazionale_per_l_inclusione_di_rom_e_sinti_ha_gia_il_fiato_corto_-137306733/

Bibliography

AffariItaliani.it. (2017). Rom scatenati denunciano Minniti e Raggi [Angry Romanies denounce Minniti and Raggi]. Retrieved from http://www.affaritaliani.it/roma/rom-scatenati-denunciano-minniti-raggi-a-castel-romano-ci-lasciano-morire-496176.html?refresh_ce

Agamben, G. (1998). *Homo Sacer: Sovereign power and bare life* (trans: Heller-Roazen, D.). Stanford: Stanford University Press. (Original work published 1995).

Allievi, S. (2010). Immigration and cultural pluralism in Italy: Multiculturalism as a missing model. *Italian Culture, 28*(2), 85–103. https://doi.org/10.1179/016146210X12790095563020.

Amnesty International. (2010). The wrong answer. Italy: The 'Nomad Plan' violate the housing right of the Romani people in Rome. Retrieved from https://www.crin.org/en/docs/AI_the_wrong_answer_Italy_nomad%20plan.pdf

Amnesty International. (2012a). Italy: Briefing to the UN Committee on the Elimination of Racial Discrimination 80th session February 2012. Retrieved from http://www2.ohchr.org/english /bodies/cerd/docs/ngos /AI_Italy_CERD80.pdf

Amnesty International. (2012b). On the edge: Roma forced evictions and segregation in Italy. Retrieved from http://www.amnesty.ch/de/laender/europa-

© The Author(s) 2018
R. Armillei, *The 'Camps System' in Italy*, Mapping Global Racisms,
https://doi.org/10.1007/978-3-319-76318-7

zentralasien/italien/dok/2012/amnesty-fordert-das-ende-der-diskriminier-ung-von-roma/bericht-on-the-edge-roma-forced-evictions-and-segregation-in-italy.-september-2012.-16-seiten

Amnesty International. (2016). Roma on the margins: Housing rights denied. Retrieved from https://www.amnesty.org/en/latest/campaigns/2016/04/roma-on-the-margins-housing-rights-denied/

Amnesty International. (2017). Italy 2016/2017. Retrieved from https://www.amnesty.org/en/countries/europe-and-central-asia/italy/report-italy/

Amnesty International, Associazione 21 Luglio, & European Roma Rights Centre (2016). Italy: The national strategy for Roma Inclusion: A short-lived hope for Roma in Italy. Retrieved from https://www.amnesty.org/en/documents/eur30/3520/2016/en/

AnalisiPolitica. (2008). I campi nomadi? Gli italiani li vogliono chiudere. Il sondaggio di AnalisiPolitica. [Nomad camps? Italians want to shut them down. A survey by AnalisiPolitica]. Retrieved from http://affaritaliani.libero.it/static/upll/sond/sondaggio-analisi-politica-campi-nomadi.pdf

Angeli, F., Forgnone, V., & Giannoli, V. (2014, December 2). 'Mafia a Roma, 37 arresti per appalti del Comune. Indagato Alemanno'. [Mafia in Rome, 37 people arrested for the subcontracting inquiry. Alemanno investigated.] *La Repubblica*. Retrieved from http://roma.repubblica.it/cronaca/2014/12/02/news/perquisizioni_alla_pisana_e_in_campidoglio-101923254/

Anheier, H. K., & Salamon, L. M. (2006). The nonprofit sector in comparative perspective. In W. W. Powel & R. Steinberg (Eds.), *The non-profit sector. A research handbook* (pp. 89–116). New Haven/London: Yale University Press.

Arendt, H. (1962). *The origins of totalitarianism*. Cleveland/New York: Meridian Books.

Armillei, R. (2014a). 'Emergenza nomadi': Institutional continuities in Italian government policy towards the Romanies. *Australian and New Zealand Journal of European Studies, 6*(1), 28–42.

Armillei, R. (2014b). Neither included, nor excluded: The paradox of government approaches towards the Romanies in Italy. *Citizenship and Globalisation Research Paper Series, 5*(3), 1–22.

Armillei, R. (2015). A multicultural Italy? In F. Mansouri (Ed.), *Cultural, religious and political contestations: The multicultural challenge* (pp. 135–151). Cham: Springer International Publishing.

Armillei, R. (2016). Reflections on Italy's contemporary approaches to cultural diversity: The exclusion of the 'Other' from a supposed notion of 'Italianness'. *Australia New Zealand Journal of European Studies, 8*(2), 34–48.

Bibliography **227**

Armillei, R. (2017a). The 'Piano Nomadi' and its pyramidal governance: The hidden mechanism underlying the 'camps system' in Rome. *Romani Studies, 27*(1), 47–71.

Armillei, R. (2017b). The Romani 'camp-dwellers' in Rome: Between state control and 'collective-identity closure'. In C. Agius & D. Keep (Eds.), *Identity making, displacement and rupture: Performing discourses of belonging, being and place* (pp. 107–122). Manchester: Manchester University Press.

Armillei, R., & Lobo, M. (2017). 'Parallel emergencies' in Italy and Australia: Marginalised and racialised Romani and Aboriginal 'camp dwellers'. *Journal of Intercultural Studies, 38*(5), 560–575.

Armillei, R., & Maestri, G. (forthcoming). Camps, civil society organisations and the reproduction of marginalisation: Italian and French 'solidarity/integration' villages for Romani people. In I. Katz, D. Martin, & C. Minca (Eds.), *Camp geographies today: Contemporary spatialities of a modern political technology*. London: Rowman & Littlefield International.

Armillei, R., & Mansouri, F. (2017). 'Ethnic Democracy' and authoritarian legacies in Italy's and Australia's contemporary policies towards 'Boat people'. *Journal on Ethnopolitics and Minority Issues in Europe, 16*(2), 13–40.

Armillei, R., Marczak, N., & Diamadis, P. (2016). Forgotten and concealed: The emblematic cases of the Assyrian and Romani Genocides. *Genocide Studies and Prevention: An International Journal, 10*(2), 98–120.

Arrigoni, P., & Vitale, T. (2008). Quale legalità? Rom e gagi a confronto. [Which legality? A comparison between Romani and Gadje peoples]. *Aggiornamenti Sociali, 59*(3), 182–194.

Asséo, H. (1989). Pour une histoire des peuples-Résistances [For a history of resistance-peoples]. In P. Williams (Ed.), *Tsiganes: identité, évolution* (pp. 121–127). Paris: Syros.

Associazione 21 Luglio. (2010). Esclusi e ammassati: Rapporto di ricerca sulla condizione dei minori rom nel villaggio attrezzato di via di Salone a Roma [Excluded and massed: Report on the condition of under-age Romanies in the equipped village of Via Salone in Rome]. Retrieved from http://www.21luglio.org/index.php/report/12-esclusi-e-ammassati

Associazione 21 Luglio. (2011a). Casilino 900, parole e immagini di una diaspora senza diritti [Casilino 900, words and images of a diaspora with no rights]. Retrieved from http://www.21luglio.org/index.php/report/13-casilino-900

Associazione 21 Luglio. (2011b). Linea 40: Lo scuolabus per soli bambini rom [Line 40: The school bus for Romani children only]. Retrieved from http://www.21luglio.org/index.php/notizie/9-lassociazione-21-luglio-presenta-la-ricerca-qlinea-40q

228 Bibliography

Associazione 21 Luglio. (2012a). Anime Smarrite. Il piano degli sgomberi a Roma: Storie quotidiane di segregazione abitativa e di malessere [Lost souls. The evictions plan in Rome: Ordinary stories of housing segregation and sickness]. Retrieved from http://www.21luglio.org/images/anime_smarrite_def.pdf

Associazione 21 Luglio. (2012b). Cinque associazioni chiedono pubblicamente l'obiezione di coscienza alle organizzazioni romane che lavorano dentro i 'campi nomadi' [Five organisations publicly ask the organisations that work in the 'nomad camps' in Rome to opt for conscientious objection]. Retrieved from http://www.21luglio.org/index.php/comunicati-stampa/107-19-giugno-2012-cinque-associazioni-chiedono-pubblicamente-lobiezione-di-cosci-enza-alle-organizzazioni-romane-che-lavorano-dentro-i-qcampi-nomadiq

Associazione 21 Luglio. (2012c). Lavoro Sporco: Il Comune di Roma, i rom e le 'borse-lavoro' [Dirty job: The Municipality of Rome, the Romani people and the 'paid traineeships']. Retrieved from http://www.21luglio.org/images/Report/lavorosporco.pdf

Associazione 21 Luglio. (2012d). Memorandum per il Comitato per l'Eliminazione della Discriminazione Razziale dell'ONU [Memorandum to the United Nations Organisation Committee for the Elimination of Racial Discrimination]. Retrieved from http://www.21luglio.org/images/Memorandum_richiesta_protezione_def.pdf

Associazione 21 Luglio. (2013a). Campi Nomadi s.p.a. [Nomad Camps Ltd.]. Retrieved from http://www.21luglio.org/21luglio/campi-nomadi-s-p-seg-regare-concentrare-allontanare-i-rom-i-costi-roma-nel-2013-giugno-2014/

Associazione 21 Luglio. (2013b). Questione rom: Dal silenzio dello Stato alle risposte di Regioni e Province [The Romani issue: From the government's silence to the responses of the regions and provinces]. Retrieved from http://www.21luglio.org/wp-content/uploads/2013/10/QUESTIONE-ROM.-Dal-silenzio-dello-Stato-alle-risposte-di-Regioni-e-Province.pdf

Associazione 21 Luglio. (2014). Roma e i rom, la politica "senza luce" della Giunta Marino [Rome and the Romanies, the 'no hope' politics of the Marino Mayorship]. Retrieved from http://www.21luglio.org/21luglio/roma-i-rom-la-politica-senza-luce-della-giunta-marino/

Associazione 21 Luglio. (2016a). La Giunta Raggi e i rom: 12 milioni per un nuovo "sistema campi" [The Raggi's administration and the Romani people: €12 million for a new 'camps system']. Retrieved from http://www.21luglio.org/21luglio/la-giunta-raggi-e-i-rom-12-milioni-per-un-nuovo-sistema-campi/

Associazione 21 Luglio. (2016b). Rapporto annuale 2016 [Annual report 2016]. Retrieved from http://www.21luglio.org/21luglio/wp-content/uploads/2017/04/RAPPORTO-ANNUALE_2016_WEB.pdf

Associazione 21 Luglio (2016c). Ultimo Banco [Last school desk]. Retrieved from http://www.21luglio.org/21luglio/wp-content/uploads/2017/03/abstract-Last-Desk.pdf

Associazione 21 Luglio (2017). 21 Luglio: ecco la situazione di Rom e Sinti in Italia [21 Luglio: The situation of the Rom and Sinti in Italy]. Retrieved from https://cild.eu/blog/2017/04/07/titolo-21-luglio/

Associazione 21 Luglio, Associazione per gli Studi Giuridici sull'Immigrazione, Amnesty International, Human Rights Watch, & Open Society Justice. (2012). Italy: Leave 'Nomad Emergency' in the past. Retrieved from http://www.statewatch.org/news/2012/may/italy-nomad-emergency-press-release.pdf

Associazione Carta di Roma. (2014). Zingaro chi? Rom, romeni e rom romeni nei media [Who's the Gypsy: Rom, Romanians and Romanian Romanies in the media]. Retrieved from https://www.cartadiroma.org/news/zingaro-chi-rom-romeni-e-rom-romeni-nei-media/

Associazione per gli Studi Giuridici sull'Immigrazione. (2010). Convegno internazionale: La condizione giuridica di Rom e Sinti in Italia [International conference: The legal status of Roma and Sinti in Italy]. Retrieved from http://www.asgi.it/home_asgi.php?n=918

Associazione Thèm Romanó. (2010). Un evento da non sottovalutare [An event which is not to be underestimated]. Retrieved from http://www.associazione-themromano.it/albumquattrosettembre.htm

Azadé, A. (2016). Life in the new shanty town taking root on Paris's abandoned railway. Retrieved from https://www.theguardian.com/cities/2016/jan/05/life-shanty-town-paris-abandoned-railway-petite-ceinture

Bagnoli, L. (2010, September 7). Opera Nomadi, il teatrino dell'indecenza continua... [Opera Nomadi, the indecency farce continues…]. U Velto. Retrieved from http://sucardrom.blogspot.it/2010/09/opera-nomadi-il-teatrino-del-lindecenza.html

Balibar, E. (2009). Foreword. In N. Sigona & N. Trehan (Eds.), *Romani politics in contemporary Europe: Poverty, ethnic mobilization, and the neoliberal order* (pp. viii–xiii). New York, NY: Palgrave Macmillan.

Barany, Z. (1998). Ethnic mobilization and the state: The Roma in Eastern Europe. *Ethnic and Racial Studies, 21*(2), 308–327.

Barbetta, G. P. (2000). Italy's third sector on consolidation course. *German Policy Studies, 1*(2), 136–160.

230   Bibliography

Barbetta, G. P., Cima, S., & Zamaro, N. (2003). *Le istituzioni nonprofit in Italia: Dimensioni organizzative, economiche e sociali* [Not-for-profit institutions in Italy: Organisational, social and economic dimensions]. Bologna: Il Mulino.

Barnes, A. (2003). Gypsy law: Romani legal traditions and culture. *Marquette Law Review, 86*(4), 823–844.

Barry, A. (2006). Technological zones. *European Journal of Social Theory, 9*(2), 239–253.

Bartlett, W., Benini, R., & Gordon, C. (2011). Measures to promote the situation of Roma EU citizens in the European Union. Brussels: European Union. Retrieved from http://www2.lse.ac.uk/businessAndConsultancy/LSEConsulting/pdf/Roma.pdf

Basso, P., Di Noia, L., & Perocco, F. (2016). Disuguaglianze combinate: Il caso dei Rom in Italia. In L. Di Noia (Ed.), *La condizione dei Rom in Italia*. Venice: Edizioni Ca' Foscari.

Bauman, Z. (2007). *Consuming life*. Cambridge: Polity Press.

Bechis, F. (2014, December 3). Roma, inchiesta Mafia Capitale [Rome, 'Capital Mafia' inquiry]. *Libero Quotidiano*. Retrieved from http://www.liberoquotidiano.it/news/roma/11729234/Roma--inchiesta-Mafia-Capitale-.html

Bellucci, P. (2007). *Rom e Sinti in Italia: Profili storici e culturali* [Roma and Sinti in Italy: Historical and cultural profiles]. Urbino: Università degli Studi di Urbino.

Benedetto, I. (2011). Le minoranze Rom e Sinte: Alla ricerca di uno status giuridico [Roma and Sinti minorities: The pursuit of legal status]. Doctoral dissertation. Retrieved from http://www.stranieriinitalia.it/briguglio/immigrazione-e-asilo/2011/dicembre/tesi-irene-benedetto.pdf

Benvenuti, S., & Martini, S. (2017). La crisi del welfare pubblico e il "nuovo" Terzo settore [The crisis of the welfare state and on the 'new' Third Sector]. Retrieved from http://www.osservatorioaic.it/la-crisi-del-welfare-pubblico-e-il-nuovo-terzo-settore-la-via-tracciata-dalla-legge-delega-n-106-2016.html

Berizzi, P. (2012, June 5). Fascisti del terzo millennio è la Cosa Nera in cerca d'autore [Fascists of the third millennium are the Black thing in search of an author]. *La Repubblica*. Retrieved from http://inchieste.repubblica.it/it/repubblica/rep-it/2012/06/05/news/fascisti_e_post-fascisti_del_terzo_millenino-36171750/

Berman, J. (2013). Utility of a conceptual framework within doctoral study: A researcher's reflections. *Issues in Educational Research, 23*(1), 1–18.

Bisbiglia, V. (2017a, May 31). Campi rom, Raggi presenta "piano di superamento" [Romani camps, Raggi launches her plan]. *Il Fatto Quotidiano*. http://

www.ilfattoquotidiano.it/2017/05/31/campi-rom-raggi-presenta-piano-per-il-superamento-patto-di-responsabilita-su-servizi-e-casa-prime-chiusure-in-24-mesi/3627998/

Bisbiglia, V. (2017b, March 13). Roma, dal comune ok a un nuovo campo rom [Rome, the city council approves the building of a new camp]. *Il Fatto Quotidiano*. Retrieved from http://www.ilfattoquotidiano.it/2017/03/13/roma-dal-comune-ok-un-nuovo-campo-rom-campidoglio-misure-temporanee-obiettivo-e-superare-villaggi/3447711/

Bisbiglia, V. (2017c, August 26). Roma, i numeri dell'emergenza abitativa [Rome, the figures about the housing emergency]. *Il Fatto Quotidiano*. Retrieved from https://www.ilfattoquotidiano.it/2017/08/26/roma-i-numeri-dellemergenza-abitativa-la-regione-al-comune-avete-40-milioni-ma-non-ci-avete-mai-risposto/3816067/

Bisbiglia, V. (2017d, May 31). Roma, tra tensioni, roghi ed esempi virtuosi [Rome, between tensions, blazes and best practices]. *Il Fatto Quotidiano*. Retrieved from http://www.ilfattoquotidiano.it/2017/05/31/roma-tra-tensioni-roghi-ed-esempi-virtuosi-ecco-la-mappa-dei-19-campi-che-accolgono-i-rom/3580993/

Bonaccorsi, M., & Vazzana, R. (2011, February 18). Sui rom si fanno i milioni [Making millions out of Romanies]. Left. Retrieved from http://www.arci-solidarietaonlus.eu/content/sui-rom-si-fanno-i-milioni

Bonetti, P. (Ed.). (2011). *La condizione giuridica di Rom e Sinti in Italia: atti del convegno internazionale. Università degli studi di Milano-Bicocca.* Milano: Giuffrè Editore.

Bonetti, P. (2012, April 24). Launch of the book 'The legal status of Roma and Sinti in Italy'. Speech presented at the Fondazione Adriano Olivetti, Rome.

Bonifazi, C., Heins, F., Strozza, S., & Vitiello, M. (2009, March). Italy: The Italian transition from an emigration to immigration country. Idea working papers. Retrieved from http://www.idea6fp.uw.edu.pl/pliki/WP5_Italy.pdf

Bontempelli, S. (2006). La tribù dei gagè: Comunità Rom e politiche di accoglienza a Pisa (1988–2005) [The tribe of the Gadje people: Romani communities and integration policies in Pisa (1988–2005)]. *International Journal of Migration Studies, 43*(164), 947–967.

Bontempelli, S. (2012). Roma policies in Italy: Good practices for housing. Retrieved from https://www.academia.edu/3279580/Roma_policies_in_Italy_Good_Practices_for_Housing

Boose, J. W. (2012). Democratization and civil society: Libya, Tunisia and the Arab Spring. *International Journal of Social Science and Humanity, 2*(4), 310–315.

232   Bibliography

Boscoboinik, A. (2009). Challenging borders and constructing boundaries: An analysis of Roma political processes. In V. Ciubrinskas & R. Sliuzinskas (Eds.), *Identity politics: Histories, regions and borderlands* (pp. 181–193). Klaipeda: Klaipeda University.

Bravi, L. (2006). *Porrajmos, altre tracce sul sentiero di Auschwitz* [Porrajmos, new traces along the path towards Auschwitz]. Mantova: Istituto di Cultura Sinta.

Bravi, L. (2009). The history of the Roma and Sinti in Nazi-Fascism. Retrieved from http://www.theforgotten.eu/index.php?option=com_content&view=article&id=58%3Ala-storia-dei-rom-e-sinti-nel-nazi-fascismo-di-luca-bravi&lang=en

Bravi, L., & Sigona, N. (2006). Educazione e rieducazione nei campi per 'nomadi': Una storia [Education and re-education inside camps for 'nomads': An overview]. *International Journal of Migration Studies, 43*(164), 857–874.

Brogi, P. (2012, September 28). Nomadi, raso al suolo Tor de' Cenci: Scontro Campidoglio-governo [Nomads, razed Tor de' Cenci: Clash between local and national governments]. *Corriere della Sera*. Retrieved from http://roma.corriere.it/roma/notizie/cronaca/12_settembre_28/tor-de-cenci-cancellato-campo-nomadi-2112023098792.shtml

Brunello, P. (Ed.). (1996). *L'urbanistica del disprezzo. Campi rom e società Italiana* [The urban scorn. Romani camp and Italian society]. Roma: Manifestolibri.

Bryman, A. (2012). *Social research methods* (4th ed.). Oxford: Oxford University Press.

Calabrò, A. R. (2008). *Zingari: Storia di un'emergenza annunciata* [Gypsies: The history of an announced emergency]. Naples: Liguori.

Camera dei Deputati. (2014). Adesione della Repubblica italiana alla Convenzione delle Nazioni Unite sulla riduzione dei casi di apolidia, fatta a New York il 30 agosto 1961 [Accession of the Italian Republic to the convention on the reduction of statelessness, adopted in New York on 30 August 1961]. Retrieved from http://www.camera.it/_dati/leg17/lavori/schedela/apriTelecomando_wai.asp?codice=17PDL0028110

Canettieri, S. (2014, November 22). Marino: "Chiudere i campi e dare una casa alle famiglie rom" [Marino: 'Closing the camps while giving a house to the Romani families']. *Il Messaggero*. Retrieved from http://www.ilmessaggero.it/roma/cronaca/comune_roma_marino_chiusura_campi_rom_case-709842.html#

Carbotti, G., & Maffia, C. (2017, January 2). 'Campi nomadi a Roma, la montagna ha partorito un topolino [Nomad camps in Roma, so much promise, so little delivery]. Agenzia Radicale. Retrieved from http://www.agenziaradicale.com/index.php/diritti-e-liberta/4370-campi-nomadi-a-roma-la-montagna-ha-partorito-un-topolino

Carrasco, O. (2011, August 23). Racist removal: The ongoing hate of Roma peoples in Europe. *POOR Magazine*. Retrieved from http://poormagazine.org/node/4049

Casilino 900, brucia. (2008, December 12). Casilino 900, brucia la 'casa dei sogni' [Casilino 900, the 'dream house' burned down]. *La Repubblica*. Retrieved from http://roma.repubblica.it/dettaglio/casilino-900-brucia-la-casa-dei-sogni/1560445

Castri, C., & Aversano, L. (2011). Piano Nomadi: Questione di integrazione o di ordine pubblico? [Nomad Plan: A matter of integration or rather public order?]. *Reti solidali, 1*, 21–35. Retrieved from http://it.calameo.com/read/000605228b53276e869f6

Cecchini, C. (2012). Oltre il campo: Tavola rotonda con testimonianze sulla condizione dei Rom a Roma [Beyond the camp: Round-table on the condition of the Romanies in Rome]. Speech presented at Palazzo Valentini, Rome.

Cefisi, L. (2011). Bambini ladri: Tutta la verità sulla vita dei piccoli rom, tra degrado e indifferenza [Children thieves: All the truth about the life of the Romani children, between decay and indifference]. Rome: Newton Compton Editori.

Cellai, F. (2003). Camminanti siciliani [Sicilian Travellers]. Città di Torino, Rivista Informagiovani, 4. Retrieved from http://www.comune.torino.it/infogio/rivista/archivio/04_03/a0403p34.htm

Cemlyn, S. (2000a). Assimilation, control, mediation or advocacy? Social work dilemmas in providing anti-oppressive services for traveller children and families. *Child & Family Social Work, 5*(4), 327–341.

Cemlyn, S. (2000b). From neglect to partnership? Challenges for social services in promoting the welfare of traveller children. *Child Abuse Review, 9*, 349–363.

Cemlyn, S., & Briskman, L. (2002). Social (dys)welfare within a hostile state. *Social Work Education, 21*(1), 49–69.

Centre on Housing Rights and Evictions, European Roma Rights Centre, Open Society Institute, Roma Civic Alliance in Romania, Romani Criss. (2008). Security a la Italiana: Fingerprinting, extreme violence and harassment of Roma in Italy. Retrieved from http://www.errc.org/cms/upload/file/m00000428.pdf

Chiarini, R. (2011). The extreme right in Italy. In N. Langenbacher & B. Schellenberg (Eds.), *Is Europe on the 'right' path? Right-wing extremism and right-wing populism in Europe* (pp. 141–157). Berlin: Friedrich-Ebert-Stiftung.

Chiodi, A., & Latini, M. (2016). Promessa cittadinanza [Promising citizenship]. Retrieved from http://reportage.corriere.it/cronache/2016/promessa-cittadinanza/

234 Bibliography

Ciani, P. (2011). I rom e i sinti in Italia: Una foto in corsa [Roma and Sinti in Italy: A picture in motion]. In T. Santoriello (Ed.), Ho visto anche degli zingari felici: Di chi parliamo quando parliamo di rom [I've also seen happy Gypsies: Who we mean when we speak of the Romanies]. Retrieved from http://www.associazionegiornalisti.it/public/files/rom_vademecum.pdf

Cittalia. (2011). Le politiche di integrazione urbana e la marginalità: Il caso dei Rom e Sinti in Italia [Integrating urban planning and marginality: The case of the Roma and Sinti in Italy]. Retrieved from http://www.lavoro.gov.it/NR/rdonlyres/67FB0B61-D7A8-4923-9E7C-1DB0DD9C2934/0/INTEGRAZIONE_URBANA.pdf

Clough Marinaro, I. (2003). Integration or marginalization? The failures of social policy for the Roma in Rome. *Modern Italy, 8*(2), 203–218.

Clough Marinaro, I. (2009). Between surveillance and exile: Biopolitics and the Roma in Italy. *Bulletin of Italian Politics, 1*(2), 265–287.

Clough Marinaro, I. (2014). Rome's 'legal' camps for Roma: The construction of new spaces of informality. *Journal of Modern Italian Studies, 19*(5), 541–555.

Clough Marinaro, I. (2015). The rise of Italy's neo-ghettos. *Journal of Urban History, 41*(3), 368–387.

Clough Marinaro, I., & Daniele, U. (2011). Roma and humanitarianism in the Eternal City. *Journal of Modern Italian Studies, 16*(5), 621–636.

Clough Marinaro, I., & Sigona, N. (2011). Introduction Anti-Gypsyism and the politics of exclusion: Roma and Sinti in contemporary Italy. *Journal of Modern Italian Studies, 16*(5), 583–589.

Colebrook, C., & Maxwell, J. (2016). *Agamben.* Milton: John Wiley & Sons.

Commissione straordinaria per la tutela e la promozione dei diritti umani. (2011). Rapporto conclusivo dell'indagine sulla condizione di Rom, Sinti e Camminanti in Italia [Final report of the survey on the status of Roma, Sinti and Travellers in Italy]. Retrieved from http://www.senato.it/service/PDF/PDFServer/DF/233751.pdf

Commissioner for Human Rights. (2012). Report by Nils Muižnieks Commissioner for Human Rights of the Council of Europe following his visit to Italy from 3 to 6 July 2012. Retrieved from https://wcd.coe.int/com.instranet.InstraServlet?command=com.instranet.CmdBlobGet&InstranetImage=2143096&SecMode=1&DocId=1926434&Usage=2

Committee on the Elimination of Racial Discrimination. (2012, March). Eightieth session. Consideration of reports submitted by States parties under article 9 of the convention. Concluding observations of the Committee on the Elimination of Racial Discrimination: Italy. Retrieved from http://www2.ohchr.org/english/bodies/cerd/docs/CERD.C.ITA.CO.16-18.pdf

Committee on the Elimination of Racial Discrimination. (2016a). Committee on the Elimination of Racial Discrimination examines the report of Italy. Retrieved from http://www.ohchr.org/EN/NewsEvents/Pages/DisplayNews.aspx?NewsID=20978&LangID=E

Committee on the Elimination of Racial Discrimination (2016b). Concluding observations on the nineteenth and twentieth periodic reports of Italy http://www.cidu.esteri.it/resource/2016/12/49098_f_CERD_C_ITA_CO_1920_26015_E.pdf

Comune di Asti. (2014). Sportello Stranieri e Nomadi [Immigrants and nomads office]. Retrieved from http://trasparenza.comune.asti.it/archivio16_procedimenti_-1_9330_22_1.html

Comune di Padova. (2015). Servizio sociale per i nomadi [Social services for nomads]. Retrieved from http://www.padovanet.it/informazione/servizio-sociale-i-nomadi

Comune di Palermo. (2016). U.O. Nomadi e Immigrati [Nomads and immigrants division]. Retrieved from https://www.comune.palermo.it/noticext.php?id=9953

Comune di Reggio Emilia. (2017). Ufficio nomadi prostituzione e carcere [Nomads, prostitution and prison office]. Retrieved from http://www.municipio.re.it/retecivica/urp/retecivi.nsf/PESUfficiTabellaWeb/8B6E6C5F9230DCB6C1256698003A08CC?opendocument

Comune di Roma. (2008). Capitolato per l'affidamento della realizzazione del progetto di scolarizzazione per i bambini e gli adolescenti rom per il triennio scolastico 2008–2011 [Terms of contract regarding the schooling project for Romani children and adolescents in the 3-year period 2008–2011]. Retrieved from http://62.77.53.204/repository/ContentManagement/information/P1914591917/CAPITOLATO_ROM.pdf

Comune di Roma. (2009a, October 22). 'Contro ogni discriminazione', protocollo Comune-Dipartimento Pari Opportunità [Against any discrimination: Agreement between City Council and the Department of Equal Opportunity]. Retrieved from http://www.comune.roma.it/wps/portal/pcr?contentId=NEW110254&jp_pagecode =newsview.wp&ahew=contentId:jp_pagecode

Comune di Roma. (2009b). Il piano nomadi [The nomad plan]. Retrieved from http://briguglio.asgi.it/immigrazione-e-asilo/2009/agosto/slides-piano-nomadi-rm.pdf

236   Bibliography

Comune di Roma. (2011a). Allegato 7 allo schema del Piano Regolatore Sociale 2011–2015: Interventi per le popolazioni rom [Social Town Plan 2011–2015 of the city of Rome: Interventions on behalf of the Romani people]. Retrieved from http://www.oasisociale.it/myDesk/_temp/All%207%20PRS-Popolazioni%20 Rom.pdf

Comune di Roma. (2011b). Capitolato per l'affidamento della realizzazione del progetto di scolarizzazione per i minori appartenenti alle comunita' rom dei campi non attrezzati di Roma Capitale 1 Gennaio 2011–31 dicembre 2011 [Terms of contract regarding the schooling project for Romani children inside non-equipped camps between 1 January 2011 and 31 December 2011]. Retrieved from https://www.comune.roma.it/PCR/resources/cms/ documents/CAPITOLATO.pdf

Comune di Roma. (2014). Capitolato Speciale di Appalto per l'affidamento del Servizio di scolarizzazione dei minori appartenenti alle comunità rom, sinti e caminanti dei Villaggi attrezzati e dei Campi non attrezzati di Roma Capitale periodo 1 settembre 2014–31 agosto 2015 [Terms of contract regarding the schooling project for Romani children inside non-equipped camps and equipped villages between 1 September 2014 and 31 August 2015]. Retrieved from https://www.comune.roma.it/PCR/resources/cms/documents/bando_ rom_2014_capitolato.pdf

Comune di Roma. (2016a). Procedura aperta per l'affidamento del servizio di gestione sociale, formazione lavoro, di interventi di piccola manutenzione e del servizio di vigilanza dei villaggi di Roma capitale [Open procedure for the assignment of the services of social management, work and training, small-scale maintenance and surveillance inside the capital's villages]. Retrieved from https://www.comune.roma.it/resources/cms/documents/Procedura_aperta_ affidamento_servizio_gestione_villaggi_di_Roma_Capitale_BANDO_DI_ GARA.pdf

Comune di Roma. (2016b). Scolarizzazione dei minori rom, sinti e caminanti residenti nel territorio di Roma Capitale: Anno Educativo 2016–2017 [Terms of contract regarding the schooling project for Romani Children in the 2016–2017 Period]. Retrieved from http://www.comune.roma.it/pcr/ do/jpsite/Site/home

Comune di Roma. (2017a). Campi rom: al lavoro per superamento villaggi Monachina e La Barbuta [Romani camps: Work is underway to close the Monachina and La Barbuta villages]. Retrieved from https://www.comune. roma.it/pcr/it/newsview.page?contentId=NEW1428937

Comune di Roma. (2017b). Ordinanza Sindacale n. 102 del 4 luglio 2017 [Mayoral Law no. 102 of July 4, 2017]. Retrieved from https://www.comune. roma.it/pcr/it/dip_sss_ufficio_nomadi.page

Comune di Torino. (n.d.). Informa Stranieri e Nomadi [Information desk for immigrants and nomads]. Retrieved from http://www.comune.torino.it/stranieri-nomadi/nomadi.htm

Conclave, M. (2017). La vera valutazione dell' impresa sociale [The real evaluation of the social enterprise]. Retrieved from http://www.nuovi-lavori.it/index.php/sezioni/502-la-vera-valutazione-dell-impresa-sociale

Cosentino, R., & Fico, A. (2012, November 2). Deportazioni, sprechi e illegittimità: Così è fallito il piano nomadi di Roma [Expulsions, inefficiencies and illegitimacy: This is how the Nomad Plan has failed]. La Repubblica. Retrieved from http://inchieste.repubblica.it/it/repubblica/rep-it/2012/11/02/news/il_fallimento_del_piano_nomadi-45769127/

Council of Europe. (1997). European convention on nationality: Explanatory report. Retrieved from http://conventions.coe.int/Treaty/EN/Reports/Html/166.htm

Council of Europe. (2008). Go beyond prejudice, discover the Roma! Retrieved from http://www.coe.int/t/dg3/romatravellers/jp3/arc/EnglishDOSTA.pdf

Council of Europe. (2012a). Descriptive glossary of terms relating to Roma issues. Retrieved from http://a.cs.coe.int/team20/cahrom/documents/Glossary%20Roma%20EN%20version%2018%20May%202012.pdf

Council of Europe. (2012b). Human rights of Roma and Travellers in Europe. Retrieved from https://www.coe.int/t/commissioner/source/prems/prems79611_GBR_CouvHumanRightsOfRoma_WEB.pdf

Council of Europe. (2016a). Fourth opinion on Italy adopted on 19 November 2015. Retrieved from https://rm.coe.int/16806959b9

Council of Europe. (2016b). Stop evictions of Roma and Travellers. Retrieved from https://www.coe.int/en/web/portal/roma-latest-news/-/asset_publisher/Wf2OtrKpyHUY/content/stop-evictions-of-roma-and-travelle-3?_101_INSTANCE_Wf2OtrKpyHUY_languageId=en_GB

Council of Europe (2017). Resolution CM/ResCMN(2017)4 on the implementation of the Framework Convention for the Protection of National Minorities by Italy. Retrieved from https://search.coe.int/cm/Pages/result_details.aspx?ObjectId=090000168073038c

Council of Europe Romani Projekt. (ca. 2005). Institutionalisation and emancipation [Fact Sheet]. Retrieved from http://romafacts.uni-graz.at/index.php/history/prolonged-discrimination-struggle-for-human-rights/institutionalisation-and-emancipation

Council of the European Union. (2000). Council Directive 2000/43/EC of 29 June 2000: Implementing the principle of equal treatment between persons irrespective of racial or ethnic origin. Retrieved from http://eur-lex.europa.eu/LexUriServ/LexUriServ.do?uri=OJ:L:2000:180:0022:0026:EN:PDF

238 Bibliography

Crepaldi, C., & Boccagni, P. (2009). The Roma in Europe: Socio economic condition and policies of integration. Paper presented at the 7th ESPAnet conference 2009 Session 11 – Migrants and the Welfare State. Retrieved from http://www.espanet-italia.net/conference2009/paper/11%20-%20Crepaldi.pdf

Crescenzi, M. (2008). La qualità del non profit e dell'impresa sociale: Casi esemplari del Terzo Settore italiano [The quality of not-for-profit sector and of social enterprise: Case models of the Italian Third Sector]. Rome, Italy: ASVI Edizioni.

Creswell, J. W., & Plano Clark, V. L. (2011). *Designing and conducting mixed methods research* (2nd ed.). Thousand Oaks: Sage.

Croce Rossa Italiana. (2010). Rom: CRI – Campidoglio, protocollo su presidi nei campi nomadi [Romani people: CRI – City Council, protocol agreement regarding the nomad camps]. Retrieved from https://www.cri.it/flex/cm/pages/ServeBLOB.php/L/IT/IDPagina/5773

Croce Rossa Italiana. (2013). Croce Rossa, i volontari eleggono Francesco Rocca nuovo presidente Nazionale [Red Cross, the volunteers elect Francesco Rocca new national president]. Retrieved from https://www.cri.it/flex/cm/pages/ServeBLOB.php/L/IT/IDPagina/15706

Croce Rossa Italiana. (2017). Chi siamo [Who we are]. Retrieved from https://www.cri.it/chisiamo

Cucinotta, G. (2012, September 11). 'Case popolari ai Rom? Se le scordino': Belviso infiamma la querelle sgomberi ['Council house to Romani people? They can forget about it': Belviso sets the dispute about evictions on fire]. Corriere della Sera. Retrieved from http://roma.corriere.it/roma/notizie/cronaca/12_settembre_11/nomadi-case-popolari-belviso-2111775738259.shtml

Cugusi, M. C. (2011, May 18). 'Generazioni rom rovinate dall'assistenzialismo': Intervista a Dijana Pavlovic [Romani generations damaged by welfare dependency: Interview of Dijana Pavlovic]. Diritto di critica. Retrieved from http://www.dirittodicritica.com/2011/05/18/rom-pavlovic-assistenzialismo-57035/

Daniele, U. (2010). Zingari di carta: Un percorso nella presa di parola rom ai tempi dell'emergenza [Paper Gypsies: A route towards the empowerment of Romanies during the emergency]. *Zapruder, 22*, 56–72.

Daniele, U. (2011a). 'Nomads' in the eternal city. *Géocarrefour, 86*(1), 15–24. Retrieved from http://geocarrefour.revues.org/8230

Daniele, U. (2011b). *Sono del campo e vengo dall'India: Etnografia di una collettività rom ridislocata* [I live in a camp and I come from India: Ethnography of a re-displaced Romani community]. Rome: Meti Edizioni.

David, A. (2008, September 21). Thousands without a country make Italy their home: Lack of papers places lives in limbo. *The Washington Post.* Retrieved from http://www.unhcr.org/cgi-bin/texis/vtx/refdaily?pass=463ef21123&date=2008-09-22&cat=Europe

Délégation Interministérielle à l'hébergement et à l'accès au lodgement. (2011). French government strategy for Roma integration within the framework of the communication from the Commission of 5 April 2011 and the Council conclusions of 19 May 2011. http://ec.europa.eu/social/BlobServlet?docId=8969&langId=en

Di Blasi, F. (2010, July 28). Campi rom, Opera Nomadi lancia l'allarme su Castel Romano [Romani camps, Opera Nomadi sounds the alarm regarding Castel Romano]. Retrieved from http://www.suglizingari.it/rassegna-stampa/campi-rom-opera-nomadi-lancia-lallarme-su-castel-romano

Di Giovan Paolo, R. (2012, April). Presentazione del volume 'La condizione giuridica di Rom e Sinti in Italia' [Book launch 'The legal status of Roma and Sinti in Italy']. Speech presented at the Fondazione Adriano Olivetti, Rome.

Di Grazia, D. (2017, September 9). Rom, quando è la stampa a diffondere gli stereotipi. Ultima Voce. Retrieved from https://www.ultimavoce.it/rom-quando-e-la-stampa-a-diffondere-gli-stereotipi/

Di Maggio, P. J., & Powell, W. W. (1991). The iron cage revisited: Institutional isomorphism and collective rationality in organizational fields. In W. W. Powell & P. J. Di Maggio (Eds.), *The new institutionalism in organizational analysis* (pp. 63–82). Chicago: University of Chicago Press.

Di Noia, L. (Ed.). (2016). *La condizione dei Rom in Italia.* Venezia: Edizioni Ca'Foscari.

Di Toro, M. (2017). Castel Romano, rom denunciano emergenza sanitaria [Castel Romano, the Romani people denounce the health emergency]. Retrieved from http://www.ilcorrieredellacitta.com/primo-piano/castel-romano-rom-denunciano-emergenza-sanitaria.html

Doytcheva, M. (2016). Between infra-right and public hospitality: Ambiguity in local policies towards Roma migrant families in France. *International Journal of Migration and Border Studies, 2*(4), 365–381.

Drogo, G. (2017, April 04). 'Il fantastico piano di Virginia Raggi per (fingere di) superare i Campi Rom'. NeXt Quotidiano. Retrieved from https://www.nextquotidiano.it/virginia-raggi-campi-rom/

Eumetra Monterosa. (2016). L'opinione degli italiani sull'arrivo degli immigrati [The opinion of Italians on the arrival of immigrants]. Retrieved from https://www.eumetramr.com/it/lopinione-degli-italiani-sullarrivo-degli-immigrati

240   Bibliography

Euractiv. (2012, May 24). 'Brussels urges EU countries to act on Roma integration'. Euractiv. Retrieved from http://www.euractiv.com/socialeurope/brussels-urges-eu-countries-act-news-512944

European Commission (n.d.). Study on Volunteering in the European Union: Country Report Italy. Retrieved from http://ec.europa.eu/citizenship/about-the-europe-for-citizens-programme/studies/index_en.htm

European Commission. (2009). Vademecum: The 10 common basic principles on Roma inclusion. Retrieved from http://www.coe.int/t/dg4/youth/Source/Resources/Documents/2011_10_Common_Basic_Principles_Roma_Inclusion.pdf

European Commission. (2011). An EU framework for national Roma integration strategies up to 2020. Retrieved from http://ec.europa.eu/justice/policies/discrimination/docs/com_2011_173_en.pdf

European Commission. (2012). National strategies. Retrieved from http://ec.europa.eu/justice/discrimination/roma/national-strategies/index_en.htm

European Commission. (2013). Roma platform. Retrieved from http://ec.europa.eu/justice/discrimination/roma/roma-platform/index_en.htm

European Commission. (2016a). Country report non-discrimination Italy. Retrieved from http://www.equalitylaw.eu/downloads/3736-2016-it-country-report-nd

European Commission. (2016b). 10th Meeting of the European Platform for Roma Inclusion: "Mutual accountability of all". Retrieved from http://ec.europa.eu/newsroom/just/item-detail.cfm?item_id=36992

European Commission. (2017). Communication from the Commission to the European Parliament and the Council: Midterm review of the EU framework for national Roma integration strategies. Retrieved from http://eur-lex.europa.eu/legal-content/EN/TXT/PDF/?uri=CELEX:52017DC0458&from=EN

European Commission Against Racism and Intolerance. (2012). ECRI report on Italy (fourth monitoring cycle). Retrieved from http://www.coe.int/t/dghl/monitoring/ecri/country-by-country/italy/ITA-CbC-IV-2012-002-ENG.pdf

European Commission Against Racism and Intolerance. (2016). ECRI report on Italy (fifth monitoring cycle) Adopted on 18 March 2016. Retrieved from https://www.coe.int/t/dghl/monitoring/ecri/Country-by-country/Italy/ITA-CbC-V-2016-019-ENG.pdf

European Committee of Social Rights. (2010). Centre on Housing Rights and Evictions (COHRE) v. Italy Complaint No. 58/2009. Retrieved from http://www.coe.int/t/dghl/monitoring/socialcharter/complaints/CC58Merits_en.pdf

European Parliament. (2017). Parliamentary questions 30 May 2017 E-001180/2017: Answer given by Ms Jourová on behalf of the Commission. Retrieved from http://www.europarl.europa.eu/sides/getAllAnswers.do?reference=E-2017-001180&language=EN

European Public Health Alliance. (2011). European Commission adopts EU Framework for National Roma Integration Strategies. Retrieved from http://www.epha.org/spip.php?article4500

European Roma and Travellers Forum. (2015). Fact sheet on the situation of Roma and Sinti in Italy. Retrieved from http://barabal.eu/images/The_situation_of_Roma_in_Italy_13062015.pdf

EUropean ROma MApping. (2008). Castel Romano Report. Retrieved from http://www.eu-roma.net/dblog/data.asp?s=Castelromano

European Roma Rights Centre. (2000). Campland: Racial segregation of Roma in Italy. Retrieved from http://www.errc.org/cms/upload/media/00/0F/m0000000F.pdf

European Roma Rights Centre. (2013). End of the road for Italy's illegal state of emergency. Retrieved from http://www.errc.org/article/end-of-the-road-for-italys-illegal-state-of-emergency/4137

European Roma Rights Centre. (2017). Parallel report: For Consideration by the Human Rights Committee at its 119th session (6 – 29 March 2017). Retrieved from http://www.errc.org/cms/upload/file/italy-iccpr-8-february-2017.pdf

European Roma Rights Centre, osservAzione, & Amalipé Romanò. (2010). Submission of the European Roma Rights Centre, osservAzione and Amalipé Romanò concerning Italy for consideration under the universal review by the United Nations Human Rights Council at its 7th session February 2010. Retrieved from http://www.errc.org/cms/upload/media/04/29/m00000429.pdf

European Union Agency for Fundamental Rights. (2017a). Fundamental Rights Report 2017. Retrieved from http://fra.europa.eu/en/publication/2017/fundamental-rights-report-2017

European Union Agency for Fundamental Rights. (2017b). Roma. Retrieved from http://fra.europa.eu/en/theme/roma

EveryOne Group. (2009). Imminent camp clearance of 700 Roma citizens. Retrieved from http://www.everyonegroup.com/EveryOne/MainPage/Entries/2009/12/16_Imminent_camp_clearance_of_700_Roma_citizens.html

Falcioni, D. (2010a, July 29). Piano Nomadi di Roma: Il punto dopo un anno [Nomad Plan in Rome: The situation after a year]. InviatoSpeciale. Retrieved from http://www.inviatospeciale.com/2010/07/piano-nomadi-di-roma-il-punto-dopo-un-anno/

Falcioni, D. (2010b, December 16). Roma: Il 'Piano Nomadi' in mano alla Croce Rossa. Anzi, ad Alemanno [Rome: The 'Nomad Plan' in the hands of

242   Bibliography

the Red Cross, or rather of Alemanno]. Inviato Speciale. Retrieved from http://www.inviatospeciale.com/giornale/2010/12/il-piano-nomadi-in-mano-alla-croce-rossa-anzi-ad-alemanno/

Favero, P. (2010). Italians, the 'good people': Reflections on national self-representation in contemporary Italian debates on xenophobia and war. *Outlines – Critical Practice Studies, 2*, 138–153.

Fazzi, L. (2011). L'innovazione nelle cooperative sociali in Italia [Innovation in social cooperatives in Italy]. Retrieved from http://www.forumterzosettore.it/multimedia/allegati/Innovazione%20nelle%20cooperative%20sociali.pdf

Federico, V. (2012). Impresa sociale e terzo settore: esperienze europee [Social enterprise and Third Sector: European experiences]. In V. Federico, D. Russo, & E. Testi (Eds.), *Impresa sociale, concorrenza e valore aggiunto. Un approccio europeo* (pp. 89–131). Lavis: LEGO spa.

Fekete, L. (2008). The Italian general election and its aftermath. *European Race Bulletin, 64*, 2–15.

Ferrazza, D., & Menghi, B. (2010). La popolazione di Roma [Rome's population]. Retrieved from http://www.comune.roma.it/PCR/resources/cms/documents/Doc_Dati_demografici.pdf

Fiano, F., & Sacchettoni, I. (2016, June 16). Tangenti sui campi rom [Bribes regarding the Romani camps]. *Corriere della Sera*. Retrieved from http://roma.corriere.it/notizie/cronaca/16_giugno_29/tangenti-campi-rom-indagati-15-dirigenti-campidoglio-819c44c6-3d66-11e6-922f-98d199acd386.shtml#

Fiaschetti, M. E. (2017, September 28). Dieci campi rom (legali) da chiudere [Ten Romani (legal) camps need to be closed]. *Corriere della Sera*. Retrieved from http://roma.corriere.it/notizie/cronaca/17_settembre_28/dieci-campi-rom-legali-chiudere-piano-comune-appena-partito-9a49eda0-a3ba-11e7-a066-220c02125bda.shtml

Fico, A. (2012, November 2). Dopo lo sgombero di Tor de Cenci é rottura tra Alemanno e mondo cattolico [The forced eviction of Tor de Cenci lead to a breakup between Alemanno and the Catholic world]. *La Repubblica*. Retrieved from http://inchieste.repubblica.it/it/repubblica/rep-it/2012/11/02/news/alemanno_isolato-45768915/

Fioretti, C. (2011). Do-it-yourself housing for immigrants in Rome: Simple reaction or possible way out. In F. Eckardt & J. Eade (Eds.), *The ethnically diverse city* (pp. 535–558). Berlin: Berliner Wissenschaftsverlag.

Fiorucci, M. (2010). Un'altra città è possibile. Percorsi di integrazione delle famiglie Rom e Sinte a Roma: Problemi, limiti e prospettive delle politiche di inclusione sociale. [Another city is possible. Integration trajectories of Roma and Sinti families in Rome: Problems, limitations and perspectives of social inclusion policies]. Roma, Italia: Geordie onlus.

Fischer, A. M. (2011). Between nation and state: Examining the International Romani Unions. Senior Projects Spring, Paper 12. Retrieved from http://digitalcommons.bard.edu/senproj_s2011/12

Fondazione ISMU. (2011). Alunni con cittadinanza non italiana: Verso l'adolescenza. Rapporto nazionale A.s. 2010/2011 [Students with no Italian citizenship: Towards adolescence. National report academic year 2010/2011]. Quaderni ISMU, 4. Retrieved from http://www.ismu.org/index.php?page=85

Forgacs, D. (2015). *Margini d'Italia: l'esclusione sociale dall'Unità a oggi* [Italian margins: Social exclusion from political unity now]. Gius: Laterza & Figli Spa.

Forti, M. (2008, October 25). Una Croce Rossa sotto controllo di stato [A Red Cross under state control]. *Il Manifesto*. Retrieved from http://www.lettera22.it/showart.php?id=9818&rubrica=193

Fosztó, L. (2003). Diaspora and nationalism: An anthropological approach to the international Romani movement. *REGIO Minorities, Politics, Society, 1*, 102–118.

Foucault, M. (1977). *Discipline and punish* (trans: Sheridan, A.). London: Allen Lane.

Foucault, M. (1990). *The history of sexuality: An introduction* (trans: Hurley, R.). New York: Vintage Books.

Francese, I. (2015, April 8). Il sindaco veneto vara il "divieto di sosta ai nomadi" [The Venetian Mayor launches 'no-parking zones' for nomads]. *Il Giornale*. Retrieved from http://www.ilgiornale.it/news/cronache/sindaco-veneto-vara-divieto-sosta-ai-nomadi-mio-paese-non-li-1114331.html

FrancoAngeli. (2011, February). Norme redazionali [editorial rules]. Sociologia e Politiche Sociali. Retrieved from https://www.francoangeli.it/riviste/NR/Sp-norme.pdf

Frignani, R. (2012, January 20). Piano nomadi: 'No' di Sant'Egidio [Nomad Plan: S. Egidio says 'no']. Retrieved from http://www.santegidio.org/pageID/64/langID/cs/itemID/7234/Piano_nomadi_no_di_Sant_Egidio.html

Gago-Cortés, C., & Novo-Corti, I. (2015). Sustainable development of urban slum areas in Northwestern Spain. *Management of Environmental Quality: An International Journal, 26*(6), 891–908.

Gaita, L. (2017, January 29). Emergenza abitativa, in Italia nel 2015 oltre 57mila sfratti per morosità [Housing emergency in Italy, in 2015 more than 57,000 evictions for rent arrears]. *Il Fatto Quotidiano*. Retrieved from http://www.ilfattoquotidiano.it/2017/01/29/emergenza-abitativa-in-italia-nel-2015-oltre-57mila-sfratti-per-morosita-roma-in-testa-fuori-casa-1-famiglia-ogni-272/3348138/

244 Bibliography

Galati, M. (2007). *Rom cittadinanza di carta: Metodologie di ricerca e di intervento sociale per apprendere parola e rappresentanza.* [Romani citizenship made of paper: Methodologies of research and social practice to learn self-representation]. Soveria Mannelli: Edizioni Rubbettino.

Geertz, C. (2001). *The Interpretation of cultures.* New York: Basic Books.

Gheorghe, N., & Acton, T. (2001). Citizens of the world and nowhere: Minority, ethnic and human rights for Roma. In W. Guy (Ed.), *Between past and future: The Roma of Central and Eastern Europe* (pp. 54–70). Hatfield: University of Hertfordshire Press.

Giannini, S. (Writer), & Gabanelli, M. (Director). (2010). *La croce in rosso* [The cross in red] [Television series episode]. In Bisogni, P. (Producer), Report. Rome: Rai 3.

Goffman, E. (1961). *Asylums: Essays on the social situation of mental patients and other inmates.* New York: Doubleday Anchor.

Grilli, F. (2011, August 4). Tor de' Cenci: Da Campo Nomadi 'modello' a Campo 'tollerato'. Ecco cos'è cambiato [Tor de' Cenci: From being an 'ideal' nomad camp to a 'tolerated' camp. This is what has changed]. *Roma Today.* Retrieved from http://eur.romatoday.it/campo-nomadi-modello-campo-toll-erato.html

Grilli, F. (2012, July10). Tor de' Cenci: 'Mantenete le promesse sul campo nomadi' [Tor de' Cenci: 'Keep the promises you have made regarding the nomad camp']. *Roma Today.* Retrieved from http://eur.romatoday.it/tor-de-cenci-residenti-chiedono-sindaco-mantieni-promesse.html

Gruppo Attivo WWF Roma XI. (2005). Sgombero di Vicolo Savini: Fu vera gloria? [The evacuation of Vicolo Savini: Was it really something to be proud of?]. Retrieved from http://www.wwfroma11.it/documenti/decima/interv-ista%20antonini%20nomadi%20decima.htm

Gruppo Intercultura CdB S. Paolo. (2011). Parliamo dei Rom solo se ne muore qualcuno tra le fiamme? [We talk about Romani people only when some of them die in a fire]. Retrieved from http://www.amicoqua.org/?p=3304

Hancock, I. (2000). Speech presented at the panel discussion 'The Romani movement: What shape, what direction?', Budapest. Retrieved from http://www.errc.org/cikk.php?cikk=1292

Hancock, I. (2009). Responses to the Porrajmos: The Romani Holocaust. In A. Rosenbaum (Ed.), *Is the Holocaust unique?* (3rd ed., pp. 39–64). Boulder: The Westview Press.

Hancock, I. (2010). *We are the Romani* [Ame Sam E Rromane Džene]. Hatfield: The University of Hertfordshire Press (Original work published 2002).

Hepworth, K. (2012). Abject citizens: Italian 'nomad emergencies' and the deportability of Romanian Roma. *Citizenship Studies, 16*(3-4), 431–449.

Honig, B. (2009). *Emergency politics: Paradox, law, democracy.* Princeton: Princeton University Press.

Honig, B. (2014). Three models of emergency politics. *Boundary 2, 41*(2), 45–70.

Howard, M. M. (2010). Civil society and democracy. In H. K. Anheier & S. Toepler (Eds.), *International encyclopedia of civil society* (pp. 186–192). New York: Springer.

Howe, B., & Cleary, R. (2001, January). *Community building: Policy issues and strategies for the Victorian Government.* Melbourne: Victorian Department of Premier and Cabinet.

Human Rights Watch. (2011). Everyday intolerance: Racist and xenophobic violence in Italy, Human Rights Watch. Retrieved from http://www.hrw.org/sites/default/files/reports/italy0311WebRevised.pdf

Il Fatto Quotidiano. (2015, February 26). Appalti pubblici, il 60% dei contratti viene affidato senza gara. A Roma l'80% [Public contracts, 60% of them are entrusted without competition. In Rome 80%]. *Il Fatto Quotidiano.* Retrieved from http://www.ilfattoquotidiano.it/2015/02/26/corruzione-60-dei-contratti-pubblici-viene-affidato-gara-roma-l80/1458396/

International Federation of Red Cross and Red Crescent Societies. (n.d.). Our vision and mission. Retrieved from http://www.ifrc.org/en/who-we-are/vision-and-mission/

Isin, E. F., & Rygiel, K. (2007). Abject spaces: Frontiers, zones, camps. In E. Dauphinee & C. Masters (Eds.), *Logics of biopower and the war on terror* (pp. 181–203). Houndmills/Basingstoke: Palgrave.

Istituto per gli Studi di Politica Internazionale. (2015). Gli italiani e le migrazioni: percezione vs realtà [Italians and migration: perception vs. reality]. Retrieved from http://www.ispionline.it/it/articoli/articolo/emergenzesviluppo-europa-italia-global-governance/gli-italiani-e-le-migrazioni-percezione-vs-realta-13562

Istituto per gli Studi sulla Pubblica Opinione. (2008). Italiani, Rom e Sinti a confronto: Una ricerca quali-quantitativa. [A comparison between Italians, Roma and Sinti: A quali-quantitative research]. European Conference on the Roma Population, Scuola Superiore dell'Amministrazione dell'Interno. Retrieved from http://www.interno.gov.it/mininterno/export/sites/default/it/sezioni/sala_stampa/documenti/minoranze/0999_2008_01_22_conferenza_rom.html_1411422173.html

246   Bibliography

Italian National Institute for Statistics. (2016). La rilevazione sulle istituzioni non-profit: un settore in crescita [The survey of non-profit institutions: A rising sector]. http://www.istat.it/en/files/2013/07/05-Scheda-Non-Profit_DEF.pdf

Jones, A. (2011). *Genocide: A comprehensive introduction* (2nd ed.). New York: Routledge.

Keane, J. (2010). Civil society, definitions and approaches. In H. K. Anheier & S. Toepler (Eds.), *International encyclopedia of civil society* (pp. 461–464). New York: Springer.

Keller, R. (2016). Cañada Real Galiana, Madrid the largest slum in Europe. Retrieved from https://www.ethz.ch/content/dam/ethz/special-interest/conference-websites-dam/no-cost-housing-dam/documents/Keller_final.pdf

Kington, T. (2008, May 17). 68% of Italians want Roma expelled: Poll. The Guardian. Retrieved from http://www.guardian.co.uk/world/2008/may/17/italy

Kjaerum, M. (2012). Making a tangible difference to Roma people's lives. Retrieved from http://fra.europa.eu/en/speech/2012/making-tangible-difference-roma-peoples-lives

Klímová-Alexander, I. (2005). *The Romani voice in world politics: The United Nations and non-state actors*. Aldershot: Ashgate Publishing Limited.

La Repubblica. (2011, March 3). Protesta del terzo settore. [The protest of the Third Sector]. *La Repubblica*. Retrieved from http://roma.repubblica.it/cronaca/2011/03/03/news/nomadi-13135597/?refresh_ce

La Repubblica. (2017, January 27). Italia non-profit, arriva la piattaforma per far conoscere gli enti del Terzo settore [Italian non-profit, soon the launch of the platform to know Third Sector organization]. *La Repubblica*. Retrieved from http://www.repubblica.it/economia/miojob/2017/01/27/news/italia_non_profit_arriva_la_piattaforma_per_far_conoscere_gli_enti_del_terzo_settore-156861576/

La Stampa. (2017, May 11). Rom e Sinti in Italia. *La Stampa*. Retrieved from http://www.lastampa.it/2017/05/11/multimedia/italia/cronache/rom-e-sinti-in-italia-DQyWN5m5PGilUEqGhvnzJK/pagina.html

Laboratorio Arti Civiche. (n.d.). Savorengo ker. Retrieved from http://www.articiviche.net/LAC/works___savorengo_ker.html

Lee, R. (2002). Roma ande Kalisferia: Roma in limbo. In S. Montesi (Ed.), *Terre Sospese: Vite di un campo rom* [Suspended Worlds: Lives of a campo rom]. Roma: Prospettiva Edizioni Srl. Retrieved from http://kopachi.com/articles/

Leeson, P. T. (2010). Gypsy law. Retrieved from http://www.peterleeson.com/Gypsies.pdf

Levy, C. (2010). Refugees, Europe, camps/state of exception: 'Into the Zone', the European Union and extraterritorial processing of migrants, refugees and Asylum-Seekers (theories and practice). *Refugee Survey Quarterly, 29*(1), 92–119.

Lewis, D. (2014). *Non-governmental organizations, management and development* (3rd ed.). Abingdon: Routledge.

Lintner, C. (2014). Overcoming the "nomad camps" by initiating a new learning process on the example of Bolzano (Italy). *Procedia – Social and Behavioral Sciences, 116*, 775–779.

Lodigiani, R. (Ed.). (2010). *Rapporto Sulla Città Milano 2010: Welfare ambrosiano, futuro cercasi* [Report on the city of Milan 2010: Ambrosiano Welfare, looking for future]. Milano: Franco Angeli.

Lori, M. (2010, July). Autonomous or dependent: Isomorphic effects of public regulation on voluntary organisations. Paper presented at 9th International Conference of the International Society for Third Sector Research (ISTR), Istanbul. Retrieved from http://www.istr.org/?WP_Istanbul

Lunaria. (2011). *Chronicles of ordinary racism: Second white paper on racism in Italy* (trans: Di Pietro, D. & Marshall, C.). Rome: Edizioni dell'Asino.

Lunaria. (2013). Segregare costa: La spesa per i 'campi nomadi' a Napoli, Roma e Milano [Segregating is costly: The expenditure for 'nomad camps' in Naples, Rome and Milan]. Retrieved from http://www.lunaria.org/wp-content/uploads/2013/09/segregare.costa_.pdf

Lynch, M. (2005). Lives on hold: The human cost of statelessness. Retrieved from http://www.refintl.org/policy/in-depth-report/lives-hold-human-cost-statelessness

Mackinson, T. (2017, July 25). UNAR, il numero antidiscriminazioni costa 800 euro a chiamata [UNAR, the anti-discrimination number costs €800 per call]. *Il Fatto Quotidiano*. Retrieved from http://www.ilfattoquotidiano.it/2017/07/25/unar-il-numero-antidiscriminazioni-costa-800-euro-a-chiamata-ed-e-un-doppione/3750752/

Maestri, G. (2016). Persistently temporary. Ambiguity and political mobilisations in Italy's Roma camps: A comparative perspective. Durham theses, Durham University. Retrieved from Durham E-Theses Online: http://etheses.dur.ac.uk/11881/

Maestri, G. (2017). Struggles and ambiguities over political subjectivities in the camp: Roma camp dwellers between neoliberal and urban citizenship in Italy. *Citizenship Studies, 21*(6), 640–656.

Maggian, R. (2011). *Guida al welfare italiano: Dalla pianificazione sociale alla gestione dei servizi* [A guide to Italian welfare: From social planning to service management]. Santarcangelo di Romagna, Rimini: Maggioli Editore.

248 Bibliography

Malinowski, B. (2002). *Argonauts of Western Pacific*. London: Routledge & Kegan Paul Ltd.

Marcenaro, P. (2012a, February 08). Rapporto conclusivo dell'indagine sulla condizione di Rom, Sinti e Camminanti in Italia [Final report of the survey on the status of Roma, Sinti and Travellers in Italy]. Retrieved from http://www.pietromarcenaro.it/index.php?option=com_content&task=view&id=1029&Itemid=247

Marcenaro, P. (2012b, May 15). Regolarizzazione dei Rom provenienti dalla ex Jugoslavia [Regularisation of the Romani peoples from former Yugoslavia]. Retrieved from http://www.pietromarcenaro.it/index.php?option=com_cont ent&task=view&id=1325&Itemid=247

Mariani, F. (2017). I nomadi ci costano duecento milioni [Nomads cost €200 million]. Retrieved from http://www.iltempo.it/roma-capitale/2017/05/11/news/i-nomadi-ci-costano-duecento-milioni-1028298/

Marotta, V. (2011a). Home, mobility, and the encounter with otherness. In F. Mansouri & M. Lobo (Eds.), *Migration, citizenship, and intercultural relations: Looking through the lens of social inclusion* (pp. 193–209). Aldershot: Ashgate.

Marotta, V. (2011b). The idea of the in-between subject in social and cultural thought. In M. Lobo, V. Marotta, & N. Oke (Eds.), *Intercultural relations in a global world* (pp. 179–199). Champaign: Common Ground Publishing LLC.

Martini, L. (2017, January 25). La Corte dei Conti "spara" sulla Croce Rossa [The Court of Auditors "shoots" at the Red Cross]. Business Insider Italia. Retrieved from https://it.businessinsider.com/la-corte-dei-conti-spara-sulla-croce-rossa/

Martirano, D. (1997, February 14). Criminalità: Il sindaco chiede aiuto allo Stato per l'emergenza nomadi [Criminality: The mayor asks the government for help in relation to the Romani emergency]. *Corriere della Sera*. Retrieved from http://archiviostorico.corriere.it/1997/febbraio/14/Rutelli_Roma_molto_piu_sicura_co_10_9702144012.shtml

Marzoli, D. (Ed.). (2012). Rom, Sinti e Camminanti in Italia [Roma, Sinti and Travellers in Italy]. Retrieved from http://www.fedevangelica.it/documenti/2/17d6721180962c67446aec731479cde2.pd

Mason, M. (2010, September). Sample size and saturation in PhD studies using qualitative interviews. *FQS, 11*(3), art.8. Retrieved from http://www.qualitative-research.net/index.php/fqs/article/view/1428/3027

Matras, Y. (2004). The role of language in mystifying and demystifying Gypsy identity. In N. Saul & S. Tebbutt (Eds.), *The role of the Romanies: Images and counter-images of 'Gypsies'/Romanies in European cultures* (pp. 53–78). Liverpool: The University Press.

Matras, Y. (ca. 2007). Roma culture: An introduction. Retrieved from http://romafacts.uni-graz.at/index.php/culture/introduction/roma-culture-an-introduction

McCulloch, G. (2004). *Documentary research in education, history and the social sciences*. London/New York: Routledge Falmer.

Mills, M. R., & Bettis, P. J. (2015). Using multiple theoretical frameworks to study organizational change and identity. In V. A. Anfara Jr. & N. T. Mertz (Eds.), *Theoretical frameworks in qualitative research* (pp. 96–118). Thousand Oaks: SAGE Publications.

Ministero del Lavoro e delle Politiche Sociali. (2010). Senza Dimora: Storie, vissuti, aspettative delle persone senza dimora in cinque aree metropolitane [Of no fixed abode: Stories, experiences and expectations of homeless people in five metropolitan areas]. Retrieved from http://www.lavoro.gov.it/NR/rdonlyres/CE06FD73-D361-4414-96D8-8EB7E5243058/0/QRS10_senzadimora.pdf

Ministero del Lavoro e delle Politiche Sociali. (2014). Italy's Operational Programme (OP) For Social Inclusion ESF – European Social Fund 2014–2020. Retrieved from http://www.lavoro.gov.it/temi-e-priorita/europa-e-fondi-europei/focus-on/pon-Inclusione/Documents/Sintesi-Pon-Inclusione-inglese.pdf

Ministero dell'Interno. (2006). La pubblicazione sulle minoranze senza territorio [The publication on stateless minorities]. Retrieved from http://www1.interno.gov.it/mininterno/export/sites /default/it/assets/files/13/La_pubblicazione_sulle_minoranze _senza_territorio.pdf

Ministero dell'Interno. (2008). Linee guida per l'attuazione delle ordinanze del presidente del consiglio dei ministri del 30 maggio 2008, n. 3676, 3677 e 3678, concernenti insediamenti di comunità nomadi nelle regioni Campania, Lazio e Lombardia [Guidelines for the implementation of the ordinances issued by the President of the Council of Ministries of 30 May 2008, nos. 3676, 3677 and 3678]. Retrieved from http://www.statewatch.org/news/2008/jul/italy-roma-ministry-guidelines-italian.pdf

Ministero dell'Interno. (2009a). Censimento dei campi nomadi: Gli interventi adottati per superare lo stato di emergenza [Census of the nomad camps: Interventions implemented to overcome the state of emergency]. Retrieved from http://www1.interno.gov.it/mininterno/export/sites/default/it/sezioni/sala_stampa/speciali /censimento_nomadi/

250 Bibliography

Ministero dell'Interno. (2009b). Third report submitted by Italy pursuant to article 25, paragraph 2 of the framework Convention for the Protection of National Minorities. Retrieved from http://www.coe.int/t/dghl/monitoring/minorities/3_fcnmdocs/PDF_3rd_SR_Italy_en.pdf

Ministero dell'Interno. (2011). Dichiarazione dello stato di emergenza in relazione agli insediamenti di comunita' nomadi nel territorio delle regioni Campania, Lazio e Lombardia [Declaration of the state of emergency in relation to the settlements of the nomads communities in the territory of the Campania, Lazio and Lombardia]. Retrieved from http://www.governo.it/Governo/Provvedimenti/testo_int.asp?d=39105

Ministero dell'Interno. (2012). Le comunità sprovviste di territorio [Stateless communities]. Retrieved from http://www1.interno.gov.it/mininterno/export/sites/default/it/temi/minoranze/sottotema002.html

Ministero dell'Interno. (2014). IV rapporto dell'Italia sull'attuazione della convenzione quadro per la protezione delle minoranze nazionali [IV Report on the implementation of the Framework Convention for the Protection of National Minorities]. Retrieved from http://www.interno.gov.it/sites/default/files/allegati/2014_05_12_iv_rapporto_it.pdf

Ministero dell'Interno. (2016). Pubblicazione sfratti 2016 [The publication on the evictions in 2016). Retrieved from http://ucs.interno.gov.it/ucs/contenuti/Andamento_delle_procedure_di_rilascio_di_immobili_ad_uso_abitativo-168224.htm

Ministero dell'Interno. (2017). Minoranze [Minorities]. Retrieved from http://www.interno.gov.it/it/temi/cittadinanza-e-altri-diritti-civili/minoranze

Ministero dell'Istruzione. (2009). Firmato protocollo d'intesa tra Miur e Opera Nomadi [The agreement between MIUR and Opera Nomadi has been signed]. Retrieved from http://hubmiur.pubblica.istruzione.it/web/ministero/cs240409

Molero-Mesa, J., & Jiménez-Lucena, I. (2013). (De)legitimizing social, professional and cognitive hierarchies. Scientific knowledge and practice in inclusion-exclusion processes. *Dynamis: Acta Hispanica ad Medicinae Scientiarumque Historiam Illustrandam, 33*(1), 13–17.

Morelli, B. (2006). *L'identità zingara* [The Gypsy identity]. Rome: Anicia.

Musgrave, S., & Bradshaw, J. (2014). Language and social inclusion: Unexplored aspects of intercultural communication. *Australian Review of Applied Linguistics, 37*(3), 198–212.

Nessun luogo è lontano. (2008). Rom e Sinti, dalla legalità alla coesione sociale [Roma and Sinti, from legality to social cohesion]. Appunti Aranconi, 4.

Retrieved from http://www.nessunluogoelontano.it/nuovosito/index.php?option=com_docman&task=searchresult&order=dmname&ascdesc=ASC&Itemid=48

Nicola, V. (2011). *I ghetti per i rom. Roma, via Di Salone 323. Socianalisi narrativa di un campo rom* [The ghettos for Romani people. Rome, Di Salone road, 323. Socio-analysis account of a Romani camp]. Cuneo: Sensibili alle Foglie.

Noi Consumatori. (2007). Diritto alla casa: Italia sotto accusa all'Onu [Housing rights: Italy is under UN indictment]. Retrieved from http://www.noiconsumatori.org/articoli/articolo.asp?ID=1138

Nozzoli, G. (2013, July 5). Campo Castel Romano e gli incendi dei rom: 'Non solo guerra etnica' [Castel Romano camp and Romanies' fires: 'Not simply an ethnic war']. *Roma Today*. Retrieved from http://eur.romatoday.it/campo-castel-romano-incendi-perche.html

Nye, M. (2007). The challenges of multiculturalism. *Culture and Religion, 8*(2), 109–123.

Office for Democratic Institutions and Human Rights. (2009). Assessment of the human rights situation of Roma and Sinti in Italy: Report of a fact-finding mission to Milan, Naples and Rome on 20–26 July 2008. Retrieved from http://www.osce.org/odihr/36374

Officina Genitori. (2008). La questione rom a Milano [The Romani issue in Milan]. Retrieved from https://www.officinagenitori.org/index.php?option=com_content&view=article&id=1968:la-questione-rom-a-milano&catid=90&lang=it&Itemid=248

Open Society European Policy Institute. (2017). Revisiting the EU Roma framework: Assessing the European dimension for the post-2020 future. Retrieved from https://www.opensocietyfoundations.org/sites/default/files/revisiting-eu-roma-framework-20170607.pdf

Open Society Foundations & Open Society Justice Initiative. (2010). Roma in Italy: Briefing to the European Commission October 2010. Retrieved from http://www.soros.org/sites/default/files/memorandum-italy-ec-20101018.pdf

Osservatorio Sociale Regionale. (2007). Il presidente dell'Opera Nomadi Abruzzo ai dirigenti nazionali: 'Dimettetevi e consegnate l'associazione a Rom e Sinti' [The president of Opera Nomadi Abruzzo to the national leadership: 'Resign and hand over the organisation to Romani people']. Retrieved from http://www.osr.regione.abruzzo.it/do/index?docid=3857

OsservAzione. (2006). Political participation and media representation of Roma and Sinti in Italy: The case studies of Bolzano-Bozen, Mantua, Milan and Rome. Retrieved from http://www.osservazione.org/documenti/osce_italy.pdf

Otieno, M. (2015, December 8). Poverty is big business in the West: A new documentary savages the philosophy of foreign aid. *MercatorNet*. Retrieved from https://www.mercatornet.com/harambee/view/poverty-is-big-business-in-the-west/17311

Paris, M. (2017, June 15). Ius soli, all'ultimo miglio in Senato. Ecco le regole negli altri Paesi Ue [Ius soli, last mile in the Italian Senate. Here are the rules in other EU countries]. Il Sole 24 Ore. Retrieved from http://www.ilsole24ore.com/art/notizie/2017-06-07/lo-ius-soli-tenta-l-ultimo-miglio-italia-come-francia-ma-guarda-modellotedesco--151755.shtml?uuid=AErfjLaB&refresh_ce=1

Parlamento Italiano. (2000). Legge 20 luglio 2000, n. 211: 'Istituzione del "Giorno della Memoria" in ricordo dello sterminio e delle persecuzioni del popolo ebraico e dei deportati militari e politici italiani nei campi nazisti' ['The institution of "Remembrance Day" for the commemoration of extermination and the persecutions of the Jewish people and the Italian soldiers and politicians deported to the Nazi camps']. Retrieved from http://www.camera.it/parlam/leggi/00211l.htm

Parra, J. (2011). Stateless Roma in the European Union: Reconciling the doctrine of sovereignty concerning nationality laws with international agreements to reduce and avoid statelessness. *Fordham International Law Journal, 34*(6), 1666–1694.

Patanè, S. (2003). The Third Sector in Italy. EuroSET Report, Rome: European Social Enterprise Training, Centro Italiano di Solidarietà di Roma.

Pavesi, F. (2013). Tutti gli sprechi della Croce Rossa italiana [All the CRI's squandering]. http://www.ilsole24ore.com/art/notizie/2013-02-04/conti-rosso-croce-rossa-190429.shtml?uuid=AbHUbBRH

Pecini, C. (2016, January 18). Esercenti dello spettacolo viaggiante: i tratti di un'identità incerta [Travel business owners: the traits of an uncertain identity]. Parksmania. Retrieved from https://www.parksmania.it/articoli-tecnici/esercenti-dello-spettacolo-viaggiante-i-tratti-di-unidentita-incerta/

Per i Diritti Umani. (2017, March 27). Il percorso di superamento dei campi rom deciso dal Comune di Roma [The process for overcoming the Romani camps set by the Municipality of Rome]. Per i Diritti Umani. https://www.peridirittiumani.com/2017/03/27/il-percorso-di-superamento-dei-campi-rom-deciso-dal-comune-di-roma/

Peró, D. (1999). Next to the dog pound: Institutional discourses and practices about Rom refugees in left-wing Bologna. *Modern Italy, 4*(2), 207–224.

Peró, D. (2007). *Inclusionary rhetoric/exclusionary practices. Left-wing politics and migrants in Italy*. New York: Berghahn Books.

Pew Research Center. (2016). Europeans fear wave of refugees will mean more terrorism, fewer jobs. Retrieved from http://assets.pewresearch.org/wp-content/uploads/sites/2/2016/07/14095942/Pew-Research-Center-EU-Refugees-and-National-Identity-Report-FINAL-July-11-2016.pdf

Piasere, L. (1985). Les pratiques de voyage et de stationament des nomades en Italie [Travel and short-stay practices of the nomads in Italy]. In A. Reyniers (Ed.), *Les pratiques de deplacement, de halte de stationament des populations tsiganes et nomades en France* (pp. 143–195). Paris: Centre de Recherches Tsiganes.

Piasere, L. (2004). *I Rom d'Europa: Una storia moderna* [The Roma of Europe: A modern history] Rome: Laterza.

Piasere, L. (2005). *Popoli delle discariche: Saggi di antropologia zingara* [Peoples of the dumps: Essays in Gypsy anthropology] (2nd ed.). Rome: CISU.

Picker, G. (2010). Nomad's land? Political cultures and nationalist stances vis-à-vis Roma in Italy. In M. Steward & M. Rovid (Eds.), *Multidisciplinary approaches to Romany studies* (pp. 211–227). Budapest: Central European University Press.

Picker, G. (2011). Welcome 'in'. Left-wing Tuscany and Romani migrants (1987–2007). *Journal of Modern Italian Studies, 16*(5), 607–620.

Pierucci, A. (2014, July 10). 'Mille euro per una baracca ai rom': Accusati di corruzione due vigili urbani [A thousand Euros for a shanty house: Two municipal officers investigated for corruption]. *Il Messaggero*. Retrieved from http://www.ilmessaggero.it/ROMA/CRONACA/mille_euro_baracca_rom_accusati_corruzione_vigili_urbani/notizie/789408.shtml

Piotrowski, T. (2017, February 26). The seeds of volunteering. *The Grassroots Journal*. Retrieved from http://www.thegrassrootsjournal.org/single-post/2017/02/25/The-Seeds-of-Volunteering

Pissacroia, M. (1998). *Trattato di psicopatologia della adolescenza* [Essay on psychopathology of adolescence]. Padua: Piccin-Nuova Libraria.

Pittini, A., Ghekière, L., Dijol, J., & Kiss, I. (2015). The State of Housing in the EU 2015: A Housing Europe Review. Retrieved from http://www.housingeurope.eu/resource-468/the-state-of-housing-in-the-eu-2015

Pividori, C., & de Perini, P. (2016). Tendenze e prospettive per il «sistema diritti umani» in Italia: a che punto siamo? *SUDEUROPA, 1*, 17–40.

Pogány, I. (2004). Legal, social and economic challenges facing the Roma of Central and Eastern Europe. Queen's Papers on Europeanisation, 2, Queen's University Belfast, Belfast.

Pogány, I. (2012). Pariah peoples: Roma and the multiple failures of law in Central and Eastern Europe. *Social & Legal Studies, 21*(3), 375–393. https://doi.org/10.1177/0964663911429152.

Bibliography

Ponziano, G. (2014, December 9). Avevo denunciato il malaffare a danno dei rom [I reported the bad management of the Romani issue, but nobody listened]. *Italia Oggi*. Retrieved from http://www.italiaoggi.it/giornali/dettaglio_giornali.asp?preview=false&accessMode=FA&id=1945077&co

Portanova, M. (2016, June 22). Roma, le tangenti in diretta nell'ufficio del Comune [Rome, bribes live inside the office of the city council]. *Il Fatto Quotidiano*. Retrieved from http://www.ilfattoquotidiano.it/2016/06/22/roma-le-tangenti-in-diretta-nellufficio-del-comune-scusate-se-ho-interrotto-qualcosa/2849711/

Puliafito, A. (2011). *Croce Rossa: Il lato oscuro della virtù* [Red Cross: The dark side of virtue]. Rome: Alberti Editore.

Pulzetti, A. M. (2010). I campi Rom: Le nuove sfide umanitarie [Romani camps: New humanitarian challenges]. Retrieved from http://www.crocerossachepassione.com/index.php?option=com_docman&task=cat_view&gid=12&Itemid=8

Quinto, V. (2017, February 28). Roma, ancora proteste contro i campi rom. Soluzione forse nel dialogo? [Rome, new protests against the Romani camps. Maybe dialogue is the solution?]. Aris Notiziari. Retrieved from http://www.arisnotiziari.it/wordpress/?p=5400

Rainews. (2017, May 31). Roma, cosa prevede il piano Raggi per il superamento dei campi rom [Rome, Raggi's plan to overcome the Romani camps]. *Rainews*. Retrieved from http://www.rainews.it/dl/rainews/articoli/roma-cosa-prevede-piano-raggi-per-superamento-campi-rom-ff1552ee-b1b5-424e-900d-05cb921c9f0e.html?refresh_ce

Ramadan, A. (2013). Spatialising the refugee camp. *Transactions of the Institute of British Geographers, 38*(1), 65–77.

Ranci, C. (1994). The third sector in welfare policies in Italy: The contradictions of a protected market. *International Journal of Voluntary and Nonprofit Organizations, 5*(3), 247–271.

Ranci, C. (2015). The long-term evolution of the government – Third Sector partnership in Italy: Old wine in a new bottle? *VOLUNTAS: International Journal of Voluntary and Nonprofit Organizations, 26*(6), 2311–2329.

Re, L. (2010). Italians and the invention of race: The poetics and politics of difference in the struggle over Libya, 1890–1913. *California Italian Studies, 1*(1), 1–58.

Redattore Sociale. (2014, February 7). Immigrati, a Roma finisce l'avventura dei consiglieri comunali aggiunti [Immigrants, end of the road for the added councilors in Rome]. Redattore Sociale. Retrieved from http://www.redattoresociale.it/Notiziario/Articolo/454202/Immigrati-a-Roma-finisce-l-avventura-dei-consiglieri-comunali-aggiunti

Renzi, L. (2010). Roma people in Europe: A long history of discrimination. European Social Watch Report 2010. Retrieved from http://www.socialwatch.eu/wcm/documents/Roma_a_long_history_of_discrimination.pdf

Rete di Sostegno Mercatini Rom. (2012). Comunicato stampa rovistatori [Press release garbage bin pickers]. Retrieved from http://retedisostegnomercatinirom.over-blog.it/

Riccardo, F., & Gruis, V. (2007, June). Social housing renovation in Italy: Which solutions can be found in the Dutch housing management model? Paper presented at the International Conference 'Sustainable Urban Areas', Rotterdam.

Ricordy, A., Trevisani, C., Motta, F., Casagrande, S., Geraci, S., & Baglio, G. (2012). La salute per i rom: Tra mediazione e partecipazione [The health of the Romanies: Between mediation and participation]. Bologna: Edizioni Pendragon. Retrieved from http://www.libertaciviliimmigrazione.interno.it/dipim/export/sites/default/it/assets/pubblicazioni/La_salute_per_i_rom_giugno2012.pdf

Riniolo, V., & Marcaletti, F. (2013). Active participation of Roma: An experience of participatory planning towards labour integration. Retrieved from http://www.errc.org/article/roma-rights-2012-challenges-of-representation-voice-on-roma-politics-power-and-participation/4174/6

Rivera, A. (2003). *Estranei e nemici* [Aliens and enemies]. Rome: DeriveApprodi.

Roma Education Fund. (2012, July 20). A good start: An upcoming revolution in Roma education in Eastern Europe? TOL Chalkboard. Retrieved http://chalkboard.tol.org/a-good-start-an-upcoming-revolution-in-roma-education-in-eastern-europe

Roma Soc!al Pr!de. (2010). Perché è nato il Roma Soc!al Pr!de? [Why was the Roma Soc!al Pr!de born?]. Retrieved from http://romasocialpride.wordpress.com/perche/

Romano Lil. (2007, September 8). Spinelli e Guarnieri: Il pre-giudizio degli 'zingari' [Spinelli and Guarnieri: The prejudice of the 'Gypsies']. *Romano Lil*. Retrieved from http://romanolil.blog.tiscali.it/2007/09/08/spinelli_e_guarnieri__il_pre_giudizio_degli__zingari__1797483-shtml/

Rondinelli, G. (2008, March 12). Rutelli riscopre l'emergenza-rom [Rutelli retrieves the Romani emergency]. *Il Giornale*. Retrieved from http://www.ilgiornale.it/news/rutelli-riscopre-l-emergenza-rom.html

256   Bibliography

Rossi, M. (2010). The city and the slum: An action research on a Moroccan and a Roma Xoraxanè community in Rome. Doctoral dissertation. Retrieved from http://etheses.bham.ac.uk/1263/

Rövid, M. (2011). Cosmopolitanism and exclusion: On the limits transnational democracy in the light of the case of Roma. Doctoral dissertation. Retrieved from http://pds.ceu.hu/doctoral-school-phd-dissertations

Saletti-Salza, C. (2003). *Bambini del campo nomadi: Roma' bosniaci a Torino* [*Children of the nomad camps: Bosnian Romanies in Turin*]. Roma: CISU.

Santilli, C. (2017). I rom che raccolgono il ferro a Roma [Romanies collect metal in Rome]. *ANUAC, 6*(1), 141–163.

Schmitt, C. (2005). Political theology: Four chapters on the concept of sovereignty. Edited and translated by Schwab, G. Chicago: University of Chicago Press.

Sciortino, G. (2010). Diversity and the European public sphere: The case of Italy, Eurosphere Country Reports, Online Country Report No. 13. Retrieved from http://eurospheres.org/files/2010/06/Italy.pdf

Scutellà, A. (2016a, January 27). Giornata della memoria, il Senato ricorda rom e i sinti deportati, confinati e sterminati [Remembrance Day, the Senate commemorates Roma and Sinti people deported, detained and exterminated]. *La Repubblica.* Retrieved from http://www.repubblica.it/solidarieta/diritti-umani/2016/01/27/news/giornata_della_memoria_il_senato_ricorda_rom_e_i_sinti_deportati_confinati_e_sterminati-132172210/

Scutellà, A. (2016b, October 5). Rom, i campi non chiudono [Romanies, camps are not shut down]. *La Repubblica.* Retrieved from http://www.repubblica.it/solidarieta/diritti-umani/2016/10/05/news/rom_i_campi_non_chiudono_21_luglio_ecco_il_sistema_a_5_stelle_-149182944/

Senato della Repubblica. (2015). Atto Camera n. 2802 XVII Legislatura [Chamber Act No. 2802 XVII Legislature]. Retrieved http://www.senato.it/leg/17/BGT/Schede/Ddliter/45140.htm

Senato della Repubblica. (2016). Disposizioni concernenti la procedura per il riconoscimento dello status di apolidia in attuazione della Convenzione del 1954 sullo status delle persone apolidi [Provisions concerning the procedure for the recognition of stateless status in compliance with the 1954 Convention on the Status of Stateless Persons]. Retrieved from http://www.senato.it/japp/bgt/showdoc/17/DDLPRES/967066/index.html?stampa=si&spart=si&toc=no

Shore, C., & Wright, S. (1997). *Anthropology of policy.* London: Routledge.

Sigona, N. (2002). *Figli del ghetto: Gli italiani, i campi nomadi e l'invenzione degli zingari* [Sons of the ghetto: Italians, nomad camps and the invention of the Gypsies]. Civezzano: Nonluoghi.

Sigona, N. (2005). Locating 'The Gypsy problem'. The Roma in Italy: Stereotyping, labelling and 'nomad camps'. *Journal of Ethnic and Migration Studies, 31*(4), 741–756.

Sigona, N. (2007). Lo scandalo dell'alterità: Rom e sinti in Italia [The scandal of otherness: Roma and Sinti in Italy]. In S. Bragato & L. Menetto (Eds.), *E per patria una lingua segreta: Rom e sinti in provincia di Venezia* (pp. 17–32). Portogruaro: Nuovadimensione.

Sigona, N. (Ed.). (2008). The 'latest' public enemy: Romanian Roma in Italy. The case studies of Milan, Bologna, Rome and Naples. Retrieved from http://www.osservazione.org/documenti/OSCE_publicenemy.pdf

Sigona, N. (2009). The 'Problema Nomadi' vis-à-vis the political participation of Roma and Sinti at the local level in Italy. In N. Sigona & N. Trehan (Eds.), *Romani politics in contemporary Europe: Poverty, ethnic mobilization, and the neoliberal order* (pp. viii–xiii). New York: Palgrave Macmillan.

Sigona, N. (2010). 'Gypsies out of Italy!': Social exclusion and racial discrimination of Roma and Sinti in Italy. In A. Mammone & G. Veltri (Eds.), *Italy today: The sick man of Europe* (pp. 143–157). London: Routledge.

Sigona, N. (2011). The governance of Romani people in Italy: Discourse, policy and practice. *Journal of Modern Italian Studies, 16*(5), 590–606.

Sigona, N. (2015). Campzenship: Reimagining the camp as a social and political space. *Citizenship Studies, 19*(1), 1–15.

Sigona, N. (2016). Everyday statelessness in Italy: Status, rights, and camps. *Ethnic and Racial Studies, 39*(2), 263–279.

Sigona, N., & Monasta, L. (2006). Imperfect citizenship: Research into patterns of racial discrimination against Roma and Sinti in Italy. Retrieved from http://www.osservazione.org/documenti/OA_imperfectcitizenship.pdf

Silverman, C. (1995). Persecution and politicization: Roma (Gypsies) of Eastern Europe. *Cultural Survival Quarterly, 19*(2), 43–49. Retrieved from http://www.culturalsurvival.org/publications/cultural-survival-quarterly/albania/persecution-and-politicization-roma-gypsies-eastern

Simon, P. (2012). Collecting ethnic statistics in Europe: A review. *Ethnic and Racial Studies, 35*(8), 1366–1391.

Sina, Y. (2012, April 3). Rom: Il governo ci riprova [Roma: The government tries again]. *Il Manifesto*. Retrieved from http://www.giustizia-amministrativa.it/rassegna_web/120403/1d3exz.pdf

Smooha, S. (2009). The model of ethnic democracy: Response to Danel. *The Journal of Israeli History, 28*(1), 55–62.

Solimano, N. (1999). Immigrazione, convivenza urbana e conflitti locali [Immigration, urban coexistence and local conflicts]. *La Nuova Citta, 2*(4), 135–140.

258 Bibliography

Solimano, N., & Mori, T. (2000, June). A Roma ghetto in Florence. *The UNESCO Courier.*

Solimene, M. (2013). Undressing the gağé clad in state garb: Bosnian xoraxané romá face to face with the Italian authorities. *Romani Studies, 23*(2), 161–186.

Solopescara. (n.d.). Pescara citta' storia: Gli zingari. Retrieved from http://www.solopescara.com/content/knowledgebase/kb_view.asp?kbid=201

Spinelli, S. (2005). *Baro romano drom.* Rome: Meltemi Editore.

Spinelli, S. (2012). *Rom, genti libere: Storia, arte e cultura di un popolo misconosciuto* [Roma, free people: History, art and culture of an unrecognized people]. Milan: Dalai Editore.

Springhetti, P. (2009). Le zone grigie del Terzo Settore [The grey area of the Third Sector]. Retrieved from http://www.volontariato.lazio.it/documentazione/documenti/RetiSolidali_2_09_ZoneGrigieDelTerzoSettore.pdf

Stasolla, C. (2012). *Sulla pelle dei Rom: Il Piano Nomadi della giunta Alemanno* [On the skin of the Romani People: The Nomad Plan of the Alemanno administration]. Rome: Edizioni Alegre.

Stasolla, C. (2017a, July 13). Campi rom e sgomberi, a Roma la musica è davvero cambiata. *Il Fatto Quotidiano.* Retrieved from http://www.ilfattoquotidiano.it/2017/07/13/campi-rom-e-sgomberi-a-roma-la-musica-e-davvero-cambiata-purtroppo/3726875/

Stasolla, C. (2017b, September 28). Roma, il campo rom deve chiudere? Il Comune gli cambia nome e gli ospiti restano lì. *Il Fatto Quotidiano.* Retrieved from http://www.ilfattoquotidiano.it/2017/09/28/roma-il-campo-rom-deve-chiudere-il-comune-gli-cambia-nome-e-gli-ospiti-restano-li/3882570/

Teolato, L. (2016, June 24). Roma, arrestato per corruzione su appalti gestione campi nomadi [Rome, arrested for bribery in relation to tender procurement contracts for the management of nomad camps]. *Il Fatto Quotidiano.* Retrieved from http://www.ilfattoquotidiano.it/2016/06/24/roma-arrestato-per-corruzione-su-appalti-campi-nomadi-aveva-affidato-bene-sequestrato-alla-mafia/2857090/

Tomasone, M. (2012). Il genocidio nazista dei Rom [The Nazi Genocide of the Romanies]. Retrieved from www.istoreto.it/amis/micros/rom_micros.rtf

Tonkens, E., & Hurenkamp, M. (2011, July 7–9). The nation is occupied, the city can be claimed. Paper presented at the Annual Conference of the Sociology of Urban and Regional Development of the International Sociological Association, University of Amsterdam, The Netherlands.

Townley, B. (1997). The institutional logic of performance appraisal. *Organization Studies, 18*(2), 261–285.

Transparency International. (2012). Italy needs anti-corruption watchdog. Retrieved from http://www.transparencyinternational.eu/wp-content/uploads/2012/08/2012-03-30-TI-Italy-ENIS-PR_EU.pdf

U Velto. (2008, March 7). Sucar Drom chiede misure urgenti al Ministero dell'Interno [Sucar Drom demands urgent measures from the Ministero dell'Interno]. *U Velto*. Retrieved from http://sucardrom.blogspot.com.au/2008/03/sucar-drom-chiede-misure-urgenti-al.html

U Velto. (2012a, February 28). L'Italia presenta la 'Strategia nazionale d'inclusione dei Rom, Sinti e Camminanti' [Italy presents the 'National Strategy for the Inclusion of the Roma, Sinti and Camminanti']. *U Velto*. Retrieved from http://sucardrom.blogspot.it/2012/02/litalia-presenta-la-strategia-nazionale.html

U Velto. (2012b, May 15). Rom e Sinti, Fornero: Uscire da gestione emergenziale [Roma, Sinti, and Fornero: Let's drop the emergency approach]. *U Velto*. Retrieved from http://sucardrom.blogspot.com.au/2012/05/rom-e-sinti-fornero-uscire-da-gestione.html

U Velto. (2012c, May 28). Rom e Sinti, l'associazionismo: Parliamo di interazione [Romani associationism: Let's talk about social interaction]. *U Velto*. Retrieved from http://sucardrom.blogspot.com.au/2012/05/rom-e-sinti-lassociazionismo-parliamo.html

Ufficio Nazionale Antidiscriminazioni Razziali. (2011a). Relazione al Parlamento sull'effettiva applicazione del principio di parità di trattamento e sull'efficacia dei meccanismi di tutela [Report to Parliament concerning enforcement of the principle of equal treatement and of the effectiveness of legal mechanism]. Retrieved from http://sbnlo2.cilea.it/bw5ne2/opac.aspx?WEB=ISFL&IDS=18688

Ufficio Nazionale Antidiscriminazioni Razziali. (2011b). Vai oltre i pregiudizi, scopri i Rom: Go beyond prejudice, discover the Roma. Retrieved from http://www.cominrom.it/wordpress/wp-content/uploads/2011/11/Volume_Campagna-Dosta_UNAR.pdf

Ufficio Nazionale Antidiscriminazioni Razziali. (2012). Brutte notizie: Come i media alimentano la discriminazione [Bad news: How media fuel discrimination]. LIL Quaderni di Informazione Rom. Roma: ISTSSS Editore

Ufficio Nazionale Antidiscriminazioni Razziali. (2014). Strategia Nazionale d'inclusione dei Rom, dei Sinti e dei Caminanti: Attuazione comunicazione commissione europea n.173/2011 [National Strategy for the inclusion of Roma, Sinti and Camminanti communities: European Commission communication no. 173/2011]. Retrieved from http://www.unar.it/unar/portal/wp-content/uploads/2014/02/Strategia-Rom-e-Sinti.pdf

260   Bibliography

Ufficio Nazionale Antidiscriminazioni Razziali. (2017). Bando di gara per l'affidamento di servizio 'Interventi pilota per la creazione di tavoli e network di stakeholder coinvolti con le comunità RSC' [Call for tenders for the assignment of the service 'Pilot actions for the creation of stakeholders' networks involved with RSC communities]. Retrieved from http://www.unar.it/unar/portal/?p=8519

Un rom delegato di Alemanno. (2010, July 27). Un rom delegato di Alemanno [A Romani person as Alemanno's delegate]. La Repubblica. Retrieved from http://roma.repubblica.it/cronaca/2010/07/27/news/nomadi-5869812/

UN-Habitat. (2016). Urbanization and development: Emerging futures. Retrieved from http://wcr.unhabitat.org/wp-content/uploads/2017/02/WCR-2016-Full-Report.pdf

United Nations. (2011). Guidance note of the secretary general: The United Nations and Statelessness. Retrieved from https://www.un.org/ruleoflaw/files/FINAL%20Guidance%20Note%20of%20the%20Secretary-General%20on%20the%20United%20Nations%20and%20Statelessness.pdf

United Nations Global Compact. (2010). Civil society. Retrieved from https://www.unglobalcompact.org/howtoparticipate/civil_society

United Nations High Commissioner for Refugees. (2017). Executive Committee of the High Commissioner's Programme Standing Committee 69th Meeting. Retrieved from http://www.refworld.org/pdfid/59a58d724.pdf

Uzunova, I. (2010). Roma integration in Europe: Why minority rights are failing. *Arizona Journal of International and Comparative Law, 27*(1), 283–323. Retrieved from http://academos.ro/sites/default/files/biblio-docs/845/roma_integration_in_europe.pdf

van Baar, H. (2005). Romany Countergovernmentality through transnational networking. Paper presented at the Oxford Symposium on (Trans-) Nationalism in South East Europe, University of Oxford, Oxford.

van Baar, H. (2014). The emergence of a reasonable Anti-Gypsyism in Europe. In T. Agarin (Ed.), *When stereotype meets prejudice: Antiziganism in European societies* (pp. 27–44). Stuttgart: Ibidem.

van Baar, H. (2015). The perpetual mobile machine of forced mobility: Europe's Roma and the institutionalization of rootlessness. In Y. Jansen, J. de Bloois, & R. Celikates (Eds.), *The irregularization of migration in contemporary Europe: Deportation, detention, drowning* (pp. 71–86). London/New York: Rowman & Littlefield.

Vannucci, A., & Della Porta, D. (2011). Countries at the crossroads 2011: Italy. Retrieved from http://www.freedomhouse.org/sites/default/files/inline_images/ITALYfinal.pdf

Verbruggen, S., Christiaens, J., & Milis, K. (2011). Can resource dependence and coercive isomorphism explain nonprofit organizations' compliance with reporting standards? *Nonprofit and Voluntary Sector Quarterly, 40*(1), 5–32.

Verhoeven, I., & Bröer, C. (2015). Contentious governance: Local governmental players as social movement actors. In J. W. Duyvendak & J. M. Jasper (Eds.), *Breaking down the state protestors engaged* (pp. 95–110). Amsterdam: Amsterdam University Press B.V..

Vermeersch, P. (2001). Roma identity and ethnic mobilisation in Central European politics. Paper prepared for the workshop on identity politics at the ECPR, Grenoble.

VII Commissione Cultura, Scienza e Istruzione della Camera dei Deputati. (2011). Indagine conoscitiva sulle problematiche connesse all'accoglienza degli alunni con cittadinanza non italiana nel sistema scolastico italiano [Cognitive study on issues related to the reception of foreign pupils in the Italian school system]. Retrieved from http://documenti.camera.it/_dati/leg16/lavori/stencomm/07/indag/alunni/2011/0112/INTERO.pdf

Vitale, T. (2010). Rom e sinti in Italia: Condizione sociale e linee di politica pubblica [Roma and Sinti in Italy: Social conditions and guidelines of public policies]. Osservatorio di Politica Internazionale, 21. Retrieved from http://www.parlamento.it/documenti/repository/affariinternazionali/osservatorio/approfondimenti/Approfondimento_21_ISPI_RomSinti.pdf

Vitale, T., & Caruso, L. (2009). Conclusioni. Ragionare per casi: dinamiche di innovazione nelle politiche locali con i Rom e i Sinti [Conclusions. Case by case analysis: Innovation dynamics in local politics with Rom and Sinti]. In T. Vitale (Ed.), *Politiche possibili: Abitare le città con i rom e i Sinti* (pp. 265–288). Rome: Carocci editore.

Volpi, F. (2017, April 7). The judicial statelessness determination procedure in Italy. LitigAction. Retrieved from http://www.litigaction.com/the-judicial-statelessness-determination-procedure-italy/

Wacquant, L. (2011). A Janus-Faced institution of ethnoracial closure: A sociological specification of the ghetto. In R. Hutchison & B. Haynes (Eds.), *The ghetto: Contemporary global issues and controversies* (pp. 1–31). Boulder: Westview Press.

Walters, W. (2011). Foucault and frontiers: Notes on the birth of the humanitarian border. In U. Bröckling, S. Krasmann, & T. Lemke (Eds.), *Governmentality: Current issues and future challenges* (pp. 138–164). New York: Routledge.

Warmisham, J. (2016). The situation of Roma and Travellers in the context of rising extremism, xenophobia and the refugee crisis in Europe. Retrieved from https://rm.coe.int/1680718bfd

262 Bibliography

Weyrauch, W. O. (1999). Unwritten constitutions, unwritten law. *Washington and Lee Law Review, 56*(4), 1211–1244.

Woodcock, S. (2009). What's in a name? How Romanian Romani were persecuted by Romanians as Tigani in the Holocaust, and how they resisted. Interstitio. Retrieved from http://www.academia.edu/207265/Whats_in_a_name_How_Romanian_Romani_were_persecuted_by_Romanians_as_Tigani_in_the_Holocaust_and_how_they_resisted

World Bank. (2013). Defining civil society. Retrieved from http://web.worldbank.org/WBSITE/EXTERNAL/TOPICS/CSO/0,,contentMDK:20101499~menuPK:244752~pagePK:220503~piPK:220476~theSitePK:228717,00.html

Wotherspoon, T., & Hansen, J. (2013). The "Idle No More" movement: Paradoxes of First Nations inclusion in the Canadian context. *Social Inclusion, 1*(1), 21–36.

Zandonini, G. (2016, April 16). Rom e Sinti, arrivata a metà corsa, la Strategia Nazionale per l'inclusione ha già il fiato corto. *La Repubblica*. Retrieved from http://www.repubblica.it/solidarieta/diritti-umani/2016/04/10/news/rom_arrivata_a_meta_corsa_la_strategia_nazionale_per_l_inclusione_di_rom_e_sinti_ha_gia_il_fiato_corto_-137306733/

Zema, A. (2012, April 3). In città, il prefetto: 'La casa è la vera emergenza' [In the city, according to the prefect: 'The house is the real emergency']. *Roma Sette*. Retrieved from http://www.romasette.it/modules/news/article.php?storyid=8363

Zincone, G. (Ed.). (2001). *Secondo rapporto sull'integrazione degli immigrati in Italia* [Second report on the integration of immigrants in Italy]. Bologna: Il Mulino.

Index

A

Abject space, 14
(Taking) advantage, 8, 21, 102, 136, 176, 189, 196–199
Adzovic, Najo, 116, 116n2, 152, 163, 168–174, 184, 196–201
Agamben, Giorgio, 11, 13, 15, 19–22, 81
Alemanno, Gianni, 84–87, 90, 113–118, 125, 127–129, 132, 135–137, 140–143, 147, 148, 151, 152, 163, 168–172, 196–199
Alien/aliens, 44, 61, 88, 177, 217
Alleanza Nazionale (National Alliance), 88, 115
Antagonism/antagonist, 9, 22, 23, 179
Arci Solidarietà Lazio, 52, 128, 131, 136, 138, 146
Arendt, Hannah, 13

B

Baraccati (shanty-dwellers), 53
(Camps as) battlefield, 20, 174
Belviso, Sveva, 139, 143, 148
Berlusconi, Silvio, 81–83, 87–89, 212
Blocchi Precari Metropolitani, 25
Boycott, 129, 132
Brazzoduro, Marco, 99, 100, 185
Buzzi, Salvatore, 153

C

Camminanti (travellers), 6, 42, 43, 46, 56, 64, 66, 82, 91, 94, 139n10, 213
'Camp-dweller', 6, 10–13, 19–22, 27, 53, 82, 84, 88, 97, 120, 133, 134, 152, 173, 174, 183, 185, 186, 197, 198, 201

© The Author(s) 2018
R. Armillei, *The 'Camps System' in Italy*, Mapping Global Racisms,
https://doi.org/10.1007/978-3-319-76318-7

264 Index

Camping River (equipped village), 25, 196

Campi nomadi (nomad camps), 1, 10–15, 18–20, 23, 46, 48, 49, 53, 57, 90, 99, 114–117, 125, 134–137, 140, 149, 153, 164, 169, 182, 188–190, 197, 200, 212, 216, 218, 219

Campizzazione (campisation), 92, 141, 184

'Camps policy', 7, 12–14, 18, 46, 56, 91–92, 117, 127, 132, 134, 135, 138, 142, 151, 174, 184, 185, 210, 214, 215

'Camps system', 10–23, 115, 117, 120, 122, 126, 134, 151, 153, 168, 189, 192, 200, 210, 215–219

Candoni (equipped village), 25, 189, 192, 193, 196

Caritas Diocesana di Roma, 101, 115, 116, 135n9, 136–139, 169

Casa Dei Diritti (House of Social Rights)/CDS, 52, 101, 128, 146, 152, 169, 170

Casilino 900, 53, 54, 57, 90, 135, 170, 194, 196

Castel Romano (equipped village), 25, 53, 86, 86n2, 114, 146, 186, 187

Catholic, 51, 127, 135–139, 210

Centre-left, 79, 90, 113, 114

Centre-right, 89, 90

Cesare Lombroso (equipped village), 25, 199

Citizenship, 10, 43, 45, 50, 60, 61, 84, 95, 97, 161, 188

Civil society organisations (CSOs), 8, 12, 16–23, 85, 95, 101, 114n1, 118–127, 140–144, 146, 147, 149, 153, 162, 166, 170, 176, 187–191, 199–201, 210, 211, 214, 215n1, 218

Collective-identity closure, 161, 174, 216

Comunità di S. Egidio, 135–139

Contentious space, 23

Convention on the Rights of the Child, 143

Converso, Massimo, 52, 165

Cooperativa Rom a Roma (Romani Cooperative in Rome), 169, 171, 172

Cooperativa 29 Giugno, 153

Coordinamento Rom a Roma (Co-ordination of the Romani People in Rome), 168, 171

Corruption, 9, 19, 53, 132, 144, 150–152, 165, 172, 187, 200, 215, 217

Croce Rossa Italiana/Italian Red Cross (CRI), 57, 83, 113–116, 128–131, 136–138, 141, 196, 216

D

Declaration on the Rights of Persons Belonging to National or Ethnic, Religious and Linguistic Minorities, 96

Di Maggio, Salvatore, 153

Document Authorising Temporary Stay (DAST), 84

Dyswelfare, 13

Index **265**

E

Emergenza Nomadi (Nomad Emergency), 6–8, 10, 14, 15, 27, 79–83, 85, 89, 103, 116, 128, 136, 141, 149, 150, 215, 217

Ermes Cooperativa Sociale, 128, 131, 133, 137, 146, 153, 215

Eureka I Onlus, 128, 131, 146

Evicted/evictions, 2, 5n1, 7, 13, 23, 49, 55, 80, 85, 91, 141, 142, 151, 186, 213–215

Extraordinary actions, intervention, measure(s), powers, 6, 14, 55, 80, 81, 83, 103, 114, 121, 142, 149, 211, 217, 219

F

Fascist, 5, 64, 84, 87, 88, 88n3, 175, 212

Federazione Romani (Romani Federation), 100, 165–167, 171

Fighters, 21, 174, 176, 184

Fondazione Romani (Romani Foundation), 98, 131, 131n8

Forza Italia (Forward Italy), 88

Foucault, Michel, 11, 12, 22, 58, 216

Framework Convention for the Protection of National Minorities, 96

G

Gadje (non-Romani people), 21, 22, 167, 174–180, 196, 197, 200, 219

'Gadjikane' (being non-Romani), 175–177

Genocide, 65, 66, 185

Gheorghe, Nicolae, 103, 167, 168, 175, 176, 180, 183, 201

Ghetto/ghettoisation, 7, 20, 46, 56, 124, 127n4

Gordiani (equipped village), 190, 196

Gruppo di Coordinamento e Garanzia del Piano Nomadi (Group for the Co-ordination and Protection of the Nomad Plan), 113, 135–139

Guarnieri, Nazzareno, 53, 90, 98, 99, 101, 102, 127, 131n8, 134, 164–168, 171, 216

H

Halilovic, Graziano, 165, 168, 169, 172

Holocaust, 65, 66

I

Illegal/illegally/illegality, 2, 5, 14, 21, 43, 64, 80, 83–85, 130, 142, 147–149, 186, 191, 192, 195

Institutional isomorphism, 12, 18, 19, 23, 214

International Convention on the Elimination of All Forms of Discrimination, 143

International Federation of Red Cross and Red Crescent Societies (IFRC), 121

Invisible/invisibility, 44, 95, 177, 201

Irregular(s), 10, 82, 89–92

266 Index

L

La Barbuta (equipped village), 85, 132, 141, 193, 194
Lack of transparency, 9, 119, 152
Left/left-wing/left-winger/leftist, 6, 8, 86, 88–91, 113, 114, 118, 129, 133, 136, 137, 139–142, 148, 150, 151, 171, 197, 199, 210

M

Mafia, 192, 195
Mafia Capitale (capital mafia), 18, 19, 144, 147, 153, 215
Marino, Ignazio, 91
Metropoliz, 25
Municipality of Rome/municipality, 18, 52, 85, 113, 114n1, 115–120, 122, 124, 125, 127, 128, 131, 136, 137, 141, 146, 150, 164, 168, 171, 174

N

'National Strategy', 6, 7, 9, 10, 14, 56, 66n4, 82, 92–95, 97–105, 189, 200, 210
'No-camps', 127, 131–135
Nomadism/nomadic, 5, 15, 42, 43, 46, 49, 50, 62, 66, 149, 178, 196, 211–213

O

Observatory for the Protection Against Discriminatory Acts (OSCAD), 94, 104

Opera Nomadi, 50–53, 164, 165, 172
'Oppressor' and 'oppressed', 20, 174

P

Pacchetto Sicurezza (Security Package), 88
Pavlovic, Dijana, 96, 152, 162–164
Piano Nomadi (Nomad Plan), 83–87, 90, 92, 116, 120, 127, 133–142, 148, 168, 170–172
Popica Onlus, 25, 131
Porrajmos, 65
Problema Nomadi (Nomads Problem), 6, 49, 212
'Pro-camps', 127–129, 127n4, 132, 134, 137, 162, 216
Prodi, Romano, 79, 88
Pro-Roma/Romani, 52, 98, 137, 164–167, 193

R

Race/racism/racialised/racialisation, 6, 12, 20, 56–59, 64, 65, 87, 88, 97, 100, 103, 104, 121, 146, 163, 168, 173, 184, 185, 192, 201, 211–217, 219
Raggi, Virginia, 54, 91, 139
Reggiani, Giovanna, 79, 88
Resistance, 8, 9, 11, 12, 20–23, 174, 178, 183, 200, 201, 210–218
Right/right-wing/righist, 6, 8, 88, 113–116, 126–128, 137, 138, 140, 142, 148, 151, 199
Rocca, Francesco, 113, 115, 121

'Rom', 42, 45, 46, 56, 62, 85, 133, 194–196
Romanes (the Romani language), 20, 21, 57, 66, 67, 174
Romani associationism/ organizations/movement, 85, 93, 97–99, 101–103, 129, 137, 163–171, 181, 182, 186, 187, 199, 200, 210, 218
'Romanipen' (Roma-being), 175, 176
Rutelli, Francesco, 89–91, 113, 114, 148, 151, 171, 195

Salone (equipped camp), 133, 135, 186, 192, 196
Segregation/segregational/segregated, 7, 9, 20, 41, 46–49, 56, 62–64, 91, 127, 132, 145, 163, 174, 176, 182, 212, 213
Self-determination, 99, 161, 164
Self-ghettoisation, 20, 218
'Sinti', 6, 42–46, 48, 51, 52, 56, 62–64, 66, 82, 92, 94, 96, 97, 166, 175, 193–196, 213
Slum/slummification, 1, 2, 9
Solidarity villages/*villaggi della solidarità*, 5n1, 10, 25, 86, 128, 140, 145–147
Spinelli, Santino, 51, 67, 162–166, 178
Stasolla, Carlo, 116, 122, 127, 136, 147, 168–172, 176, 183, 185, 214
Stateless/statelessness, 44, 46, 50, 54, 57–61, 142, 212
'Systemic disease', 23

Third Sector/*Terzo Settore*, 7–9, 12, 13, 16–19, 22–27, 57, 99, 116–119, 125–128, 131, 134–139, 152, 162–164, 168, 188, 210, 211, 215, 218
Top-down, 4, 7, 23, 143, 151, 181, 201
Tor De' Cenci (tolerated camp), 25, 140, 143, 148, 150, 151, 167, 183, 184

UNAR (the National Office against Racial Discrimination), 7, 43, 44, 47, 62, 82, 93, 93n4, 96, 97, 99–101, 104

V Department, 'Ufficio Nomadi' (Nomads Office), 139–145, 213
Veltroni, Walter, 79, 86, 88, 90, 114, 129, 134, 142, 147, 151, 152, 171
Via Amarilli (homeless shelter), 197

Warriors, 21, 176
Welfare dependency/funding dependence, 8, 12, 18, 19, 23, 58, 80, 96, 103, 145, 153, 163, 183, 214, 216, 218

268 Index

X

XI Department, Education and Schooling Policy Office, 139, 144

XII Municipal Hall, Culture Office, 139, 140, 148, 150

Z

Zingaro/i (Gypsies), 21, 41–43, 45, 46, 48, 62, 64, 164, 174, 178, 184, 185, 216, 219